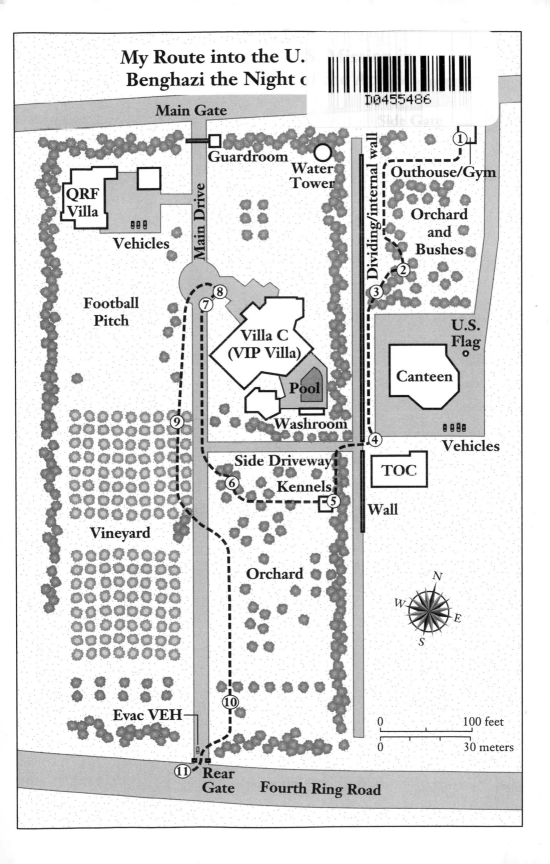

THE
EMBASSY
HOUSE

*The Explosive Eyewitness Account of the Libyan
Embassy Siege by the Soldier Who Was There*

SERGEANT MORGAN JONES
&
DAMIEN LEWIS

THRESHOLD EDITIONS
New York   London   Toronto   Sydney   New Delhi

Threshold Editions
A Division of Simon & Schuster, Inc.
1230 Avenue of the Americas
New York, NY 10020

First Threshold Editions hardcover edition October 2013

THRESHOLD EDITIONS and colophon are trademarks
of Simon & Schuster, Inc.

For information about special discounts for bulk purchases,
please contact Simon & Schuster Special Sales at 1-866-506-1949
or business@simonandschuster.com.

The Simon & Schuster Speakers Bureau can bring authors to your live event. For
more information or to book an event, contact the Simon & Schuster Speakers
Bureau at 1-866-248-3049 or visit our website at www.simonspeakers.com.

Interior design by Claudia Martinez

Manufactured in the United States of America

1   3   5   7   9   10   8   6   4   2

ISBN 978-1-4767-5113-9
ISBN 978-1-4767-5115-3 (ebook)

For Tyrone Woods and Glen Doherty, who died in the
battle for the American Embassy, Benghazi, Libya,
on the night of September 11, 2012.
In true Navy SEAL tradition they refused to
take a step backward or to leave a man behind,
and for that they paid the ultimate price.

For Sean Smith and the American ambassador to Libya,
J. Christopher Stevens, who also perished on that fateful night.

And for David Ubben and Scott Wickland,
and all the others injured in that battle.

I promised to fight by your side, and although
I did all that I could, ultimately in that I failed.
It will haunt me for the rest of my days.

AUTHOR'S NOTE

Where agents, soldiers, or private operators' real names have been published in the press coverage of the Benghazi 9/11 events, I have used their real names in this book. Where agents, soldiers, or private operators' real names have not been published in the press, or where I am unable to establish their full real names, I have used pseudonyms. I have also been asked or seen fit to use pseudonyms for some of the Special Forces and other elite operators still involved in sensitive operations, or who undertook sensitive operations during their careers in the military. Otherwise, all aspects of this story remain unchanged and as they took place on the ground.

I have done my utmost to ensure that all the events portrayed herein are factually accurate. Few written records exist covering the events described in this book. Accordingly, I have re-created conversations from how I remember them and in discussions with others.

I have used the words Embassy, Mission, Consulate, and Diplomatic Mission interchangeably, to describe the American diplomatic facility at Benghazi. When considered as a whole, the Diplomatic Mission and the (CIA) Annex in Benghazi may well have constituted America's largest such facility in Libya, and it was often referred to as "the Embassy" by those of us who worked there, especially the local staff. When the American ambassador was present at the Mission my understanding is that it was formally known as the Embassy.

PROLOGUE

Every morning I wake up feeling ashamed that I am still alive while four Americans that I served with are dead. I thought that my feelings of guilt would fade over time: they have not. If anything, they are getting worse, and at times the guilt is unbearable. I keep friends, family, and work colleagues at a distance, as I do not want to get close to anyone like I did to those I worked with at the U.S. Mission in Benghazi.

Libya is constantly on my mind. If I sit down to take a break for five minutes at work, Benghazi is instantly in my head. I am back among those fateful events of Benghazi 9/11 and it is deafening. My close friends tell me that I have changed. Unfortunately, I don't think that there is much I can do about that. I feel dead inside, and it is my son who keeps me going day to day.

People will likely ask why I have decided to write this book now. I have kept silent for nearly a year, and in spite of being approached by the media. I felt the need to tell this story first and foremost in the hope that doing so will help assuage my guilt and somehow help me to heal. I hope in writing this story down that it may offer me some kind of catharsis.

But if the truth be told, I am also angry at all the misinformation that surrounds the events of Benghazi 9/11. The families of those who lost loved ones, or had their loved ones horrifically injured during that dark night, deserve better. I hope in presenting a simple and straightforward rendering of the events as they unfolded during my six-month tenure at the U.S. Mission I may help shed light on what actually transpired, and how the U.S. Embassy in Benghazi could have ended up being as wide open as it was to such an attack. So, I have also written this book in an effort to set the record straight.

Benghazi 9/11 has become a political hot potato in America. But in the political cut and thrust the real story appears to have been forgotten, as have the crucial lessons that should have been learned. The Regional Security Officers (RSOs)—those Americans tasked with ensuring security at the Benghazi Mission—and those personnel at the Annex—the nearby CIA base collocated with the Mission—are heroes in my eyes. Having seen at firsthand what they were up against I cannot believe how many got out of Benghazi alive. Losing four Americans—Ambassador Stevens included—was horrendous, but it could so easily have been thirty-four dead Americans, the odds against them were so unbelievably high. If their loss is not to be in vain, lessons must be learned.

The men who carried out the rescue from the Annex executed one of the most amazing missions I have ever encountered. The five RSOs at the Embassy—Scotty, Dave, Alex, and the Ambassador's two close protection (CP) guys—managed to hold out for long enough against one hundred or more heavily armed attackers until their backup arrived. They were outgunned and outnumbered thirty-to-one against Islamic extremists baying for their blood: *they went to the Mission specifically to kill Americans.* It must have been utterly terrifying and is something those young RSOs will very likely keep reliving for the rest of their lives.

Two brave Americans—SEAL veterans Tyrone Woods and Glen Doherty—gave the ultimate sacrifice on that night so that others might be saved. They deserve the very highest honor, respect, and recognition for doing so. Two of the young RSOs—

Dave and Scotty—ended up seriously injured as a result of their resistance to the savagery that was unleashed against the Mission and the Annex, and as a result of their repeated efforts to rescue the Ambassador in terrifying and deadly circumstances. They deserve the highest honor and respect for doing so.

Ambassador Stevens was a fine, upstanding American and a great asset to his country and to Libya. His loss will be felt by both greatly, as it will by his family. Sean Smith was a committed professional with a young wife and family. They will doubtless feel his loss for the rest of their lives. Libyan guards stationed at the Mission were also injured and killed in the attacks, and their families will likewise live in mourning.

The lesson to be learned from Benghazi 9/11 is what security measures need to be put in place to ensure that this never happens again, or at least to reduce the risks to acceptable levels. The level of risk that the U.S. Mission in Benghazi was exposed to was unacceptable. Americans—and their allies—were put in harm's way without due safeguards: that should never be allowed to happen again.

I n the months following the Benghazi Embassy siege I learned the fuller picture of what happened during that fateful night, both at the Mission itself and at the Annex, which was only a short drive away from the Mission. Tensions were running high that evening, because of a recce mission that a Libyan policeman—or more likely a bad guy posing as a policeman—had carried out that morning. We'd caught him taking photos of the Mission's front gate and grounds, and we feared it was in preparation for some kind of an attack.

I had served at the Mission for six months as the security manager overseeing the Libyan guard force, one employed by Blue Mountain Group, a British private security company. My role was to recruit, train, and oversee the guards, but due to my extensive experience of such security operations I also worked closely with the Americans stationed at the Mission, in an effort to improve its wider security. As we were all painfully aware, the defenses at the Embassy were woefully inadequate, plus the city of Benghazi itself was becoming ever more dangerous, especially for Americans and/or their allies. As a result, the Benghazi Mission had become a place of fear for just about everyone stationed there, and especially on the day when we had what we suspected were recce photos taken of the Mission.

Even Sean Smith, the IT guy who was only days into his posting, and whose mind I had recently tried to put at rest by telling him we'd never had any real trouble at the Mission—even he was fearful. A couple of hours prior to the attack Sean was online with his friends, and one of them emailed, "see you tomorrow." Sean replied: "If I'm still here tomorrow; our security manager caught a guy taking photos of the Embassy front gate; so I hope I make it through the night." It was ominous, his foreboding of the imminent attack.

Sean was a big online computer gamer, and he was actually online as the attack began. He typed in real time: "I hear shots; we're being attacked . . . I hope I will be able to speak to you again tomorrow." Of course he never would, because Sean would die in the assault that was even then unfolding.

This is how it went down.

Shortly after nightfall fifty gunmen from the Shariah Brigade— a Libyan militia tied to Al Qaeda—rushed the Mission, and were able to gain access via the pedestrian entrance set to one side of the main gate. They did so by threatening the Blue Mountain guards with assault rifles and RPGs. Basically, the guards—who were unarmed and defenseless, *because the State Department contract dictated that they be unarmed and defenseless*—were ordered to open the side gate or else be killed.

The one thing my unarmed guard force did do was raise the alarm—either via their radios or by pressing the duck-and-cover alarm (it remains unclear which occurred). Alerted to an attack, Alex, the lead RSO, could see via the CCTV monitors in the Tactical Operations Center (TOC) what was unfolding. Scores of heavily armed gunmen were streaming into the darkened compound.

Ambassador Stevens had retired to the VIP Villa approximately thirty minutes before the attack, having finished an evening meeting with the Turkish ambassador to Libya. At the time of the attack Stevens was alone in the VIP Villa, apart from Sean, who was also billeted there, and one of the Ambassador's close protection guys, who was watching a video in the villa's common area.

The two RSOs, Dave and Scotty, were relaxing at the rear of the VIP Villa, in the outside seating area, along with the second of the Ambassador's CP guys. Dave and Scotty heard explosions and gunfire coming from the front entrance, and a warning of the attack was radioed through to them by the Blue Mountain guard force. Realizing they were under armed attack, the three of them raced to their respective positions, exactly as had been planned in the event of such an attack.

Scotty headed into the VIP Villa to secure the Ambassador and Sean. He grabbed his weaponry—a combat shotgun, M4 assault rifle, plus a SIG Sauer pistol—and got the Ambassador and Sean to don their body armor. He got them into the safe area and locked and secured it, with the three of them inside. That done, Scotty radioed through a confirmation of their whereabouts to Alex in the TOC. He then took up a defensive position inside the safe area, with a view through the steel gates covering any route of ingress of any potential enemy.

Meanwhile the Ambassador's CP guy who'd been watching the video in the Villa had sprinted for his room—in Villa B, opposite the TOC—wherein his weaponry was held. Scotty had passed his cell phone to the Ambassador, who began making calls to the U.S. Embassy in Tripoli and to other local contacts, requesting assistance. Just moments into the attack the third RSO, Alex, was also able to put a call through to the Annex, which was just a short drive away, alerting them to what had happened and asking for their help: "We're under attack. We need help. Please send help now . . ."

The dozen-strong CIA security team at the Annex—consisting of ex–Special Forces (SEALs and Delta Force) and other elite operators—were the cavalry that were called to the Mission's aid. That call was made at approximately 9:40 P.M.—so barely minutes after the attack had been launched—and similar calls were put through to the Diplomatic Security team headquarters, in Washington, alerting them to the fact that the Benghazi Mission was under attack.

Dave and the other CP guy sprinted toward the TOC and the nearby Villa B to arm themselves. Dave was that night's "TOC officer"—meaning he would sleep at and man the TOC—and his weaponry was located there. Dave linked up with Alex in the TOC, at which point the imperative was to break out the M4 carbines, shotguns, and ammo held there and don their body armor. Before doing so, they locked and barred the door to the TOC, and they could already hear the attackers trying to break in.

The Ambassador's two CP guys were now in Villa B, pulling on body armor and readying weaponry. That done, they attempted to return to the VIP Villa, where the Ambassador was locked into the safe area. As they turned onto the dirt track leading to the VIP Villa they came up against a mass of the Shariah Brigade fighters. In the ensuing firefight they quickly realized how heavily they were outnumbered and outgunned. They were forced back into Villa B, together with one of my guard force. They barricaded themselves into a back room and took up defensive positions.

But by now the Shariah fighters had blown up the guardroom at the main gate and torched the QRF Villa which lay adjacent to the main gate and housed the Quick Reaction Force made up of a local Libyan militia. They captured two of my guard force and made them kneel inside the front gate, where they beat them and carried out mock executions. Guns were put to the guards' heads, and triggers pulled on empty chambers—hence initial reports that I heard that my guards had been shot in the head and executed. Having made it clear they were "only here to kill Americans," the attackers shot one of the guards in both kneecaps before turning to their main task—the hunt.

They spread out through the wider compound searching for American targets. At around 9:50 P.M.—ten minutes after the attack began—Ambassador Stevens managed to place a call through to Tripoli using a cell phone. He managed to speak to the U.S. Embassy in Tripoli, his warning triggering the mustering of a small, ad hoc Quick Reaction Force (QRF), which was apparently all the Tripoli Embassy could manage due to the lack of available airframes to fly them to Benghazi.

The Shariah Brigade fighters converged on the VIP Villa and broke into its interior. Unable to penetrate the steel security gate barring off the safe area, they started banging on it and yelling violently and firing. Scotty made the decision not to return fire, in an effort to hide the fact that he, the Ambassador, and Sean were locked inside. He warned the Ambassador and Sean to prepare for explosions and blasts when the Shariah fighters tried to break their way through the security barrier.

Instead the Shariah fighters decided to try to burn the occupants out. They fetched cans of diesel fuel that were going to be used to power the Mission's generators—ones that were not yet in service—and were stored near the QRF Villa. They torched the Mission's armored SUVs parked by the QRF Villa before turning back to the VIP Villa itself. They went inside and threw the diesel around the villa's interior, soaking furniture with the fuel. They then set the building on fire.

As the fire took hold, the villa's interior filled with thick black diesel smoke and the fumes thrown off by the burning furniture. Scotty first realized the villa was on fire when the light became dim, as the smoke seeped into the safe area. Realizing that the Villa had been firebombed, he got the Ambassador and Sean to retreat into a room at the rear—a bathroom. The three men got down on their hands and knees in an effort to avoid the thick black diesel smoke that was billowing into the safe area.

Scotty tried to seal the bathroom door using wet towels, but the smoke kept seeping inside. He next tried opening the bathroom window, in an effort to ventilate the place, for all three of them were having problems breathing and visibility was down to near zero. But opening the window only served to create a through-flow of air in the wrong direction, drawing more smoke into the small, cramped room, which in turn made it even more difficult to breathe. The toxic fumes were building to intolerable and potentially deadly levels.

Scotty realized they couldn't last in there, and he yelled for the others to follow him as he made his way onto the roof of the villa. This involved moving into an adjacent bedroom, from where a window opened onto a patio and from there onto the roof. Crawling on his hands and knees and unable to see properly, he yelled for the others to follow. He showed them the way, banging on the floor to guide the Ambassador and Sean to the exit. Scotty managed to make the window, open the security grille, and clamber outside, collapsing onto the small patio area.

As soon as he was visible to the Shariah fighters Scotty came under fire. Realizing that neither the Ambassador nor Sean was with him, Scotty went back into the smoke-filled villa to search for them. He did this several times, each time trying to take in fresh air from outside to enable him to continue the search, and still taking fire from the enemy. But on each attempt the thick smoke and the boiling heat forced him to retreat outside in an effort to recover. He kept doing this until he was close to being rendered unconscious, at which stage he staggered up onto the villa roof and radioed for help.

In the TOC, Dave and Alex heard his radio call, but Scotty was so badly affected by the smoke that he was almost unintelligible. They finally realized what he was trying to tell them: that he didn't have the Ambassador or Sean with him, and that they were trapped in the Villa's smoke-filled interior. Outside the TOC the Shariah fighters had tried to burn the SUVs parked there, but their jerry cans of diesel were empty. They also tried to break into Villa B, where the Ambassador's two CP guys and the Libyan guard were holed up, but failed to do so.

Dave and Alex had watched all of this on CCTV. Leaving Alex in the TOC to man communications, Dave managed to fight his way across to the nearby Villa B—using a smoke grenade to cover his movements—and he reunited himself with the two CP guys. Together the three of them made their second foray into the grounds of the Embassy, trying to get from the TOC to the VIP Villa. Driven back by ferocious enemy fire, they grabbed an armored SUV parked outside the TOC and used it to break through the hordes of fighters now occupying the compound.

Dave and the two CP guys made it to the VIP Villa, whereupon they debussed and headed for the roof to put down fire onto the enemy. There they discovered Scotty, who was vomiting from severe smoke inhalation and in danger of losing consciousness. One of Scotty's last acts had been to smash open a skylight in the VIP Villa's roof in an effort to ventilate the interior and help the Ambassador and Sean trapped inside, but it didn't appear to have had much of a positive effect.

Dave and the CP guys took up positions on the villa roof, so they could put down aimed shots onto the scores of heavily armed Shariah fighters now converging on their position. This was the fallback defense plan if the compound itself was taken—the idea being to hold the VIP Villa long enough for reinforcements to arrive and break the siege, and drive off the attackers. But as Dave would make so clear in a cell phone call to me, they had little hope of any force getting to their aid in time, due to the massive numbers of enemy surging into the compound.

All three of them—Dave and the Ambassador's two CP guys—made repeated forays into the interior of the villa, using the same route through the window that Scotty had employed, searching for the Ambassador and Sean. If anything, the conditions inside were even worse. They were forced to snake along on their bellies, to try to keep below the thick and suffocating smoke. In spite of their efforts all they achieved was to make themselves violently sick, and all three ended up on the verge of losing consciousness.

While the Americans at the Mission had been fighting this desperate battle, I was doing all in my power to make good on my promise—to stand with them if the bad guys attacked. I was billeted away from the Mission compound, but just as soon as I'd got the warning call from my guards, I'd got my driver, Massoud, to head over to my place with weapons. We'd set out across the city, intent on launching a one-man rescue mission—for I doubted very much if Massoud was coming with me, and in any case I needed him to stay with the vehicle. If I did manage to rescue the trapped Americans, we'd need a driver and set of wheels to make our getaway.

Meanwhile, at the nearby Annex, the CIA's head of security had heard explosions echoing across to them from the direction of the Mission. According to some media reports the call for help from the Mission was initially denied by the Annex CIA Chief of Base (COB), though this is disputed by the CIA. Either way, a seven-man team led by ex–Navy SEAL Tyrone S. Woods assembled—grabbing weaponry, ammunition, and night vision equipment in preparation for leaving the Annex to go to the aid of those under siege at the Mission.

Tyrone Woods was a member of the Annex's Global Response Staff, former elite forces members contracted to provide security to CIA agents operating out of the Annex. Woods had served with the U.S. Navy's SEAL Team Three and had won the Bronze Star with a Combat V for valorous duty in Iraq. He'd led ten reconnaissance missions leading to the capture of thirty-four insurgents in the volatile Al Anbar Province of Iraq. He'd also completed multiple tours of Afghanistan during twenty years of service with the U.S. military.

In 2007 he'd left the military and was working in the Annex as a Global Response Staff member, and he was hugely respected in that role. Ty Woods and his team were going to the Mission's aid, with or without the COB's blessing. It took twenty-five minutes from their first being alerted to the attack for the team from the Annex to be ready to go to the Mission's rescue.

It was just after 10:00 P.M. when they set out driving two armored Toyota Land Cruisers. There were six of them, as one operator had been left to man radios—a vital role. In the time it had taken them to prepare to leave they had tried to muster support from various of the pro-government militias in Benghazi—which in part accounts for the delay—but none seemed willing to come to their aid.

It took that six-man team a good twenty-five minutes to drive the short distance to the Mission compound. This is largely because they would run into the same kind of resistance that Massoud and I would encounter—namely, scores of Shariah gunmen and their gun trucks, equipped with heavy weaponry. Roadblocks had been put in place to stop any relief force getting to the Mission, and—unlike Massoud and myself driving a local vehicle—the Annex team in their armored SUVs were highly distinctive from some distance away.

At one point the Annex team stopped to try to convince militia members—most likely 17th February Militia, who were massed around the battleground—to join them in their efforts to retake the Mission. Those requests were denied by the militias, and the QRF team were forced to move ahead with no help and taking savage fire as they drew closer to the Mission compound.

The sheer level of hostile fire that had engulfed the Mission was fearsome, but there was no way that Ty Woods and his fellows were turning aside from their tasking. At the same time, Massoud and I were converging on the battleground. After working there for so long I figured I knew of a secret route into the compound, and I was intent on launching my own rescue attempt.

This was the start of a night of sheer hell. It was a night upon which Americans would die in the most horrific of ways, and for reasons that to this day both escape and enrage me. It was a night upon which I would fight my way into the besieged Benghazi Mission three times over, and largely against orders, in an effort to find my American brothers-in-arms and to stand with them against the terrorist horde. It was a night on which I should have died many times over, along with my American buddies.

This was the blackest of nights—one that would lead me to find the American Ambassador to Libya lying dead and without a fellow American by his side. I'd discover him with a tiny cut to his forehead, but otherwise looking more or less unharmed—yet he had been murdered in the most inhuman of ways. In short, this was a night of criminal failure, of individual acts of unrivaled heroism, and of untold savagery and murderous intent on the part of America's enemies.

But when I first deployed to Benghazi, I had not the slightest inkling about the nightmare that was coming.

CHAPTER ONE

April 5, 2012,
Tripoli, Libya

No one had told me about the money. It was only once I'd flown in to the Libyan capital, Tripoli, that I got the warning. Steve O'Dair was the guy who briefed me. He was a fellow private security operator, working "the circuit" as it's called among those in the world of private military operations. Right now he was the Libyan country manager for Blue Mountain, the British private military company (PMC) that had contracted me to do the present job.

We met at the plush and glitzy Corinthian Hotel, in downtown Tripoli. With its space-age towers and golden arches the Corinthian would look more at home in Las Vegas, as opposed to Libya. Granted, there were a few bullet holes in the outer stonework, testifying to the recent fighting that had convulsed the country—fighting aimed at toppling Libya's forty-five-year rule by Colonel Muammar Gaddafi—but otherwise the place looked pristine and gleaming.

We had a coffee and chatted a bit in the glitzy, palm-fronded lobby, and then Steve sprung the surprise on me—*the thirty-thousand-dollar surprise*. Blue Mountain had two dozen Libyan guards working at the American Embassy complex in Benghazi, Libya's second city. I'd come here to put that guard force through three weeks of intensive training, to lick them into shape.

Trouble was, their wages were overdue, and the only way to get the cash to them in post-Gaddafi Libya was for someone to carry it on their person on the flight to Benghazi. As I was about to fly onward to Libya's second city, Steve had got it into his head that I'd be up for just such a mission.

It was less than six months since the Libyan "democratic revolution" had toppled Gaddafi's regime—the dictator having been captured, tortured, and executed by those who had seized him. Blue Mountain was one of the few PMCs licensed to operate in Libya, and the company ran Tripoli's Palm City residential complex, one popular with international businesspeople, United Nations workers, and the world's media reporting on the story of Libya post-Gaddafi.

It was my first time in Libya, and after seeing the news reports of the recent fighting I had expected the capital to be far more war-torn. On the cab ride from the airport to the Corinthian I'd seen a handful of government buildings that had been turned into piles of twisted metal and shattered rubble, one of which the driver had pointed out gleefully was all that remained of Gaddafi's Tripoli palace. Each had been flattened by a NATO air strike of impressive surgical precision, and there was little wider damage.

The NATO smart bombs had gone down as they are designed to—right on target. I'd soldiered in the Balkans, across Iraq and Afghanistan, and I'd been expecting a similar level of battle damage here as I'd seen in places like Sarajevo, Baghdad, or Kabul. But apart from the occasional NATO demolition of specific targets, the impression I got was that it was business as usual in Libya's capital city.

Yet as Steve was quick to point out, and as Blue Mountain's boss had warned me back in Britain, the toppling of Gaddafi had ushered in no benign new regime. The scores of rebel militias that had united under one cause—that of toppling the dictator—had just as quickly become disunited once Gaddafi was gone. At its simplest, Libya post-Gaddafi had become one massive power grab, with each militia vying to seize control of whatever moneymaking means it could.

As one of the worst examples—at least as far as I was concerned, now that I'd been asked to carry a serious chunk of cash on my next flight—the so-called Zintan Brigade had taken control of the airports. A militia that was best known for capturing Saif al-Islam Gaddafi—one of the last Gaddafi family members then at large—was now running security, customs, immigration, and passport control at some of Libya's major transport hubs.

Unsurprisingly, it had proven a recipe for insecurity and chaos, not to mention massive racketeering. My first sight of one of the Zintan mob had been upon my arrival at Tripoli International Airport. A guy dressed in gray combat-style pants, a skintight white T-shirt, and a wide-brimmed khaki jungle hat slung around his neck had been standing guard as I'd disembarked from my flight from London.

I'd noticed the Nike runners on his feet, the thick, half-length beard, and the worn AK-47 assault rifle slung over the shoulder. But most of all I'd noticed the guy's predatory, wolflike gaze, as he'd scrutinized the new arrivals for what I had to presume was lucrative prey. And that encapsulated the problem with me being the cash mule for Blue Mountain: I'd be going through Tripoli airport carrying thirty thousand dollars, while under the scrutiny of the Zintan Brigade.

Moving around with large bundles of cash wasn't so uncommon in the world of private security operations. It stands to reason that in many war zones or postconflict countries the rule of law has broken down, and the banking system with it. In such situations the only way to pay a local guard force is invariably in cash dollars.

In the past I'd carried a lot more than the thirty thousand Steve had asked me to take. Presuming it was in one-hundred-dollar bills, it would make a bundle less than an inch thick. I could slip it inside an envelope and carry it on my person, or I could conceal it inside one of the books in my hand luggage. I was plowing through the memoirs of Britain's iconic wartime leader, Winston Churchill, and one of those tomes could easily hide thirty thousand in hundred-dollar bills. Like that it would be all but undetectable and shouldn't prove a major drama.

Or so I thought.

It was Mohammed, one of Blue Mountain's local drivers, who came to take me to the airport. Shortly after I finished chatting with Steve I slipped into the rear of Mohammed's smart American Mustang, and we set off to catch my flight. Mohammed spoke excellent English and we got down to business right away.

"So, Mohammed, where's the cash?" I was expecting him to pass me an envelope.

Instead he jerked a thumb at the vehicle's rear. "In the back, my friend."

I glanced around, but all I could see was a large plastic travel bag lying on the floor.

"Where in the back?" I asked.

"There in the bag, where d'you think?"

"Which bag?"

He eyed me in the rearview mirror, irritably, like I was the one being difficult. "You haven't seen it? The bag lying at your feet."

I reached forward and unzipped it. Maybe there was an envelope of cash lying on top of a load of other Blue Mountain equipment. But no. The bag was stuffed to the brim with what I recognized immediately as the local currency—Libyan dinar. Unfortunately, thirty thousand dollars' worth of Libyan dinar fills your average travel bag to bursting—just like this one was now.

It was my turn to eye Mohammed. "*Libyan dinar.* No one said it was thirty thousand dollars in jingly money. What the hell am I supposed to do with that?"

Mohammed laughed, like it was all a big joke. "No problem! No problem, my friend."

"*No problem.* How d'you suggest I get this lot past the Zintan Brigade?"

Mohammed waved his hand dismissively. "No problem. It will be fine."

It was easy for him to say that, when he wasn't the one tasked to carry it. Thirty thousand dollars in whatever currency was the equivalent of several years' wages for someone like Mohammed, or one of the Zintan Brigade fighters. I'd heard the horror stories about what was going down at Libya's airports under their control. Two weeks earlier a private security guy had tried going through the airport with one hundred thousand dollars in cash. They'd pulled him aside and taken the money, and he'd been lucky to escape with his life.

The Zintan Brigade hailed from the Zintan region of Libya, being a loose coalition of some twenty tribal groups. They'd been brought into the capital by the Tripoli Brigade in some kind of trade-off: Zintan got the airports while the Tripoli Brigade got all the government offices. But at night the city was alive with gunfire as the rival militias fought each other in what amounted to turf wars. To a Westerner they all looked the same: Zintan, Tripoli, whatever—they all wore a hodgepodge of military equipment, plus tight T-shirts, and carried the ubiquitous AK-47. But somehow they knew how to distinguish between each other at a glance, which had to come in useful when engaging in firefights.

I glared at the bag stuffed full of dinar lying at my feet. Mohammed was prattling on about this and that, as if the small matter of a giant travel bag bulging with cash wasn't an issue. There was no way that I could refuse to carry the money. I knew how badly we needed it at the Benghazi Embassy, and more to the point I had a huge amount invested personally in the job I was tasked with doing here.

I'd taken the Benghazi contract for several reasons, the most crucial of which was Lewis. For the first time in thirty-seven years—the last twenty of which I'd spent soldiering in the world's trouble spots—I had someone else depending on me now: *my son*. Lewis had only just turned one. He was the most important thing in my life and the best thing that had ever happened to me. Of course, his mother and my partner, Laura, came a very close second.

It's all too easy to go dodging bullets in danger zones when you're a one-man band. In fact, the work is hugely addictive. Nothing comes close to the buzz of getting shot at and surviving. It makes you feel so incredibly *alive*. But having Lewis had changed all that. I'd taken the present contract because Libya post-Gaddafi promised to be far less risk-laden than working in Iraq or Afghanistan, or taking some of the antipiracy missions that I'd worked on recently, acting as an armed escort to ships plying the lawless waters off Somalia.

During the past two years I'd led scores of security teams on antipiracy operations. We'd been under serious attack three times, with Somali pirates doing their utmost to board our vessel and take us and the ship's crew hostage. Working at the U.S. Embassy's Benghazi Mission promised to be a far less risky undertaking, or so I reasoned. Having worked directly for the U.S. military and diplomatic clients, I knew how impressive the Americans' security setups tended to be. The Benghazi operation was bound to be a veritable Fort Knox, and I'd promised Laura I'd be safe as could be on this one.

The other key reason I'd taken the job—and why I couldn't refuse to carry the money—was Robert Smith, Blue Mountain's boss. I'd been brought up by a single mother in an impoverished housing project in the Welsh mountains—Wales being one of the countries that make up the United Kingdom of Great Britain (along with England, Scotland and Northern Ireland). Robert hailed from the same Welsh valley as I did, and I respected him more than just about any man in the world. I guess he was something of the father to me that I'd never had.

One of the few careers open to a boy who grew up in my hometown was joining the British Army. I'd signed up at sixteen and spent ten years soldiering in the Royal Corps of Signals, a communications-specialist unit of Britain's armed forces. But with the sport of rugby being such a strong tradition in Wales—a country with just three million inhabitants fields one of the top international rugby teams—I was snapped up to play for the British Army.

Rugby is something akin to American football, although it's played with a larger ball and with no helmets, pads, or protection of any sort. It is intensely physical and brutally tough. I'm only five feet, ten inches tall, but I'm half as wide, which is the kind of physique that made me ideal for playing as a hooker in the scrum—the guy who swings forward with his feet to grab the ball once it's thrown in.

One year we were playing the British Special Forces Team, which is made up of players from the Special Air Service (SAS)— the equivalent of Delta Force—and the Special Boat Service (SBS)—the equivalent of the Navy SEALs. Needless to say, our opponents were some of the fittest, hardest, toughest soldiers in the world. Normally we managed to beat them, but we'd win by dint of our skills only—the Special Forces boys being all over us in terms of fitness and physicality.

The opposing packs had gone for a scrum-down, locking horns in a contest of sheer power and strength. As we butted heads I'd made an appropriately insulting comment to my opposite number, but in Welsh, the national language of Wales. I'm a native Welsh speaker, English being my second language, and I didn't for one moment expect my opponent to understand. He was a couple of inches shorter than me, looked to be around thirty years old to my twenty, and he had a rock-hard barn door of a physique.

"You might be Special Forces," I growled, "but you're still full of shit. I'm gonna snap your neck . . ."

He fired right back at me: "Go screw your mother, asshole."

He was a fellow Welsh speaker! I was amazed.

We got talking as the game progressed, and it turned out he hailed from the same Welsh valley as me—Carmarthen. After the match we made our way to the bar and spent the rest of the evening downing beers and swapping stories. We stayed in touch and by the time I got out of the military in 2003, Robert had set up his own PMC—Blue Mountain Group. The company is named after a line from James Elroy Flecker's poem "The Golden Journey to Samarkand," which is the unofficial collect of Britain's Special Air Service Regiment: "Beyond that last blue mountain barred with snow . . ."

If I'd had a tough childhood, Robert's had been tougher. But what I admired about him most was that he had made it into *several* Special Forces outfits during his time in the military. Most soldiers struggled to make it into even the one. Robert had served in the British military's equivalent of the U.S. Marine Corps, the SEALs, the CIA Special Activities Division, and Delta Force. The man was a living legend in such circles, although if you met him you'd never have guessed it. He was good to everyone, no matter who they were or their background, and polite and courteous to a fault.

There's always a danger that if you work with your closest buddies and you mess up, it messes up the friendship. For that reason I'd always avoided working for Blue Mountain. But right now Robert had landed the security job to die for: he'd been contracted by the U.S. State Department to provide a guard force to the Benghazi Embassy. Needless to say it was a massive coup. If it was successful, it could go massive. But if it failed, it could spell the end of

Blue Mountain. The stakes were as high as they could be, and in that context he'd trusted me to go sort out his Libyan guard force. I'd run larger security contracts than this, but rarely with so much riding on it.

Robert had put a massive amount of trust in me, and the last thing I was about to do was let him down—hence the thirty thousand dollars' worth of Libyan dinar had to make it through the airport. That having been decided, I unloaded the cash from the travel bag and stuffed it into my khaki green day pack. Hopefully, with that slung over my shoulder it would be a little less obvious what I was carrying.

Having watched me repack the cash, Mohammed made a wiseass remark from the front seat. "Okay, so you've made sure you counted it all?"

Very funny. Mohammed the joker. I ignored him.

We were five minutes out from the airport, and I was steeling myself for whatever was to come. I was ninety percent certain I was going to get pulled. In truth, there was no way to hide such a large volume of cash. I put a call through to Steve on my cell phone, which I'd fitted out with a Libyan sim card so I could make such calls via the local network.

"I'm nearing the airport. One thing, mate: you never told me it was a suitcase full of Libyan dinar."

"No, no, mate, you'll be all right," he reassured me. "If the worst comes to the worst just hand it over."

British soldiers use the word *mate* the same way Americans use the words *buddy* or *dude*. That, it seemed, was the best advice Steve had for me. It was easy for him to take that stance. It wasn't his best friend who owned the company, a man to whom I had unshakable loyalty.

Mohammed dropped me at the airport. He cracked the driver's window. "Have a nice trip—hope to see you again soon."

I didn't detect a great deal of sincerity in those words. I wouldn't put it past the guy to be readying himself to call his friends in the Zintan Brigade and give them a heads-up that a white-eye foreigner was coming through, a green day pack stuffed full of a king's ransom in dinar slung over his shoulder. If he made that call and negotiated a third cut of the cash for himself, he'd earn a year or more of his present wages in a matter of minutes.

But either way, there was no going back now.

I stepped into the chaos of the airport. The check-in desk for the Benghazi flight was under siege. I decided to go get a brew and wait for the crowd to die down. As I made for the nearest café I spotted a familiar figure. It was Stuart Beevor, a buddy of mine from the private security world. Stuart was ex–Parachute Regiment—the equivalent of the U.S. Rangers—and he was a top operator. I knew he was here in Libya working for another PMC, but it was sheer chance to run into each other at the airport like this.

Stu and I were great friends, having worked together in Iraq. He was well-known in our circles, if for no other reason than the epic battle he'd fought when still in the "Paras," as the Parachute Regiment is known. In 2003 he'd flown in with a helicopter-load of Paras to rescue six British soldiers who were under assault from hundreds of Iraqi insurgents in the town of Majar al-Kabir. As it came in to land, the twin-rotor Chinook heavy-lift helicopter was hit by heavy ground fire, and Stu had taken three rounds in his back.

The Chinook was practically shot down, and with Stuart very seriously injured they'd lost their sergeant, the key commander as such a unit goes in to battle. At that moment they'd have had every right to call off the mission, but fellow British soldiers were surrounded and in desperate need of help. Stuart had told his men to get out there and do their job, leaving him and two other wounded to be treated as best they could on the bullet-ridden helo.

The lightly armed Paras had fought their way into Majar al-Kabir and successfully broken the siege, only to find that the six British soldiers they'd come to rescue had been overrun and executed by the Iraqi gunmen. In due course Stu was medically discharged from the Army, after which he'd taken several years to recover from his wounds. But once a Para, always a Para: he was now back on his feet and working the private security circuit.

I made the sign for a brew—hand in front of my face, tilting it like supping from a mug—and we converged on the café. Over small glasses of Libyan coffee—thick, sugary-sweet, and strong— we had a good catch-up. Stu is normally hopelessly scruffy, but today he was dressed smartly in chinos and a button-down shirt. It turned out he was collecting an important client from the airport. He'd been here since the start of the revolution, and as far as Libya was concerned Stu was an old pro.

"So, you're off to Benghazi," he remarked, "birthplace of the revolution and all that . . ."

Benghazi being the largest city and historical power base in traditionally restive eastern Libya, it had been the launch point for the 2011 uprising against Colonel Gaddafi's rule. The city had long been seen as a focus of resistance to his regime, though some claimed it was also a hotbed of Islamic extremism.

"I got a couple of good guys down there right now," Stu continued. "Word is there's a hard-line militia called the Shariah Brigade turning up on the streets. My guys figure they're coming out of Derna, which is jam-full of Al Qaeda types. They're even trying to implement Shariah law."

I rolled my eyes. "Sound like another Mosul in the making," I said. Mosul is the northern Iraqi city where Stu and I had served for years as private security operators, and it had proved a heavy posting. "I thought Benghazi was where the revolution started, so it'd be full of the good guys?"

Stu shrugged. "You'd think so. But no. Most Western companies pulled out of there before the revolution, due to insecurity. They're reluctant to return even now." Stu scribbled down the numbers of a couple of local guys he used if he ever needed anything done in Benghazi. "If you're in the shit, phone these boys.

I'll let them know you'll be there for a while, so they'll know who you are if you call."

"Cheers. Will do."

He nodded at my bulging green rucksack. "So, what's with the bag?"

"Thirty thousand dollars' worth of Libyan dinar. Wages for the guard force down at Benghazi."

I saw his face drop. "No, no, no, mate—this is bad shit. Listen, as soon as those Zintan Brigade lot ask for it—'cause, trust me, they will—you hand it over, okay? No messing, or it and you will disappear. Don't be a hero, just hand it over, okay?"

I gave a brief nod. "Yeah. Okay."

I had a great deal of respect for Stu, but he knew me well, and he was well acquainted with my ultra-stubborn, loyal-to-a-fault nature.

"Listen, mate, I mean it," he continued. "Just give it over. People have gone missing for that kind of money, so just hand it over." He paused. "What the hell were you thinking, anyway, trying to get through with that?"

I told him how the cash had been dumped on me at the last minute. I explained how I didn't have much of a choice but to give it a go, for our Benghazi guard force was overdue for getting paid.

"Whatever, mate, trust me—it ain't worth dying for." Stu drained the last of his coffee. "When you get to Benghazi give me a shout. I want to be sure you made it, plus I can fill you in on all the int from down there."

Int is military-speak for intelligence. By now Stu was sure to have a network of sources all across the country, which could prove very useful. We parted company promising to speak in a couple of hours' time.

I made my way to the check-in desk, which by now was blissfully empty. I was flying business class, and as they processed me I could see Stu shaking his head at me worriedly. He watched me all the way to the first security scanner, at which point I had to slip off the green day pack and dump it on the conveyor.

I walked through the security arch trying to keep my cool. The Zintan Brigade guy sitting on the far side let me reclaim the day pack, but as I did so he glanced up at me and smiled. I could read the look in his eyes: *he knew.* I grabbed the bag, slung it over my shoulder, and said "Shokran"—Arabic for "thank you." As I turned toward the stairs leading to departures, I saw him pull out his cell phone. No doubt about it, he was phoning through a warning to the next guys.

I made my way up the stairs feeling almost sick with nerves. What would I say to Robert if I lost the cash? What were we going to pay the Libyan guards with, if the money was taken? And if we weren't able to pay them, was the Benghazi contract about to come crashing down around our ears? We were still on the State Department's two-month probationary period, during which time they could cancel the contract at a moment's notice. In fact, Blue Mountain had won the business for the simple reason it was one of only two companies with a license to run private security operations in Libya. We were treading on thin ice as it was, without having a guard force in open revolt over unpaid wages.

The second security check was just prior to the boarding gate. I could see five Zintan Brigade guys up ahead clustered around the scanners, dressed in a ragtag of assorted half-uniforms. Five sets of eyes were glued to the day pack as I swung it into the scanner. I stepped through the body arch and went to grab the bag as if all was as it should be. As I shouldered it, a small, skinny guy about five feet, six inches tall stepped forward and blocked my way.

"Sir, you follow me, please." He gestured to a corridor that lay off to one side. "This way, please."

I felt another figure behind me. I glanced around and there was a monster of a Libyan taking up the rear. He was six feet four and barrel-chested, if a little overweight. Still, the only way to beat him would be to get in close and get him down on the ground quickly. More important, he had an AK-47 slung over his shoulder.

"Sure. No problem," I told the skinny guy, who was obviously in charge here.

I followed him in a tense and heavy silence. We turned this way and that, twisting down a series of corridors. I felt as if we'd been walking through the airport for a good thirty minutes, time was dragging so slowly. Then Skinny Guy stopped before a steel door, unlocked it, and walked in.

He held the door open for me. "Come, come."

I stepped inside and felt as much as heard the big guy slam the metal door behind me.

"Sit down," Skinny Guy ordered.

There was only the one bare desk and chair, so I knew where I was to sit. I plunked myself down, the bag of cash on the floor between my feet. Little and Large didn't sit down. Skinny Guy stood before me, ready to start the questioning. The big guy stood behind me where I couldn't quite see him, but could feel him staring at the back of my head.

"Where are you going?" Skinny Guy began.

"Benghazi."

"What for?"

"I'm a paramedic. I'm going to Benghazi to train some of the Red Cross staff, and pay some of their wages."

Whenever I was traveling on private security contracts I was always a "paramedic" to the locals. Being a medic didn't seem to rub them the wrong way so much as being a private military contractor might.

He indicated the bag. "What is in there? Please, place it on the table."

Here we go, I told myself. I had no choice but to obey.

Skinny Guy nodded at the bag. "Please, empty the contents."

I started to haul out the big slabs of Libyan dinar. Skinny Guy was trying to act as if all this money was no big deal to him, like he'd seen this amount and more every day since they'd taken over at the airport.

"How much?" he asked me, once I was done unloading.

"Thirty thousand dollars' worth."

"What for?"

"To pay the Red Cross workers."

"Okay," he announced. "You can go."

I started to put the money back into the bag. *Christ, they couldn't be letting me go that easily.*

"No: *you* can go," he snapped. "The fucking money—it stays!"

I shook my head. "Sorry, no, I can't do that."

"Listen to me," he hissed, "you leave the money."

I was trying to avoid making eye contact, so as not to provoke him, while at the same time standing my ground. "I can't leave it. I signed for the money . . ."

"You don't seem to understand," he snarled. "You leave the money because nasty things can happen in here. Very nasty things. So, you fucking leave the money."

I was still staring at the floor as I continued to argue. From out of nowhere he stepped forward and punched me right in the face. For a small guy he swung with power and hit as hard as he could. I'm used to how Arabs tend to fight. They have a way of slapping each other open-handed, as opposed to using the clenched fist of a Westerner. This guy was different. His bunched knuckles caught me just above the jaw. My head snapped back and for a moment I saw stars. I spat out a mouthful of blood as Skinny Guy turned away to his side of the desk. He was nursing his right hand, and I figured the punch must have hurt.

In a fair fight I'd flatten the guy with one blow, then rip his head off with my bare hands, but I was powerless with Jaws standing behind me cradling his AK-47. Skinny Guy turned to face me again. I spat out some more saliva mixed with blood.

"Right, I offer you a deal." He gestured at the heap of Libyan dinar. "We keep half. You take half."

"You're getting fuck-all."

I had no idea where that had come from. I was so angry that he'd punched me and that I couldn't fight back, and the words had just come from out of nowhere. Somewhere in the back of my mind there was also a little, stubborn voice reminding me that today, April 5, was my thirty-ninth birthday, and I was having to put up with this kind of shit from the likes of him.

Skinny Guy exploded. "Right, that's fucking it! I've tried being reasonable! We're taking it all! You—fuck off! Get out while you still can."

Without saying a word I stood up and pulled out my cell phone. I pressed the last-call redial. I wasn't sure which number I was dialing and I didn't really care. This was a piece of pure theater and it was all about ratcheting up the pressure and calling the guy's bluff.

"What are you doing?" he screamed, angry spittle flecking his lips. "Who are you phoning?"

"The British ambassador."

I saw a moment's doubt flash through his eyes. "Why?"

I shrugged. "It's his money you're stealing."

I still wasn't making eye contact, in part because I didn't want him to see that I was bluffing. Without warning he sprang forward and punched me for a second time in exactly the same spot. I was standing with a wide, boxer's stance, so I didn't so much as flinch, but boy did it hurt. As I spat out yet more blood he snatched my cell phone and slammed it down on the table. He was practically dancing around with rage now.

I saw him pull a pistol out of his belt, cock it, and place it on the desk, the muzzle pointed at my groin area. Keeping one hand on the weapon he yelled out some rapid orders at Jaws, in Arabic. Jaws came around from behind me and stood shoulder to shoulder with Skinny Guy, as he continued to jabber away furiously. If I took a punch from Jaws I knew it wasn't going to be pretty and that I probably was going down.

I can understand Arabic pretty well, but at the speed Skinny

Guy was talking most of it was going over my head. I felt in my pocket for my wallet. I fished inside and pulled out my British Embassy ID card. It was three years out of date, and it was from when I'd run a private security team for the Foreign and Commonwealth Office—the British equivalent of the State Department—in war-torn Afghanistan. On first glance it looked fairly impressive, with the British Embassy's coat of arms, plus the red, white, and blue Union Jack flag.

I flicked it down on the desk, knowing that this was my last-gasp chance. Most Arabs who can speak English can't actually read it, just as I can speak Arabic but can barely read a word. With the alphabets being so completely different—our own being Roman lettering, Arabic being Abjad script—reading and writing are the real challenge. Arabic is even written the other way around—from right to left—from how we write.

I was banking on the fact that Skinny Guy would recognize the symbols—the flag, the coat of arms—and miss the fact that it was an ID card for the wrong country and well out of date. If I'd misjudged him, I was finished, but this was last-chance saloon kind of stuff right now.

Skinny Guy tightened his grip on the pistol. He glared at the ID card, then back at me. "What is this?"

"British Embassy ID card. Like I said, you steal the money it's the British Ambassador you'll have to answer to."

He picked up the pistol and for a moment I thought—*Here it comes, I'm gonna get pistol-whipped.* It was a big, heavy, Soviet-era Makarov, and a few blows from that would be seriously bad news. Pistol-whipping breaks bones, and I wasn't keen on having my face rearranged for the sake of thirty thousand dollars in Libyan dinar. For a second or so Skinny Guy seemed to weight the weapon in his hand, before he inverted it and slipped it back into the holster at his side.

He stared at me. "Go. Get out. *Now.*"

I started stuffing the money back into the bag, cursing the fact there was so much that it was a struggle to make it fit. I kept my eyes downcast so as not to give him the slightest excuse to change his mind. I heard Jaws open the door behind me. I feared it could be one last act to really mess with my head—show me the way to freedom, before kicking seven bales of shit out of me.

I turned to leave. "Shokran," I muttered. Thank you.

I moved toward the big guy, my heart beating like a machine gun.

The door stayed open and I slipped through, practically sprinting down the corridor.

CHAPTER TWO

I turned the final corner leading to the departure gate, green day pack griped tight to my shoulder. A crowd of people was milling about—my fellow passengers. Thank God I hadn't missed the flight. I wanted out of Tripoli as soon as. I couldn't wait to get to Benghazi and the Embassy, where we'd have a screen of American security all around, and I'd be away from the power-crazed, gun-toting militias.

But as I strode toward the gate, in every direction I looked people were staring. My fellow passengers were gazing at me mouths agape. Did they all somehow know about the money? I wondered. I was starting to get paranoid. But no doubt, people were staring. I felt like saying: *What the hell are you lot looking at?*

I head a voice speaking in what sounded like an Australian accent. "Best get to the toilet, mate. You've got blood all over your face. That's why everyone's eyeballing you." The speaker was a crew-cut white guy in his early forties. He nodded at a bathroom that was adjacent to the gate.

I thanked him for the tip. In the bathroom mirror I could see why I'd got all the looks. My face was a mess of split lips and dried blood. I filled a sink with warm water and did my best to sponge it off. I'd taken worse beatings than this and more often than not on the rugby pitch, but I hated the fact that such scum as those Zintan Militia boys had had the power of life or death over me.

My face cleaned up a little, I called Steve, the country manager. "I'm at the departure gate and I've still got the money," I told him, "but I've taken a beating in the process."

He assured me that Dan Barnfield, the Blue Mountain Benghazi rep, would be waiting for me at the other end, and that there were no more security checks ahead of me. I guessed he'd been banking on the fact that I wouldn't hand the cash over without a fight, so there was a good chance it would make it through.

I returned to the gate, and got a nod from the Aussie guy who'd given me the heads-up. I figured he had a good idea what had just happened, and he was letting me know I looked half presentable again. A few minutes later the flight was called and I was settling down in my seat for the hour-long trip to Benghazi.

I felt a wave of relief wash over me as we took to the skies. Until the moment of takeoff things could still have gone horribly wrong. Had Skinny Guy realized the bluff I'd just pulled, I could have been hauled off the flight and I'd have taken a horrific beating or worse, plus the money would have been gone. As it was I'd made it through with a mixture of luck, front, and pure guile.

As I relaxed into the flight, I reflected upon the fact that that was about the worst Libya was likely to throw at me. Compared to Iraq and Afghanistan, this place should be a breeze. There had been few if any IEDs—improvised explosive devices; roadside bombs or car bombs—and no suicide bombings here yet. Presumably, we—the Brits and Americans—were seen as being on the side of right, which wasn't always the case in Iraq or Afghanistan.

It was our NATO warplanes that had bombed Colonel Gaddafi's forces into oblivion, and our Special Forces soldiers who had helped battle his troops on the ground. It was our governments that had armed the rebel militias—though how wise that had been I was starting to doubt, especially after my airport beating.

Even so, in Libya we should be seen as those who'd helped topple a decades-long dictatorship, and by rights that should make us and the Libyan people the best of friends.

My expectations of the Benghazi Embassy were based upon what I'd experienced in other U.S. missions over the years. At the height of the conflict in Iraq, the U.S. Embassy in Baghdad was massive, with hundreds of Americans based there, and it even came complete with fast food outlets like Burger King and Pizza Hut, plus shopping malls. The U.S. Embassy in the Afghan capital, Kabul, is pretty flash as well, with hundreds of staff posted there. I knew the Benghazi Mission wasn't anything like those operations in scale, but still I expected it to be tight and slick.

I figured the Mission, being a small slice of America, would be suitably fortresslike, with security of the type that said to the bad guys—*You are not getting in*. By rights, my Tripoli airport beating should be the worst the present contract held in store for me. Ahead lay a cushy gig training the Libyan guard force, interspersed with all that a U.S. Mission normally has to offer—great food, a top gym, and some fine American colleagues to work with.

Having soldiered alongside most nationalities in the security business, I preferred the Americans even over my fellow Brits. I tend to get on with Americans fantastically. Generally, they are openhearted, genuine, warm, and trusting—especially where the British are concerned—and loyal to a fault. Most have been brought up with guns as a constant in their lives, so they've got great weapons-handling skills, as opposed to the majority of Brits, whose first experience of weaponry is when they join the Army.

The Americans also tend to be less obsessed about unit or cap badge. In the British private security world everyone wants to be able to say they're ex-SAS. The Americans didn't seem to care much what unit you hailed from—they just wanted to be certain you knew how to do your job. They seemed more willing to take an operator at face value. I'd worked a lot with American Special

Forces and they were fantastic. They were matchless soldiers, and they were always happy to pass on their elite experience and specialist skills.

A part of me wondered why the Americans needed a diplomatic mission in Benghazi, when they already had an embassy in Tripoli. But the British and most other key players had established missions there, so I guessed the Americans needed one, too. Benghazi lay in the heart of Libya's oil-producing zone, so in a sense it was where the wealth and the real power lay.

I was being sent in to train a Libyan guard force to secure the American Mission—or at least to augment the Americans based there. I presumed the Libyans would provide the outer ring of defense, with American operators providing an inner core. From my experience of other U.S. missions that was how things were done. I was expecting a tight operation, with a sizable American security contingent and a well-guarded, inviolable perimeter. The challenge was going to be to get the Libyan guards up to such exacting standards, and quickly.

Thankfully, I breezed through arrivals at Benghazi airport with barely a hint of trouble. In fact, there were no passport or baggage checks at all, and I couldn't see that any were being made for the departing passengers, either. If Tripoli International Airport had been dangerous and chaotic, this place was sheer anarchy. It didn't bode well for anyone who might be flying out of the country, myself included, when three weeks from now it came my time to leave.

I'd never worked with Dan Barnfield, Blue Mountain's Benghazi security rep, but I knew him by reputation. He was a good fifteen years older than I, and a grizzled veteran of British Army operations. He'd been best man at the wedding of one of the most famous SAS soldiers of all time—Andy McNab. Dan and Andy has soldiered in the Royal Green Jackets, a tough infantry regiment, and McNab had gone on to undertake one of the most epic missions of the Persian Gulf War.

McNab had commanded an eight-man SAS patrol—call sign Bravo Two Zero—sent into the Iraqi desert to hunt down Saddam Hussein's Scud missiles. They had been compromised when a goatherd had stumbled across their place of hiding. Barely an hour later they'd had half the local population coming after them with guns, not to mention the Iraqi military. The patrol had been scattered and forced to go on the run. Three men died, four were captured, and only one escaped. With Dan Barnfield sharing some of that pedigree, I didn't doubt he was a top operator.

He greeted me with a raised eyebrow. "Good to have you here, mate, but what's with the face?"

I shrugged. "I took a good pasting at Tripoli airport. They were after the money."

He steered me toward a waiting vehicle, shaking his head, worriedly. "Tell me you *have* got it . . . It's a new contract, the first time we're paying them and we're late. It's not even our guard force—it's one we took over from the Americans. But we've still got to pay them, as they're Blue Mountain staff . . ."

"I've got the money," I reassured him. "But they'd better be bloody thankful. I've taken a good beating so they can get paid."

Dan snorted. "Fat chance. They've held a protest outside the Embassy already. They've even sprayed graffiti over the T-walls."

T-walls are concrete barriers used to protect vital installations from explosions.

"Just how late is it?" I asked.

"Twenty-four hours."

"You what? Their wages are a day late and already they're up to that kind of shit?"

Dan looked uncomfortable. "You haven't seen the half of it, mate. Wait till you meet 'em . . ."

He shoveled me into the waiting vehicle, a cream-colored Chrysler. His interpreter-cum-driver was seated at the wheel. He looked very Libyan, but his name was actually Tom Ghazi, and it turned out he had a British mother and a Libyan father. Tom had spent half his life in the United Kingdom and half in Libya, before marrying a Benghazi girl and starting a family here. He looked to be in his mid-thirties, and he was a six-feet-four bear of a man. I was sure he'd prove immensely strong, but at the same time I could tell he was seriously out of shape.

Dan was like an imp beside him. He had to be a good fifty-five years old, with a shock of gray hair, and he had the lean and wiry physique of a runner. But he'd injured his leg on a recent contract, and he was still in some pain and limping badly. It gave the impression that he was older and less fit and capable than he really was.

He settled into the rear seat of the Chrysler and turned to me. "All I can say is—thank fuck you're here and that you've got the money."

I patted the green day pack that lay on the seat between us. "I got it. Let's go tell them it's payday."

Before heading to the Embassy, Tom needed to fuel up the Chrysler. Gas was the equivalent of twenty-five cents a gallon, so it took six dollars to fill her up. That was one of the perks of being an oil-producing nation, I guessed. We set off and I gazed about myself, trying to get a feel for the city and any security risks we might face. Apart from the odd roadblock manned by gun-toting militiamen, there was little to suggest that six months ago this was a city torn apart by civil war.

Quite the reverse seemed to be the case. My overriding impression was one of wealth. The roads were wide, multilane highways crammed full of gleaming vehicles. I spotted top-of-the-line Hummers and Audis, each being one hundred thousand dollars' worth of vehicle. Downtown Benghazi was a mass of glitzy superstores. Tom drove via the aptly named Dubai Street, which was lined with designer-label boutiques. I was amazed to see a Rolex store, plus Armani, Gucci, Bose, and other luxury brand-name outlets. I'd yet to see a single donkey cart like you'd get in Afghanistan. There was clearly a great deal of money here in Benghazi.

We drove past a massive sports stadium that was in the final stages of construction. The cranes hung dinosaur-like over the concrete sarcophagus, and work had obviously come to a standstill. Tom explained that Libyans rarely did any manual labor. Instead, it was all done by Chinese, Koreans, and Bangladeshis. The workers building the stadium had left due to the war, but they were expected back at any moment to finish the construction.

I'd been expecting a lot more gunmen on the streets, and I wasn't getting a particularly bad vibe about the place. Everyone seemed to be going about business as usual—as if toppling Colonel Gaddafi had been but a small blip in the otherwise serious matter of making money and getting ahead. Yet still I didn't feel particularly comfortable about our setup here in Benghazi.

Tom was taking no obvious security precautions as he drove us to the Mission, and it wasn't as if Dan had been able to pass me a weapon just as soon as we were in the vehicle. On just about every contract I'd ever worked you'd get a weapon in your hands from the get-go. But here in Benghazi we were going to have to go about our business *unarmed*. Under Libyan law the only foreign contractors allowed to carry weapons were those doing close protection (CP) work for diplomats. As our role was to train the Libyan guard force, it didn't allow us to carry arms.

If Benghazi turned out to be as benign as my first impressions suggested it might be, perhaps it wasn't going to be too much of an issue. But still, being weaponless didn't make me feel particularly comfortable.

We'd been on the road for a good thirty minutes when the buildings began to thin out. We were clearly entering some kind of upmarket neighborhood. To the left and right were these massive, plush-looking, white-walled villas, set amid lush groves of palm trees. All the vehicles were massive V-8 Mustangs, Chargers, and Hummers, and we had to be in among the real wealth here.

We came to a halt outside one of the white-walled compounds. There was nothing to announce that this was the American Diplomatic Mission in Benghazi. It was indistinguishable from any number of large residences that we'd driven past. I figured they were keeping everything deliberately low-profile, which was fair enough on security grounds. Tom drove past the T-wall blast barrier that funneled any official traffic into the gate, and we parked up at the far side of the entrance on the gravel roadway.

It struck me as odd that we were making our way into the compound on foot. At the entrance to the T-walls there was a manually operated barrier. It stood to reason that at least one member of the Libyan guard force ought to be manning it, so as to check any incoming vehicles, but there was no one to be seen.

I nodded at the deserted barrier. "So where's the guard?"

"Dunno." Dan shrugged. "He should be here."

We walked toward the gate, the T-walls channeling us for twenty yards against the exterior wall of the Mission. It was twelve feet high and of concrete block construction, so good for blocking visibility into the interior, but there were no additional security measures that I could see: no coils of razor wire atop the wall, or security lights, or CCTV cameras facing out at us, or watchtowers. In short, it looked as if it would be easy for a determined force of attackers to scale the wall and get inside.

The gate itself was a large, black steel structure set within an arched gatehouse. It wasn't reinforced as far as I could tell, but at least it was secured with a padlock and chain. To the right was a concrete guard hut, like a small bunker. It could be accessed only from the inside, using a doorway set to one side of the main gate, and the window was barred. But even so it would be easy enough for an attacker to poke an AK-47 assault rifle through the bars and unload on the guard force inside.

But most important, I'd yet to see any sign of the Libyan guard force—*our guard force*—that was supposedly standing security. I glanced through the window. Half a dozen guys were in there drinking tea and playing cards. They were dressed in the standard Libyan male dress—skintight T-shirt, jeans, and trainers. None of them had noticed us. If I had been carrying a weapon and I had wanted to murder them all, it would be like stealing candy from a baby.

Dan tapped on the window. One of the guards glanced up and buzzed us in via the pedestrian gate. We stepped inside and no one so much as saluted us, or even bothered to sign us in. I was starting to get a sense of just what I was up against here. As far as I was concerned these guys were finished. I was going to sack every last one of them and recruit a completely new guard force.

I turned right and poked my head into the guardroom. "So, who's on barrier duty?" I demanded. "Who's supposed to be outside?"

I was speaking English, for there was supposed to be a guard supervisor on every shift who had decent English. That was part of the State Department contract, but no one so much as bothered to volunteer a reply.

I pointed out one guy at random. "Get outside and do your job."

He just stared at me.

"That man—he doesn't speak English," one of his fellows finally volunteered.

"Then you tell him from me: he's to get outside and stand guard, or all five of you can go home."

I was fuming. For all of them to be sitting there having a cup of tea and some laughs when they were supposed to be on duty—I knew already that none of them gave a shit about their supposed tasks. This wasn't standing security at some downtown nightclub or bar: this was *the American Diplomatic Mission*, for Christ's sake.

"Either he gets outside and does his job or you can all sod off home," I repeated.

The guy who I guessed was the guard supervisor translated the basics of what I'd said. The guard I'd ordered outside glared at me sulkily, before slinking out to take up his position at the barrier.

I eyed the supervisor. "Let's get one thing straight: things are gonna change around here. It's going to be very, very different, very, very quickly."

I'd been given free rein by Blue Mountain's boss to do whatever it took to sort out the guard force. We were still within the sixty-day "bedding-in" period, and the State Department could throw us off the contract at any moment, which would mean all of Robert's investment would be down the tubes.

But I knew already that the guards hated me, and I was also wondering what Dan thought of me now.

CHAPTER THREE

I stepped out of the guardroom and surveyed the wider compound. What struck me immediately was how large the place was. It looked to be at least two hundred yards from end to end. Inside the gate were two luxurious-looking villas. The one to our front left was the VIP Villa, where the diplomats would be billeted, Dan explained. It was also the main consular building, with a swimming pool, gardens, patios, and relaxation area.

The smaller building lying immediately to our right was the Quick Reaction Force (QRF) Villa. That, I presumed, was where they'd have the QRF stationed—a force from the U.S. Marine Corps, or a similar elite unit. A mission this size would warrant a dozen such troops, and somehow I was going to have to get the Libyan guard force up to something like their exacting standards. It was going to be one hell of a challenge.

Down the center of the compound ran a wide driveway paved in brick, at the end of which was the rear gate. Parked on the driveway at the far end I could see a lone SUV.

I nodded at it. "That the evacuation vehicle?"

"Yep," Dan confirmed. "Armored SUV."

"Keys?" I queried.

Dan mimed as if he was feeling about in the roof of the SUV. "Where they always are."

"Fuel shutoff?"

Dan reached down like he was grabbing something between his knees. "The usual place."

This was the standard setup for an evacuation vehicle. Keys were kept in it at all times, for obvious reasons. If you had to flee the Embassy under attack, the last thing you needed to be doing was searching for the keys. Beneath the dashboard there would be a simple fuel cutoff switch, which should prevent the bad guys from stealing the vehicle.

To the front of the main consular building was what looked like a vineyard. It was certainly very pretty, with purple-hued grapes hanging from the branches in swollen bunches. But to me it rang alarm bells. It constituted a thick patch of vegetation like the proverbial jungle, and it would provide perfect cover for any force that had scaled the outer perimeter. All a determined enemy would need to do was place a ladder against the wall, clamber over it, drop into the vineyard, sneak through its cover, and they'd be in among the consular staff before anyone could stop them.

I motioned at the greenery. "Nice grapes. But what the hell's a vineyard doing here?"

Dan shrugged. "Yeah, I know. Bad shit."

He showed me around the rest of the Mission. It turned out to be even larger than I'd first imagined. Halfway along its length the main driveway hit a T-junction, a dirt track striking off to the left and leading to a second half of the compound. There was a solid wall about the same height as the exterior one, separating one half of the compound from the other. Hidden away behind the wall was a second group of buildings, which contained the Embassy's Tactical Operations Center (TOC)—in essence the nerve center of all security and communications—a third accommodation villa, plus the Mission's canteen.

With the dividing wall and the thick vegetation, this second half of the Mission was pretty much invisible from the main gate. But as Dan walked me around the compound I felt this growing sense of unease. I'd been sent in to whip the Libyan guards into shape, and the State Department contract stipulated that our guard force was to be *unarmed*. That was it—training and deploying an unarmed Libyan guard force was the full extent of our responsibility. But everywhere I looked I could see gaping holes in the Embassy security setup, ones that were crying out to be plugged.

A wire-mesh inner fence was being erected, but it was going to be next to useless. First off, it was too close to the outer wall. If an attacker climbed on top of the wall, they could jump from there onto the fence, and onward into the compound. It needed to be set farther back to provide a "moat effect"—so that any intruder would be forced to climb it from ground level. Second, it was going to have just the one roll of razor wire atop it, which was nowhere near enough. All an intruder needed to do was throw a carpet over it, jump onto the fence, and carry on from there.

But the worst part was this: even when finished the fence was going to be *incomplete*. For some incomprehensible reason there were significant gaps in it. Whoever had drawn up the design was either incompetent or had been given an impossible brief from which to work. In short, an incomplete security fence would provide incomplete protection. I could see CCTV cameras covering many parts of the compound, and they supposedly fed their images back to monitors in the TOC, but as Dan told me, most of the cameras weren't working.

So far, the security measures here—or rather the lack of them—struck me as woefully inadequate. I'd seen not one guard on duty, nor anyone carrying any kind of a weapon. I could see few if any physical security measures befitting what was supposedly a high-risk U.S. diplomatic facility. Basically, there was little that marked this place out as being any different from any of the other compounds that we had driven by.

I told myself that I had to be missing something. Hidden away in the TOC there was bound to be a contingent of State Department special agents, or Regional Security Officers (RSOs), as they're more commonly called. RSOs are tasked with protecting American diplomatic personnel all over the world, plus their staff and their families. It would be the RSOs' job to draw up a security plan, one designed to deal with threats posed by terrorists, criminals, and other hostile forces.

"So, let's go meet the RSOs," I suggested to Dan. "I guess they're at the TOC?"

"Yeah, but he's out at the minute."

I stopped dead and turned to Dan. "What d'you mean—*he's out? He's out.* What—*there's only one?*"

"Yeah. There's only one. One security guy."

For a moment I stared at Dan in disbelief. I knew from my briefing in England that there were two diplomatic staff here already—an IT guy and a guy I'd been told was the Deputy Chief of Mission here, the person once removed from the Ambassador. How the hell could they have one lone RSO allocated to safeguard an entire diplomatic mission? I'd presumed there would be around eight for a setup this size. In the worst-case scenario you'd need a minimum of three—so two could ride in the vehicle with the client providing mobile security, and one could remain in the TOC, monitoring CCTV and communications.

But one RSO? It was impossible. Presuming that lone individual had to ride with the diplomatic staff when they went out into Benghazi on meetings, he'd have no one to call at the Embassy if they got into trouble. He had no way to raise a warning, or to call for backup if they got hit. In short, he had nothing. The only mutual support he might have was if he could get a call through to the British Embassy, so they might come to his aid.

I was flabbergasted, and doubly so because I knew the strength of the British setup here. Two of my closest buddies were working on the British Embassy's Benghazi close protection team. One was an ex–Royal Marine, so the equivalent of a Marine Corps Force Recon operator, the other an ex-Para. They formed part of a team of eight, equally capable and battle-hardened operators. Yet here we had just the one RSO. Since when did the Americans provide a fraction of the security to their key facilities as the British did?

Nothing was making any sense.

"Okay, let's recap," I said to Dan. "The U.S. Embassy here in Benghazi has just the one security guy, is that it?"

"Yep, just the one RSO."

"That's it—just the one guy?"

"Yep."

"All I can say is the guy must be Captain bloody America if he can secure this place on his own."

"They do have a QRF," Dan volunteered.

"Great. Thank fuck for that. What are they—U.S. Marines or Rangers?"

Dan shifted about uncomfortably. "Neither. They're Seventeenth February Militia."

"You—are—fucking—kidding me." I spat out the words slowly, and in total disbelief. "You're saying the same kind of people who tried to rob me at the airport are the Embassy's QRF?"

Dan nodded. "Militia."

"What the hell? How many?"

"Four. And it's worse than that. You wait till you see them."

I was stunned into total silence.

The 17th February Militia had fought in and around Benghazi to drive out Gaddafi's forces. They'd received significant military aid from the British, French, and American governments, but it was the Qataris who had given them the most sophisticated military hardware, including heavy machine guns and surface-to-air missiles. Yet in spite of being so well armed, they had performed poorly in battles against Gaddafi's military. In reality, it was NATO air strikes and our Special Forces that had toppled Gaddafi's regime.

And now that the revolution was over, there was little to distinguish the 17th February Militia from any of the other militias, including those who had tried to rob me at Tripoli airport.

Yet they were the QRF.

I was struggling to get my head around all that Dan had told me, but there was no escaping the fact that the American Mission in Benghazi had just one lone American protecting it. I couldn't stop swearing. A string of curses erupted from my lips. I'd been slammed about by a bunch of thuggish, corrupt militia at the airport, risking my life to get the wages here for a bunch of useless, ungrateful local guards, it was my birthday, and now this . . .

"Dan, tell me you're joking," I practically begged him.

"Sorry, mate, I'm not. It is what it is."

Back in 2007 and 2008 I'd run a twenty-man security team in Iraq made up mostly of Brits, Europeans, and Americans. We worked for Erinys, a PMC contracted by the U.S. Army Corps of Engineers (U.S. ACE), those who were tasked with building hospitals and prisons across Iraq's Northern Sector—an area encompassing Tikrit, Mosul, Kirkuk, Tal Afar, and Kurdistan. Ours was one of the largest security contracts ever awarded in Iraq, and we were tasked to secure visiting VIPs and U.S. State Department officials.

In Afghanistan later I'd been security team leader for G4S Secure Solutions, contracted to the British Foreign and Commonwealth Office in war-torn Helmand Province. Our tasks had included securing visiting diplomats and heads of state, and operating closely with the U.S. Marine Corps, with whom we'd been in several fierce firefights against the Taliban.

In short, I was an experienced security professional and I knew how things should be done. It was in that light that the Benghazi Embassy setup so shocked me. The physical defenses that should have been in place were all but nonexistent, and there was one lone American tasked to defend the entire Mission. It was mind-boggling.

I glanced at my watch. It was past one o'clock and I'd not eaten since an early breakfast back in Tripoli. "Okay, mate, fancy showing me the canteen," I remarked to Dan. "I mean, they do have a kitchen and cook, don't they? Or don't tell me—they get the locals to send a burger van around?"

Dan gave a short bark of a laugh. No matter what, you had to try to keep your sense of humor.

The canteen lay adjacent to the TOC in the far half of the compound. Inside there were three dining tables, a large plasma-screen TV, a leather sofa set before it, and a massive fridge loaded with soft drinks. To one side were the hot plates, plus a counter laden with homemade cakes, biscuits, and chocolate. The kitchen lay off to one side, and there were two bedrooms for any visiting RSOs—not that there ever seemed to be any, Dan added.

The place seemed to be deserted, but there was bound to be some food on the go. There always was at every American base or diplomatic mission I'd ever worked on before. I could hear someone banging about in the kitchen. I figured I'd load up on the cakes while I waited for the staff to serve whatever was for lunch. But as I went to grab a muffin Dan stopped me.

"Er . . . We're not supposed to eat in here."

I did a double take. The one thing Americans were always faultless with was their hospitality.

"Sorry, we're not allowed to eat here? What's the crack with that, then?"

"Apparently, we're not budgeted to eat on-site."

"You are kidding me. Come on, mate, money doesn't come into it with the Americans."

Dan shrugged. "Apparently, they're not budgeted to feed any of us."

This really didn't add up.

Dan offered to show me around the TOC. We went in via the main entrance and took a right into the Operations Room. There were five workstations with computers, but only one terminal was occupied. There was a local girl dressed in a traditional robe and hijab—a Muslim headscarf—tapping away at a keyboard. She greeted us in a friendly enough way, and explained that she was one of the Embassy secretaries.

At the rear of the Ops Room was a row of lockers, which contained the Embassy's weaponry and ammo. They were kept locked and to be opened only in an emergency. It went without saying that the lone RSO had the only key, and right now he was out on Embassy business—so if there was an emergency we had no way to break out any of the guns.

Opposite the makeshift armory was a row of CCTV screens. They looked like high-tech, costly pieces of equipment. The trouble was, none of them seemed to be working. They showed a row of blank screens. Next to the Ops Room was the IT Room, one crammed full of computer stacks, spools of cable, and satellite communications gear. There was a lone figure in there, and it was now that I got to meet my first American at the Benghazi Embassy.

Rick Daltree introduced himself as the Embassy's IT guy. I could tell at once he didn't have a bad bone in his body. We got chatting and it turned out he had just three weeks left here, and then he was getting posted to Sri Lanka. He'd secured a three-year stint at the U.S. Embassy in Colombo, the nation's capital. I'd spent a lot of time in Sri Lanka, it being a convenient starting point for security teams boarding ships sailing into the Indian Ocean and pirate waters.

Rick was being posted there with his wife and kids, and he seemed a little apprehensive about the trouble with the Tamil Tigers, a separatist rebel group in Sri Lanka. I reassured him that the civil war was pretty much finished, and that Colombo was safe. I told Rick how Sri Lankans loved to gamble. I'd not been able to resist a visit to the two Colombo casinos named after famous Las Vegas joints—the "MGM Grand" and the "Mirage."

"I tried to play a little poker in both, but Las Vegas it was not."

Rick laughed. "Yeah, a whole long way from Vegas is my guess."

Rick seemed like a solid, noncomplaining type of guy, and I was about to ask him what the score was about using the Internet, when Dan pulled me to one side.

"We're not allowed to use it," he hissed. "The Internet. It's out of bounds."

I stared at him, incredulous. "There's wireless in here, right? And you're saying we're not allowed to use it?"

"Yep, it's wireless, but we're not allowed to use it," Dan confirmed.

"Look, Dan, there's no security to speak of, no food, no Internet, and the one lone RSO is out on business. It's pretty much pointless us being here. Mind showing me the Blue Mountain villa? We'll come back tomorrow when we can see the RSO, and maybe start to make some kind of headway."

Dan said he was good with that. We left via the main gate, the guard force giving me the daggers. The guy I'd sent out to man the barrier was still there, but sulking heavily, and as far as I was concerned his days were numbered. Tom joined us at his vehicle, and we made the short drive across Benghazi to the Garden City area of town. Garden City is a more modest, residential part of Benghazi, one that had been popular with expats prior to the war. It constituted an area of small but comfortable villas, each with its own compound.

Ours turned out to have double gates and a wall around it up to shoulder height. It would be easy enough to jump over the wall, so security left something to be desired. Inside, every window had heavy bars and the front door was very solid-looking. If someone did try to get to us, at least they'd have a problem breaking into the building itself. But as we had no weapons with which to defend ourselves, if they did get in we were going to be pretty much toast.

I asked Dan the obvious question. "So, do we have any kind of QRF here at the villa?" If we did, we could maybe keep the bad guys out long enough for the QRF to get to us.

"We don't have one, no."

"Not even the Americans?" I asked.

Dan shook his head. "There's only one of them, anyway. We're on our own."

The villa was a two-story affair. The upper floor was locked, and it was full of the owners' belongings. Apparently they had taken off at the start of the revolution, which suggested they were either friends of Gaddafi or at least associated with his regime. The ground floor had a kitchen, a lounge, a bathroom, plus two bedrooms. For the next three weeks this was where I was going to call home.

There was little food in the place, so I got Tom to fetch us some takeout barbecue chicken. Food eaten, Dan and I settled in the lounge for a proper chat. There was no beer in Benghazi, alcohol being pretty much banned, so we made do with tea. The nonexistent security measures at the Embassy were not Dan's fault, or Blue Mountain's for that matter. Even the appalling state of the Libyan guard force wasn't our doing. The present bunch had been recruited by the State Department, a month or more before Blue Mountain got the contract, so we'd inherited the lot. But even so, we needed to massively shake things up.

"No two ways about it, Dan, that lot on duty today—they have to go."

"We can't sack 'em all until we have replacements."

"Fine. So first priority is to get some new guys in. Plus the guys involved in the strikes over wages and the graffiti, they've also got to go."

Dan said he'd call a meeting with Tom and a few of the guards that we could trust, and send out word that we were recruiting.

"Uniforms is the next thing," I added, "just as soon as we've got a decent replacement force."

"The boss has got uniforms en route from the U.K.," Dan told me. "They'll be here in a matter of days."

"Great, 'cause with security the look is the half of the thing . . ."

I asked Dan outright if he'd had some kind of falling-out with the RSO. Nothing else could explain the no-food and no-Internet rules. Dan promised me that he hadn't. It had been like this ever since he'd arrived. But we agreed that something wasn't right here, and the only way to get to the bottom of it was to have a frank chat with the lone American at the Mission.

It was around eight o'clock when Dan told me he was off.

"Where you going?" I asked.

"Bed. I've been up since three A.M. If we aren't on top of this contract within the sixty days, we're finished. I've been working every hour God sends."

It was fair enough. Dan looked exhausted, and he was glad to have another pair of hands here to help. He mentioned there was a security patrol that did the rounds of the villas at night, so not to worry if I heard any noise. I'm not a big sleeper, so I watched TV until around midnight. I retired to bed and was just nodding off when I heard some voices outside. I presumed it was the security that Dan had mentioned, and drifted off into an uneasy sleep.

I woke to the deafening noise of gunshots. They sounded so close I could have sworn the bad guys were in my room, or at the very least inside the villa. I dived out of bed and crawled to the window, keeping low as more rounds sparked off into the night. I could tell now that the gunfire was coming from the compound right outside my window. More rounds sparked off, the concussions of the weapon firing hammering into the villa walls. The noise was one I would recognize anywhere. It was the distinctive *crack-crack-crack* of AK-47 fire, the chosen weapon of militias, insurgents, and terrorists the world over.

I risked a quick glance over the sill, keeping low in case any rounds came punching through. I spotted two shadowy figures standing in our compound, trying to wrestle an assault rifle off of a third. *What the hell was happening?*

As they fought over the weapon, the muzzle sparked and more rounds went flying. I didn't recognize any of the figures, though they were clearly locals. Even if I could work out what they were up to and they proved to be the enemy, what the hell was I supposed to do without any kind of a weapon?

As the firing continued, I did the only thing I could think of: I turned and leopard-crawled out of my room and across to Dan's. I spied him crouched by the window.

"Dan, what the fuck?" I hissed.

He half turned, keeping one eye on the gunmen below. "They're pissed again. Fucking jokers."

"What d'you mean—*they're pissed again? Who's pissed again?*"

Pissed is British slang for drunk.

"The security guys. Every night they get whacko on this home-made hooch. This is the first time they've started loosing off with their weapons this close, though."

I was angry now. Fuming. Every single thing about the setup here just seemed to be messed-up. But it wouldn't help right now unloading on Dan. In any case, I didn't think much of it was his fault. Dan had been dumped into a shitty situation. He was trying to make the best of it, and I liked the guy for that.

"Is it like this every night? Shooting inside the compound?"

"No. It's a first. Normally they're shooting outside." Dan paused, then pointed at something. "It's okay, Ahmed's here—the owner. They'll calm down now."

It turned out that the guy who'd been loosing off all the AK rounds was the brother of Ahmed, the guy who owned the villa we were renting. I suggested that Dan tell Ahmed getting his brother to unload a mag of 7.62mm rounds into our walls wasn't the best way to have us keep paying the rent. Dan promised that he would have words, and he reiterated that it would be fine now that Ahmed was here.

I returned to my room, but I couldn't sleep. This was the first time in my life that I'd been in a hostile environment and not been armed. It was a bad feeling. If you have a weapon at least you can let the bad guys know very quickly that they're going to get some if they keep up with their attack. Not here. The best I could manage was a knife from the kitchen, and that wasn't going to cut it.

I needed a weapon, and I vowed that night that I was going to get one. Even a pistol would do. Otherwise I figured I was going to end up in an orange jumpsuit doing a walk-on part in an Al Qaeda video. Trouble was, our contract didn't allow for us to be armed. Like the Libyan guards, we were supposed somehow to go about our tasks without a weapon. *Well, sod that.*

Either I got a gun, or I was resigning. I wasn't prepared for my family to see me going out like that.

CHAPTER FOUR

Dan and I spoke over breakfast. He'd already had words with Ahmed. He'd told the villa owner that if we had another episode of gunfighting in the compound, then we were moving out. Ahmed had promised to get it sorted out. Even so, I knew we had to get ourselves properly armed.

"Dan, we need to get some weapons," I told him.

"We can't, mate. We're not allowed."

"I don't give a damn. We need weapons."

"We can't. Libyan law doesn't allow it and neither does the State Department contract."

Dan went on to explain that while the militias who controlled the Benghazi streets seemed happy enough for every Libyan and his brother to carry a gun, it was a total no-no for foreigners. If they caught a foreigner with a weapon, it was a perfect excuse to throw you in jail and beat a serious cash bribe out of you in return for your release. And neither Dan nor I was particularly keen to see the inside of a Libyan prison cell.

Yet in spite of the risks Dan agreed with me that we needed weapons. The other issue was cost. While you could pick up an AK-47 across most of Africa for a couple of hundred dollars, for some bizarre reason it would cost you two thousand, minimum, here in Libya. As for a pistol, it was twice that kind of money—and all for a shitty Browning or Beretta that was twenty years old. Nevertheless, Dan and I were going to have to make it a priority to score some weaponry.

"Why aren't we based at the Embassy compound, anyway?" I asked Dan. "It doesn't make sense us being here. At least then we could support them if it all went noisy."

Dan shrugged. "That's how it's specified in the contract."

From all my experience of running security operations for the Americans you were collocated with them—either at their Mission, their headquarters base, or their FOB (Forward Operating Base). Billeting us outside the Benghazi Mission didn't make any sense, but there was precious little I could do about it right now.

Tom turned up to drive us to work. He was late as usual. It bugged the hell out of Dan that the Libyans were always thirty minutes late for everything. Punctuality is a big thing for any ex-soldier, for the military hammers into you the importance of precise timekeeping. Soldiers synchronize watches before an operation for a reason: it's so that all parts of the plan of attack can be executed to the exact same second—crucial when coordinating ground forces, supporting fire, airborne troops, air strikes, and various other assets.

On the drive to the Embassy I noticed a different bunch of militiamen on one of the street junctions. What drew my eye were the black flags they had flying from their Toyota gun trucks. In Afghanistan any forces flying the black flag—either plain black, or with white lettering emblazoned across it—were the really bad guys. They weren't simply Taliban, who were often as not full-time farmers and part-time insurgents. The black-flag guys were die-hard Al Qaeda.

I nodded out the window. "Those black-flag guys . . ."

"They're Shariah Brigade," Tom cut in. "Not good. We have too many of them in Benghazi now."

"And the black flags?" I queried. "They mean what I think they mean?"

Dan nodded. "Yeah. They're pretty much Al Qaeda."

I asked Dan how many of this Shariah mob there were in the city. He said that as far as he could tell they were as common as any of the other militias.

I sat back to digest this new piece of information. While the majority of the Libyan population might view us as their "liberation buddies," these guys most certainly would not. Unless I was missing something, we had a lone American tasked with defending the entire U.S. Mission in Benghazi, and the streets were crawling with a heavily armed militia allied to Al Qaeda. I wondered how it could get any worse. The Benghazi Embassy was a disaster waiting to happen. It was an invitation to an Al Qaeda massacre and/or a kidnapping.

We arrived at the Embassy gates, and one of our local guards was actually standing duty at the barrier. Tom had been earmarked as our guard force commander, for we needed a perfect English speaker as the link between the Libyan guards and the Americans. I'd noticed him making a sneaky call on his cell phone a few minutes before we arrived. I reckoned he'd been phoning through a warning: "They're coming; make sure someone's outside on guard."

In a way I could understand why he might have done so. He was trying to make the guard force—the force he would be commanding—look good. But it wasn't working. The guard at the barrier didn't even glance up as we walked past: he was too busy texting someone on his cell phone. All of this crap—*all of it*—had to stop.

We made our way through the pedestrian gate, and it was now that I got my first glimpse of what I presumed had to be one of the so-called QRF. There was a guy standing outside the QRF Villa dressed in a skintight bright yellow T-shirt, tight combat bottoms, and flip-flops, with an AK-47 slung over his shoulder.

He had what looked like fake Oakley shades on, and a smoldering cigarette hanging on his bottom lip.

I called over a greeting: "Salam alaikum, mate."

The traditional Arabic Muslim greeting is "salam alaikum"— peace be unto you. The expected reply is "alaikum salam"—and unto you, peace. This guy just blanked me completely. Not a word in response.

I didn't know it yet, but this was Mutasim, the leader of the four-man 17th February QRF. The guard force had clearly warned him that there was a new guy in town—me—and that I was trouble, hence his well-rehearsed act of snubbing me. So be it. I was up for any kind of confrontation that these kind might have on offer.

As we turned left into the dirt track leading to the TOC I caught sight of a stocky, bald-headed white guy dressed in a khaki green T-shirt and red shorts. What he was wearing was the informal uniform of the U.S. Marine Corps when doing PT, or physical training. I'd seen U.S. Marines dressed like that countless times before, when collocated on missions with them. This guy had to be the RSO.

He darted into the TOC, and a minute or so later we followed inside. He introduced himself as Lee Saunders, the Benghazi Embassy RSO. I could tell right away that he was off with us. He didn't seem to want to talk to Dan at all, and I could barely get a word out of him myself.

Dan excused himself. "I'm going next door. I've got some paperwork to do."

"Ex–U.S. Marine?" I prompted, once Dan was gone.

Lee paused for an instant. "Yeah. How d'you know?"

"PT kit."

"Oh, right, okay. Say, about that little nonsense outside the gate—not acceptable."

I presumed he was referring to our guards' demonstration over their late pay, plus the graffiti. I couldn't agree with him more—it was totally unacceptable.

"We're on it. We're getting rid of the bad guys, just as soon as we can get some new guys in to replace them. We'll get it sorted."

"Right. You'll have to excuse me—I gotta go on a mission."

"Yeah, no problem. Laters."

Our chat had lasted five minutes, if that. Of course, I knew Lee had to be horrendously busy, not to mention stressed beyond measure. The poor bugger was trying to do eight people's jobs. But I'd got not the slightest chance to raise any of my security concerns with him. More to the point, I got the strong sense that he didn't seem to like us or to rate us much.

A few minutes later I spotted Lee in a blazer and tie, escorting a smart-looking woman toward one of the Embassy's armored SUVs. She was around five feet eight, with long auburn hair and pale Irish looks. She was snappily dressed and seemed to be wearing not a scrap of makeup. I didn't know the woman's name yet, but I figured she had to be the Deputy Chief of Mission. Lee helped her into the rear of the vehicle, before taking up his place as the driver.

A figure hurried over from the direction of the QRF Villa. It was the same guy I'd seen earlier, complete with his yellow T-shirt, only now he was wearing jungle boots and a cheap and nasty chest rig of the type you'd buy from Wal-Mart. It was the sort that a teenage kid would wear, complete with oodles of ammo pouches. He went to get into the passenger seat so he could ride shotgun for Lee, with the principal—the lady diplomat—in the rear.

As he jumped in, the curved magazine of his AK-47 caught on the door frame. An instant later it had sprung off, and 7.62mm rounds were pinging all over the drive and bouncing under the vehicle. I could not believe my eyes. A mag only ever falls off an AK if you've failed to seat it in the housing properly. Otherwise, it's rigidly attached to the weapon, as it needs to be to fire. A guy who didn't know how to attach a mag properly should not have been allowed to carry a loaded weapon, let alone do so in the company of diplomats.

I watched as the yellow T-shirt guy scrabbled about on his hands and knees, trying to gather up all the spilled rounds and reload them into the empty mag. I was shaking my head in utter bewilderment: *and these guys were supposed to be the QRF.*

I heard a snort of derision from behind me. "What a total tosser." It was Dan.

I turned away from the window and cracked up laughing, Dan doing the same. We didn't want Lee to see us, for that would be disrespectful and belittling. I didn't think for one moment that Lee had selected the 17th February Militia—as opposed to a bunch of fellow U.S. Marines—as his QRF, but someone must have done so. Whoever had recruited these idiots as the Embassy's only permanently armed protection force had to bear some heavy responsibility.

I'd been on Dan's back for all the problems we were experiencing here, although I hadn't meant to be. Having a good laugh at the QRF's expense helped unite us. We had ten interviews to do that day—potential new guard force recruits. Dan had actually got to know two of the existing guards, Walid and Drizzi, pretty well. They were decent guys, and what distinguished them from the others was that they were willing to work and apply themselves. They were the first to admit that the rest of the guards were a waste of space.

The loan RSOs—Lee and his predecessor—had had zero time to get on top of the guard force, hence Blue Mountain being brought in. But without anyone pushing them, the guards had decided that it was easier to drink tea and play cards in the shade than to do what they had been hired to do—which was to patrol the compound perimeter on foot and man the guardroom and barricade.

Walid and Drizzi had put out word that we were seeking new recruits, and hence we'd got the guys in to interview. After long years working in Iraq I speak passable Arabic, and I was able to conduct the interviews in Arabic. The questions were pretty basic. Do you have any background in the military or security? How many brothers and sisters do you have, and what are their names? That question was designed so we could do an identity check against a database maintained by the Americans. What was your role in the revolution? Have you ever been abroad, and if so, where and when?

All ten of the guys seemed keen and motivated. We passed the interview forms on to the TOC so Lee could get them vetted. If all ten came back clear we'd hire the lot, and I'd be able to sack the worst of the present bunch. Truth be told, I was relishing the prospect. It would act as a warning to those who remained. There was nothing like getting rid of the worst—*pour encourager les autres.*

The interviews done, Dan and I did a walkabout of the perimeter. In addition to the main and rear gates, there was a third hidden away on the eastern side of the compound. That was strictly the tradesmen's and garbage entrance. Our guard force was supposed to be split, with one on each of the three gates, one in the guardroom manning comms, one out front on the barrier, and one walking the perimeter. Amazingly, all of the guards were in position and doing their stuff. That was what just the threat of a mass sacking had achieved.

I asked Dan to draw up a list of the ten guys he most wanted gone. That way, if all ten new recruits were positively vetted we could get rid of the worst of the present bunch. Two of the ten on Dan's list were on duty today, and I figured there was no time like the present. It made sense for me to get rid of the lot, for that way they wouldn't blame Dan—and in three weeks I'd be gone, whereas he was contracted for the long term.

I made my way to the guardroom and sacked the first two guys. I got right in their faces and told them they were done. They were only to return once, and that was to hand in their ID badges and any Blue Mountain equipment. One of the two was a big, lazy slob of a guy called Alif—the type of bad apple that could turn an entire crop rotten. He reacted to his sacking just as I suspected he would.

"I come with my tribe!" he started yelling. "Me and my tribe—we come find you and kill you!"

"Fine," I responded. "Bring it on. You know where I live. I'll be expecting you."

"Me and my tribe—we come kill you for this!"

"Listen, come on your own, man to man, and I'll be ready and waiting."

Big Tom, our driver and now guard force commander, was dancing about with worry. "He will come with his tribe and it'll be a disaster . . ."

I told him to shut it. From my experience the guys who threatened to kill you never did anything much. Al Qaeda and their ilk weren't into issuing death threats. If they came for you, they'd hit you with proper planning and with deadly, murderous intent.

Dan and I returned to our villa, ate chicken for a second night running, and again Dan was in bed by eight. I stayed up until midnight, bored out of my brain and watching the TV. Luckily, we could get CNN, the BBC, and a few other serious news networks, so at least I could kill time watching some decent current affairs programming.

Around midnight I heard Dan's phone ring. A call coming at this time of night just had to spell trouble. I walked to his bedroom and I could hear his voice through the door.

"What! Where? Who was it? You've not caught them yet . . . Any idea why?"

I tapped on the door and walked in. Dan was perched on the bed shaking his head with worry. "Any injuries? Are all the Americans okay?"

He listened for a while longer, then ended the call.

"What's up?" I asked.

"Someone's attacked the compound."

"What d'you mean—attacked like how?"

"Someone's thrown a grenade over the compound wall. Luckily, there's no reports of injuries."

"Right, give Lee a ring and see if he wants us. He's on his own up there."

We still had no weapons, but presumably Lee could arm us out of the Mission's armory if need be. Dan made the call. Lee told us he was in the process of securing "the client." Dan asked if he wanted us there.

"No," Lee responded. "Me and the QRF have it under control."

"We're here if you need us," Dan told him, and then the call was done.

Something hit home to me there and then: Lee actually thought more of the QRF than he did of us. I'd never come across such an attitude among serving or ex-Marines. I was a great believer in the American–British special relationship, and normally they and us were tight. Where was this coming from, I wondered. It was thirty minutes past midnight, the Embassy had just been hit, and who knew what the remainder of the night might bring—and all Lee had was the 17th February Militia to back him up. Yet he'd refused our help.

I returned to my room feeling seriously unsettled. The first night we'd had rounds unleashed right outside our villa walls. Now, on night two, we'd had a grenade thrown into the Embassy grounds. Something was going horribly wrong, if the first two nights were anything to go by, and yet the lone RSO holding fort at the Embassy didn't seem to want any support or help from us.

Around 4:00 A.M. we had a call from Lee. Apparently, they'd captured the attackers. One was a serving Blue Mountain guard, the other, one of those that had got the sack. They were under arrest and getting questioned by the Benghazi police. It looked as if the attack was an inside job—rogue guard force members out for revenge.

Lee ended the call by telling us he needed us in his office at 8:00 A.M. sharp. Dan and I had a long talk about it. We hadn't hired either of these clowns, so while we'd face the music in the morning this was a problem we had inherited. Still, neither of us was kidding ourselves that it was going to be an easy meeting. I was convinced by now that we'd lost the contract. I was two days in and I feared that I'd let Robert, my boss and my closest mentor, down.

I put a call through to him in the United Kingdom. I briefed him on what had happened. I could tell that he was fuming. He told me to get it sorted out or else the State Department would be rid of us fast. It was fair enough. Shaking up the guard force was what I'd been sent in to do. Somehow we were going to have to survive the coming showdown with Lee and make things right.

The drive to the Embassy the following morning was tense and largely silent. We talked the issue over briefly with Tom. There was no actual proof that the two guys had thrown the grenade, but there was no other reason for them to have been there. One had been fired already and the other was on the list of those to go. They'd been caught driving away from the scene of the attack, and in truth there was little chance that it wasn't them.

We were at the TOC early, but Lee was ready and waiting. He got us into his office and closed the door heavily. There was no offer of coffee. I felt as if I were back in the headmaster's study, on one of the numerous occasions when I'd been caught causing trouble at school. It was only going into the British Army that had straightened me out back then—and I didn't have a clue what would save us right here and now.

"Last night a grenade came over the compound wall," Lee started, in a voice like gravel. "The alarm wasn't raised as the system's not working yet, but I heard the blast, cleared the area, and secured the client, while the QRF went around the compound to check. They held two of your guard force, and they were taken away by the local police." Lee fixed us with this hard-ass look. "Make no mistake, I am not fuckin' happy with your fuckin' guard force attacking the compound, especially when one of them still works for you guys . . ."

Lee went on for a good minute in this vein. Finally, I couldn't resist saying a few words.

"I'm not being funny, mate, but they're not our guards," I cut in. "You hired them: we're in the process of getting rid of them. So don't fucking blame us. We didn't sign these guys up—you or your predecessor did."

Dan was staring at me mouth agape. But as far as I was concerned we had nothing to lose now, and anyway, this was the truth.

I plowed on. "If you're looking for someone to blame you need to look closer to home, mate. Either you hired them or the guy before you did. Period."

Lee stared at me for a long second, then he broke into the beginnings of a smile. "Fair point. You're right. You're fuckin' right. We did hire them."

I seized the initiative. "Listen, mate, we're trying to get rid of all the worst as fast as we can. But we need to get the vetting forms back from you, at which point we can get shot of ten in one go."

Lee nodded. "Gotcha. I'll get onto it. But I got one thousand and one goddamn things to do . . ."

I had rarely if ever seen a guy under so much pressure. Lee was holding the fort alone, and now he'd been up half the night dealing with a grenade attack. It was piling up on him, and I didn't for one moment blame him for wanting to unload on someone. But like a truly decent guy he'd come around pretty damn quickly.

"Okay, guys, thanks, really," he said. "If you can fix the guard force, that'd be a real help."

"You get them vetted, we'll get them sorted," I reassured him. "Plus you need to get your alarm working. There's no point the guard hitting the duck-and-cover alarm if the system doesn't work. Plus the CCTV needs to be up and running . . ."

"Don't I know it," Lee growled. "I got it on the list of things need doin' around here."

The standard attack response for our guard force was to sound the "duck-and-cover alarm," one that would alert the entire Embassy to an attack via a series of loudspeakers—only right now that system wasn't operational.

Dan and I got up to leave. "Mate, if you need us for anything—*anything*—just let us know," I added. "We're here to help."

The offer seemed to have hardly registered with Lee. We shook hands and left, but I was determined to come back and see him on my own and get to the bottom of it all.

I let a good hour go by before I returned to his office. I knocked and entered. "Any chance of a word, mate, just me and you."

"Yeah, yeah—no problem. Close the door."

This time Lee did fetch coffees. That done, I got right down to it. "So, I'm wondering, is there a problem between you and Dan?"

Lee fixed me with a look, as if he was assessing what exactly he could afford to tell me. "No, not as such. But man, Dan just looks so worn-out. He looks old and past it. He's limping about, for Christ's sake. He doesn't look up for it."

"Fine. But trust me, if you need our help you only have to ask and Dan and I will come running."

"Why? What's your background?"

"I spent fourteen years in the British Army. After that, three years in Iraq as a private operator looking after U.S. ACE. Then Helmand for three years working with U.S. Marine Corps in Garmsir and Sangin." Now I went for the killer punch. "Plus I was in charge of a team looking after a guy you may have heard of—Major General James T. Conway."

Lee nearly fell off his chair. "No shit! How come you were looking after that guy?"

I returned the smile. "James T. Conway: six feet four, looks like an American football player and a really nice guy. I looked after him in Afghan and took him around the place. We were his close protection squad in Helmand Province. I even got his coin."

"No shit!" Lee shook his head in amazement. "I met the general once . . . The Marines—we love that guy."

"Yeah, I know. I know why, too. He's a top bloke."

Major General James T. Conway was the commander of the entire U.S. Marine Corps. He had 250,000 Marines under his command, so a force almost three times the size of the entire British military.

I told Lee a story about the general. He was the only commander I'd ever known to keep a helicopter pilot waiting. It was at the end of his Afghan tour, and he'd been going around his CP team—meaning, us—shaking each man's hand. We were ten, and to each he was saying a personal thank-you plus giving us his coin—a commemorative metal disk about the size of a medal, with his personal crest and motto emblazoned on it, plus that of the Marine Corps—*Semper fidelis:* always faithful. He was halfway through when his personal assistant came hurrying over to warn the general that his helo was ready to get airborne. The general rounded on the man. "Well, you just tell the pilot he can fuckin' wait."

"That's General Conway, you betcha!" Lee enthused. "Fuck, man, it's great to have someone here who can help if the shit goes down. I got no one to watch my back." He was starting to really open up now. "You know, this is my first ever overseas postin' as an RSO, and what do they do to me—*alone in Benghazi.*"

"That's why I made the offer of help. If you need me to sleep up here on one of the couches, I'll be here watching your back. I'll happily fight alongside you, mate."

Lee didn't seem able to thank me enough. The poor bastard had been here for days on end utterly alone and unsupported. He only had two weeks left before another RSO replaced him, but he was already burned-out. Whoever had sent him out here alone—they needed to come see for themselves the level of shit they'd landed him in.

"Thank Christ, buddy. You know . . . I've been kinda struggling. It's been hard here, all alone, you know?"

"Like I said, I'm here. I'll help you—whatever you need." I felt genuinely sorry for the guy. "You should not be here on your own. It's madness. There should be four of you, minimum, and ideally eight."

Lee shrugged, exhaustedly. "Don't I know it."

He proceeded to talk me around all the weaponry and the ammo stored in the TOC. He unlocked the cases, and there were racks of folding-stock M4 assault rifles, plus pump-action combat shotguns and rakes of ammo. *Now this was more like it.* There were also enough top-of-the-range SIG pistols to arm five men. He showed me where the keys were kept and how to unlock the cases.

Game on.

Lee waved a hand over the racks of weaponry. "Buddy, you ever feel the need—here's where it all is if the bullets start to fly . . ."

I told him I'd fight back-to-back with him if need be. "I don't know if you know Dan's background, but trust me, he'd fight to the death to protect you, too. Dan did twenty-two years in the Royal Green Jackets—a top infantry regiment—plus nine years as a private operator in Iraq."

Lee looked shocked. "Man, I didn't know. Why didn't he tell me?"

"Dan's not the kind of bloke to volunteer much. He doesn't boast. But rest assured, he knows what he's doing."

Whenever I'd served alongside them I valued the U.S. Marines highly. They refused to go backward no matter what, and they were fun to be around. From now on Lee and I would greet each other with "Semper fi" whenever we ran into each other. I told him I would fight to safeguard his principal, the lady diplomat, so he didn't need to worry about standing alone anymore.

I meant every word of it, too. I'm not the kind who leaves my friends hanging.

CHAPTER FIVE

The grenade attack, plus our heart-to-heart, was the push Lee seemed to need to get the vetting done. The forms on the ten new recruits came back almost immediately with all being cleared. That done, I could start the training proper. It was all to take place at the Blue Mountain villa, for the State Department contract stipulated that we should have our own "training facility."

One guy struck me immediately as having real promise. His name was Nasir, and he was the only one not wearing a figure-hugging T-shirt and jeans. Instead he was dressed in smart trousers and a button-down shirt, which were neatly pressed and ironed. He was super keen to learn, and if his English hadn't been so poor I'd have made him the guard force commander, in preference to Tom—for there was something about Tom's attitude that was starting to grate.

Nasir was maybe thirty-five years old, five feet ten and of typical slim Libyan build. He had honest eyes above a small goatee beard, and he struck me as being a genuinely nice guy. I'm the kind of person who tends to go on first instincts. I'd warmed to Lee from the get-go, even though he hadn't particularly liked us. Likewise, I was sure I'd hit gold with Nasir.

Before the revolution Nasir had been a Caterpillar driver,

working sixteen-hour shifts and getting paid a lot less than the nine hundred dollars a month we were going to pay for eight-hour guard shifts. He couldn't be happier with his new job and I appointed him as a guard force supervisor right away.

Another diamond recruit was Mustaffa, though he and Nasir were like chalk and cheese to look at. Untypically for a Libyan, Mustaffa was a fitness and bodybuilding freak, and he was a massive hunk of honed muscle and sinew. He also sported a full-length beard, and when we'd first checked out the photos of the potential recruits Tom had tried to rule him out.

"We obviously can't have him," Tom had remarked.

I'd asked why.

"Look at his bushy beard," Tom had answered. "He could be an Islamic fundamentalist, maybe even Shariah Brigade."

I pointed out that I had a beard, but it didn't make me a terrorist. I'd grown it specifically so I could blend in better with the locals here.

I actually suspected that Tom didn't want Mustaffa around because he looked far bigger and tougher than he did. Mustaffa proved to be as imposing in the flesh as he'd looked in his photo, but above the monster beard he had honest, intelligent eyes. Mustaffa's English wasn't great but he was quick to learn, and I made him another guard supervisor, alongside Nasir. He would end up being one of my best recruits, so much so that I nicknamed him "Mr. Reliable."

Then there were three guys who'd worked as volunteers for the Red Crescent—the Islamic world's equivalent of the Red Cross. They'd been ambulance drivers all through the revolution, and anyone who volunteered to do that kind of work was a good guy in my books. Mohamed Mohamed was a big lump of a man with another monster beard, and in time he'd prove to be a top recruit.

Abd Monhein was the second Red Crescent recruit, and like Mohamed he hailed from the Khufra region in the southern deserts of Libya. The third Red Crescent guy was Sahad Mohamed, again from Khufra. Sahad was distinctly black African looking, as opposed to the others, who were Arabic in appearance.

All three of the Red Crescent guys would prove to be first-class recruits, apart from one thing: Abd and Mohamed were horrendously racist. Whenever Sahad was slow at getting anything during the training—as all the recruits were at times—Mohamed and Abd would start in on him.

"What d'you expect from Sahad—he's black!"

"No surprises there—he's a Kuffir!"

"He's stupid like all blacks!"

In fact, most of the Arab-looking recruits piled in with similar comments. It didn't matter that they were doing so in Arabic, I could still understand most of what was said. It hadn't seemed to cross their minds that I might disagree with their racist bullshit. Even Sahad himself seemed so used to the abuse that he didn't raise any objections. I couldn't believe what I was hearing.

The British Army is far from perfect, but it is one of the least racist institutions you could ever come across. Once a man or woman made it into the forces, their skin color was a complete irrelevance. I'd served alongside just about every ethnic mix you could imagine, both in the regular forces and as a private military operator. Race just didn't come into it when the bullets started to fly.

I knew I had to nip this in the bud, for the Americans would have about as much time for this as we did. The question was, how? I had decided to treat the recruits firmly, but with respect, for I knew how stubborn and prideful Arab males can be. In the British and American military you shout and scream at new recruits and it's all part of the accepted training, but if I did so with these guys they'd simply walk off the job. They might need the work and the money, but they were capable of taking offense at the smallest thing.

I tried explaining to the recruits that their key role was to protect the Americans at the Embassy, for that was who they worked for. Strictly speaking, the Benghazi Mission was a Consulate, but that distinction was lost on my recruits, and most of us who worked there referred to it as the "Embassy." They took a while to get what I was saying. They were getting paid by Blue Mountain, so what were the Americans to do with any of it? they asked me. I tried a different tack. I tried explaining that the U.S. Embassy in Benghazi was actually a slice of American soil.

"Guys, the Libyan Embassy in London—that's part of Libya; it's Libyan territory. Likewise, the U.S. Embassy here in Benghazi is part of America."

Several of them shook their heads. "No, no—it cannot be."

"But this is Libya," said another.

"Libya is Libyan territory," another said.

"Yes, guys, I know," I explained, "but the U.S. Embassy here in Benghazi *is* American soil. I know it sounds a bit odd, but that's how it is."

I explained that I was their boss, but since I worked for the Americans, that made the Americans their big boss. Next I explained that both their American and British bosses wouldn't appreciate comments of a racist nature. I tried explaining how it was wrong to call people "stupid" and "dumb" just because they were black. I tried explaining how everyone was equal, no matter what his or her skin color.

"No, no, but that's just Sahad," the guards objected.

"We only say those things 'cause he's black."

"Sahad doesn't mind—he knows he's stupid."

The very concept of racial equality seemed utterly lost on them.

I decided for now to let it lie, at least until I'd taught them the basics of what was in the State Department contract. I started off with timekeeping. I tried explaining how vital punctuality was, especially when serving in a guard force. If everyone turned up half an hour late for their shift, the whole rotation would be unworkable.

"No, no," they objected. "Is not like that. If we are all half an hour late, everything just starts half an hour later."

You couldn't fault their logic.

I told them that punctuality was still key, and it was either my way or the highway. Whoever turned up late I'd start to dock their pay, and I'd give the money to the guard they'd kept waiting. Cash talked with these guys, and I didn't just want them turning up on time for payday.

I moved on to vehicle and body checks. All vehicles were to be stopped at the barrier, and the underside searched with a mirror on a stick. The guard on the barrier was to start at one corner and go all around the vehicle, checking for explosives. That done, they were to ask everyone to dismount and they'd search the vehicle's interior. That included under the hood and in the trunk, and they were to search for concealed weapons as much as they were for bombs.

They'd search individual visitors in the classic airport style—making them assume a star shape and patting them down. They'd start with the arms, work their way down the body, and finish with the legs. Dan and I rigged up some dummy bombs, and we hid them in Tom's Chrysler, setting the recruits the task of finding them. We did the same for body searches, Dan or I hiding a weapon on our person and telling the guys to find it.

The highlight of the training so far proved to be first aid. I explained that what they were about to learn might save the lives of their children, or even a stranger on the street. I taught them how the body holds eight pints of blood, and that simply by stopping someone from bleeding you could save their life. I demonstrated how applying a simple tourniquet—a strap that fastens around a damaged limb to stem the flow of blood—could stop them bleeding out. I explained how I'd once seen a female U.S. Marine with all her limbs blown off from an IED, but how the tourniquets applied to each limb had kept her alive. They loved it that something as simple as that could magically save someone.

I demonstrated the tourniquets that the guard force would have in their medical kits—a tough canvas strap with a rod that twists to tighten it, and a clasp to hold the rod in place. I got them to practice on each other. I got them to do simple mouth-to-mouth resuscitation and CPR—using the hands to pump the chest of a victim of a heart attack, to try to keep oxygenated blood circulating. I kept it simple, the idea being that they could keep someone alive long enough for Dan or me or Lee to get to them.

The State Department contract also stipulated that we had to teach health and safety, like wearing protective goggles when at work. These guys had just lived through a civil war and a revolution, and needless to say, health and safety was completely lost on them. They stared at me like I'd beamed myself down from planet Zog.

"Don't worry about it too much," I told them. "Health 'n' safety—it's all a load of bollocks."

They didn't really get the joke. Like most Libyans, they weren't big into humor and they were totally not into sarcasm. If you tried yanking a Libyan guy's chain, he'd very likely mistake it for deliberate nastiness on your part and you'd quickly make an enemy. Libyan males were all about front, respect, and not losing face.

But I did find a way to make them lighten up. I'd pick up an Arabic word they used and slip it into the training. Perhaps it was my pronunciation, but it had them in fits of laughter. They loved it that I could speak even my level of broken Arabic, and they kept trying to get me to teach them English swear words. Dan swore like the proverbial trooper, and most of his curses were so obscure that the recruits had never heard of them, not even in the movies.

"What does *wanker* mean, Mr. Michael?" they'd ask.

No one could pronounce my first name, Morgan, so I'd become Michael to the guards. Libyans tended to call you "Mr." plus your first name, so "Mr. John" if you were called John Smith.

"Where the hell did you hear that?" I'd counter, knowing full well it had to be Dan.

Oddly enough, there are almost no curses in Welsh, my first language. If you want to swear in Welsh you actually have to use an English word. As a result it doesn't come very naturally to a Welsh-speaker to be swearing all the time.

In addition to my broken Arabic, the guards loved it that I was growing a beard. As with Muslim males the world over, no self-respecting Libyan man would be seen without a beard. In their eyes, my growing one meant that I was showing respect for their culture. I was used to this from Iraq and Afghanistan. Afghans in particular would see you with a beard, stroke their own, and say, "Good, good."

Apart from forging some common ground with the recruits, I had a secondary reason for growing one. With a beard and a good suntan most Libyans would mistake me for a swarthy Lebanese, and there were hordes of Lebanese businessmen and traders in Benghazi. Living outside of the Embassy we had to venture onto the streets for food, stationery, equipment, whatever. I wanted to be able to blend in. I spoke enough Arabic to get by, and I wanted the fewest people possible to know I was a Westerner.

On my first few trips downtown I'd taken Tom with me, and I'd learned how to get around the streets on foot without turning many heads. The city struck me as being horrendously busy, but apart from the militia who seemed to be on every street corner, it wasn't as if the place was awash with guns. For a country fresh out of a revolution there were very few weapons to be seen.

But every now and then I'd come across a black-flagged militia vehicle parked on a street corner, the gunmen eyeing the passing pedestrians and vehicles. I wore a baseball cap to shade my eyes— as many Libyan males do—and I'd keep my head well down. But all it would take was one of those Shariah Brigade guys to challenge me verbally, and my cover would be blown. They'd know immediately that I was a Westerner, which had to make me fair game, the Shariah Brigade being so closely allied to Al Qaeda.

Every time I came across them my mind would flip to the Embassy, barely thirty minutes away by car. There we had at least one high-value target (HVT), as far as Al Qaeda would see it—the female diplomat at the Mission. Right now there was only one individual who would stand and fight to protect her: Lee. And on scores of Benghazi road junctions you could find a half a dozen Shariah fighters, complete with AK-47 assault rifles, RPGs, and with 12.7mm DShK heavy machine guns mounted in the rear of their Toyota pickups.

Anyone who's ever been under fire from a DShK—as I have, in Afghanistan—knows how fearsome the weapon is. More commonly known as the Dushka—the Russian word for "sweetie"—there is nothing sweet or gentle about it. It is the equivalent of our own Browning .50-caliber heavy machine gun. It has a distinctive deep, throaty boom, and the rounds can cut through trees and walls and blow your head or your limbs clean off.

It didn't take a genius to figure out what would happen if a handful of those Shariah gun trucks hit the Embassy. My newly trained *and unarmed* guard force would be facing several dozen fighters armed to the teeth. A couple of RPG rounds would be enough to blast the unreinforced steel gates off their hinges, at which point the gun trucks would be inside the compound, tearing the villas to pieces with 12.7mm armor-piercing cannon shells.

Against all of that there would be Lee, with an M4 assault rifle, plus Dan and me—and that's if we could get there in time. The very idea of it was chilling. Somehow, there seemed to be a total disconnect here in Benghazi between the actual threat level and the State Department's assessment and preparedness for it.

The only other thing we could hope to rely on was intelligence—that somehow we'd get early warning of an impending attack. The best intelligence is human intelligence—"HUMINT"—and that was the other reason I sought to forge a bond with my guards. Each of them was a potential source of HUMINT, as was Tom. If I could bring them suitably on our side, maybe one of the guards would pick up on an impending attack and pass us a timely warning.

If that happened we'd have to evacuate the Embassy immediately, for there was no way we could mount a proper defense, and certainly not against the kind of forces the bad guys could muster. I figured we'd get everyone to the airport and from there out of

Libya, via whatever flight was going to somewhere a degree less menacing than here, which was pretty much just about anywhere.

The other trick I deployed to win the guards over was religion. One day I asked them why I never saw them praying much. I started talking about what it says in the Koran about the importance of prayers five times a day. I told the guys if they needed to break the training to pray it was fine by me.

"How do you know about this?" one of them asked.

I told them how I'd worked all over the Islamic world, and how I had many, many friends who were Muslims—especially in Afghanistan. Over time they'd taught me about their beliefs and that had made me curious—and so I had read the Koran. The guards were amazed that a Westerner might have read it. I had to explain that it was available in translation, so I'd been able to do so in English.

I told them what I'd learned about the life of the Prophet Muhammad—how he had lived in caves in the desert before riding into battle twice on his horse to win heroic victories. I told them about the hajj, the pilgrimage to Islam's holiest sites in Saudi Arabia—one that all Muslims are supposed to complete before they die. I told them that I'd been to Saudi Arabia at the time of the hajj, so although I wasn't a Muslim, still I was doing better than most of them!

The idea of a white-eye foreigner and unbeliever like me having been at the hajj, when none of them had yet managed to complete it, really tickled their fancy. Only Tom seemed unsettled and disconcerted by what I was saying.

"Why do you know so much about this?" he asked. "Why do you need to know it? Why does it even interest you?"

"I work in Muslim countries and need to know and respect what their people believe in. That's why I read the Koran. You've read it, obviously?"

Tom didn't answer.

Amazingly, a lot of Muslim males haven't read the Koran, especially if Arabic isn't their first language. Strict believers maintain that the Koran should be read only in Arabic, or else the true meaning of Muhammad's words as written down by him are lost. This puts off a lot of Muslims, for they can't read it in a language they can understand, and that's for those who can actually read.

I wondered what might lie behind Tom's apparent uneasiness with me. I suspected a large part of it was that he was the guard force commander and wanted to appear like the big man in front of "his" guards. I figured I'd have to try not to cast too heavy a shadow, for Tom was the only guy we had whose English was good enough to fulfill that part of the contract.

I turned next to what was the core of the guard force training—self-defense and weapons skills. I was acutely aware that most Arab men tend to think they're Sylvester Stallone when it comes to fighting—and especially hand-to-hand combat. I warned the new recruits that this was training only, and the idea was not to hurt anyone. I knew it was vital not to get into the whole disrespect thing by making any of them look stupid.

I showed them simple wrist-lock techniques, in slow motion. I used Tom as my dummy, locking him into moves that forced him onto the ground. The trainees loved it, but in truth I didn't think they'd ever have much cause to use such holds—for if the bad guys did attack, they were more than likely to come for us with grenades and guns.

One morning I was demonstrating a hold on Tom when he swung around and tried to grab me in a vicious headlock. I twisted free, kicked his legs out from under him, and he slammed into the ground. He was a big guy, up near three hundred pounds, and to hit the ground with that kind of mass must have hurt. He lay there groaning. I warned everyone that that was what happened if you messed around. It was a good lesson to have got in early.

Once I'd made sure Tom was all right, I took him to one side. I asked him what the hell he thought he was playing at.

He glared at me. "I'm sick and tired of you making me look stupid and weak in front of the others."

"Don't be silly. Next time you can demonstrate the holds on me, if you like. But don't ever mess around like that, 'cause I've made you look really stupid now, haven't I?"

"Well, why can't I have a better title, instead of guard force commander?" Tom demanded. "Can't I be security manager or something?"

"No, Tom, you can't," I replied, with infinite patience, "because the security manager is either Dan or me."

From now on Tom got to demonstrate all the holds on me, after which I hoped his Arab pride would be satisfied.

The final thing I had to teach the guard recruits was use of the one weapon the State Department contract *did* allow them to carry—the extendable steel baton. The baton was like a short metal club that could be flicked out to full, baseball-bat-like length. I taught them never to go in halfhearted with the baton, for if they did, it could be used against them and it could injure or kill.

If they were up against someone who was unarmed, they were to go for a knee or an elbow—which would stop the attacker, but not prove fatal. If their opponent was armed they were to go for the "red areas"—the head, chest (the heart area), and the groin. If you hit a guy properly in any of the red areas he was going down.

This raised the issue of what would happen if one of the guards killed someone. More often than not in Libya, such cases would be settled without recourse to the law. Tribe would meet with tribe, and the family of the deceased would be offered blood money as compensation. But if it happened at the Embassy and it went to the police, the guards feared they might end up in jail.

I tried explaining that what happened at the Embassy happened on American soil, so it wasn't going to be dealt with under Libyan law, or tribal practice for that matter. But still they didn't seem convinced. I agreed to double-check with Lee, and next time I ran into him at the Embassy I raised the issue.

"Semper fi, mate," I greeted him.

"Semper fi. How's it goin', brother?"

Lee was a totally positive, hardworking professional and I'd never once heard him moan about things. He'd never stated the obvious—that he hated this posting and couldn't wait to get himself gone. But it was obvious that he was counting down the days, and I could tell he was close to being totally finished.

"Listen, mate, I've got one for you," I ventured. "If someone comes at one of my guards with a knife or a club, are they free to go for the red areas?"

"Yeah, that's exactly what we want," Lee confirmed. "If they injure someone we'll deal with it from there on in. Tell your guys that they will be looked after."

"Cheers, mate, appreciate it."

"Say, how're the new guards shapin' up, anyways?"

"They're hardly Arnie Schwarzenegger, but they'll do."

Lee grinned. "Good to go, brother." He paused. "So, you know I'm almost done?"

I nodded. "We'll be sad to lose you, mate, but I'm on my way out, too, remember?"

Lee was a couple of days short of leaving, and I was scheduled to be here less than a week more. My training task was pretty much done, and if truth be told I was looking forward to getting out of there almost as much as Lee.

"We got three replacement RSOs comin' in," Lee continued. He explained that he'd sent it "up the chain" that there was a desperate need for more security staff and physical protection measures, for the Benghazi Mission was wide open to attack. "Maybe that's why they're sendin' three new RSOs, instead of only one. And hey, you know what—the head RSO, she's a woman. So what d'you think of that?"

I shrugged. "I've worked with loads of chicks in the Royal Signals, mate. They're good as gold. Often, they're a lot better than the blokes."

Lee laughed. "You better believe it with this one. Her name's Rosie, and she's got a towering reputation. She's gonna be awesome. She's volunteered for just about every shithole goin'—Iraq, Syria, Afghanistan. Man, she is the real deal."

"So if anyone can kick ass, Rosie can?"

"You got it. Plus it's a three-person team, so things are lookin' up. It should all start to change around here."

I relayed Lee's words to the trainees—that the Americans would deal with any injuries or deaths they might cause at the Embassy. It was then that Mustaffa, our bearded giant of a body-builder, raised the million-dollar question. In a sense, all through the training this had been the elephant in the room.

"Mr. Michael, what are we to do if we are attacked by men with guns?"

"Good question. Let's be clear about one thing: batons are about as much use as tits on fish in a firefight. I'll speak with the RSO, but there's no way you can be expected to fight armed attackers with batons."

I knew the answer to Mustaffa's question, but once again I figured I'd double-check with Lee. I put the question to him: what do my guards do if they're hit by guys with guns?

"If we're hit by gunmen and it's safe for them to get out and run, that's what they're to do," Lee told me. "Their only role is to raise the alarm. Once they've done that they cannot be expected to stand and fight an armed force. They're to make a run for it and find the quickest route to safety."

I relayed the instructions to my recruits. I could tell it didn't sit easy with them. They were a guard force, but if they faced a serious attack they were to run away. I tried explaining that it was the QRF's job to stand and fight, because they had the weapons. From the expressions on their faces, I could tell what they thought of that.

"But Mr. Michael," big Mustaffa objected, "the QRF will be the *first* to turn and run."

CHAPTER SIX

I feared that Mustaffa was right, and if the QRF were going to run we needed to be ready. Lee might well have to call us in and we'd need to be armed. For now we settled upon a makeshift compromise: Tom had an AK-47 at his house; we'd keep that with us, either in his Chrysler or at the villa, so at least then we'd have something with which to go to Lee's aid.

The training package done, I proceeded to sack the worst of the remaining guards. Predictably, several more threatened to kill me, but at least now we had a workable force: four teams of five, standing eight-hour shifts on a 24/7 rotation. Each team had one of the newly trained guys as a supervisor—Nasir, Mustaffa, or another—giving them a positive role model to follow. Tom was overall guard force commander, and after our rough-and-tumble during the training his bad attitude seemed to have mostly gone.

Things were starting to shape up, at least compared to the mess they had been, and all in time for the arrival of Rosie and her new RSOs. As luck would have it a DHL parcel arrived the day before the new RSOs flew in—the guard force uniforms. They consisted of beige shirts and matching trousers, displaying Blue Mountain's name and logo—a pilgrim in silhouette, carrying a staff. It came complete with matching beige desert boots, plus a black baseball cap and bomber jacket, with SECURITY emblazoned across them in white letters.

The guards loved the new gear. At least now they felt part of some kind of an official team. The afternoon before the new RSOs' arrival Dan and I did the rounds checking all was as it should be. We had to admit the guards were unrecognizable from the rabble that we'd inherited. They looked smart, alert, and on-task.

That evening Robert phoned to let us know he too was flying in. He'd be at the airport early, and he planned to spend a couple of days with us liaising with the new RSOs. The following morning we collected him and whisked him back to the villa for a quick breakfast. From there we drove to the Embassy, and out front was one of our guards dressed in his smart uniform and ready to search our vehicle.

"Great," Robert enthused. "Nice work, guys."

It was good to hear him sounding so positive and upbeat, barely a week after the grenade attack by those two renegade guards.

I took him in to meet Mustaffa, who happened to be the guard force supervisor on that day's morning shift. I tried explaining to Mustaffa that this was the boss of Blue Mountain, and that he'd flown in from Britain to see how they were coming along. I wasn't sure if Mustaffa grasped it all, but he was smart and responsive and paying close attention, which was what mattered.

As we made our way to the TOC to meet the newly arrived RSOs, Robert commented on the obvious.

"That, mate, is a pile of shit," he remarked, pointing out the security fence that was still under construction. "And where's the razor wire on the exterior walls? And what's with the vineyard, for God's sake? You could hide a bloody army in there."

I told him we'd tried to raise it with the RSOs, but up until now there had been the one alone, and he was insanely stressed and overworked.

"And why haven't I seen a single armed guard?" Robert continued. "Where are they? Where are the Americans supposedly protecting this place?"

I told him there was just the one RSO, and a QRF formed from a bunch of 17th February Militia. Robert was staring at me like I had horns growing out of my head. It was a repeat performance of how I'd reacted when Dan had first told me.

"They've got militia acting as the QRF?" he asked, incredulously. "Tell me you are shitting me."

We were nearing the TOC, so we switched to Welsh, just in case any of the RSOs overheard. I repeated for Robert's benefit all that I knew: until today there had been one lone RSO, and he constituted the entire American security contingent for their Embassy in Benghazi. Other than that, the only force mandated to carry any weaponry were the four guys from the 17th February Militia, who for some inexplicable reason were the Mission's QRF.

Robert's eyes were popping out of his head. "But that's totally insane. It's like putting the lunatics in charge of the fucking asylum."

"You got it," I confirmed.

There wasn't a lot more to be said. We were at the TOC and about to meet the new team. We switched back to English as Lee ushered us in, and we did the round of introductions. Rosie Stephenson and her team were dressed in the standard kind of "uniform" for people in our business: desert boots, North Face trousers, and collared shirts left hanging free, in an effort to better cope with the soaring heat.

Rosie was five feet seven, blond, and very athletic-looking. She had to be pushing fifty, and she was still strikingly attractive. Most noticeable of all was her manner, which was warm and approachable. I took an instant, instinctive liking to her. At the same time I could tell by the respect her two fellow RSOs held her in that Rosie was the business. I felt sure she would be more than capable of saying no when she had to, and that she got things done her way and the right way.

"Say, I gotta congratulate you guys on the guards," she told us. "Those guys—they sure look the part."

It was good to hear that.

Rosie's deputies were Adam and Jim. While Rosie was ex-police, Adam and Jim were both ex-military, but that was where the similarity ended. Adam had served in the U.S. Air Force prior to becoming an RSO, whereas Jim was an ex-Army grunt. Pretty quickly Rosie, Lee, and Robert disappeared into an adjoining office, so they could manage the handover between them, which left Dan, Adam, Jim, and me to get acquainted.

You couldn't have asked for two more different guys. Adam was six feet one, slim, and fit-looking, with dark hair and looks. When I told him I was Welsh—as opposed to a Brit—I expected the standard response from anyone who wasn't from our small island nation: *what the hell is Welsh?* But Adam seemed to be a well-read individual. He knew that the United Kingdom was a union of England, Scotland, Northern Ireland, and Wales, and he seemed to know a damn sight more about British history than I did.

By contrast Jim gave the impression of being a typical quiet, tobacco-chewing farm boy. He didn't let on about much, apart from mentioning that he'd done two tours of Iraq prior to training as an RSO. His Iraq experience was more than enough for me—that plus the build of the man. He was six two and naturally massive. As opposed to Tom, our guard force commander, Jim's bulk was all where it should be. He had this incredible V-shaped physique, with big shoulders and chest, and I figured he had to be a bodybuilder.

"So, you work out?" I ventured.

"Should see my dad," he spat. "He's massive."

I laughed. "Jesus, and you're not!"

I explained to Jim that I and the guards had rigged up a make-shift gym in one of the outhouses, adjacent to the side gate. I'm big into weights, and if I don't go training every day I start to go stir crazy. We didn't have much in the way of equipment at the gym, but it was the best we could do: there was no other gym on the entire compound. Jim and I agreed to try to catch a few sessions together when we could.

Robert popped his head around the door. "Come and join us, mate. Rosie wants a word."

I looked around for Dan. I guessed he must have popped out to use the bathroom. "Not Dan," Robert added, switching to Welsh. "Just you."

I made my excuses to Jim and Adam and went to join the others. I felt a bit uncomfortable with Dan not being there, especially as this was his contract, but this was what Robert had asked for. We made a bit of small talk, before Rosie asked me to run her through the grenade attack on the base. I told her the basics of what had happened, and then Lee had this to say.

"It was us who'd hired those guys, not Morgan and Dan. And now they've been sacked, along with all the other bad guys."

It was good of him to volunteer that information. Lee: a top guy.

"Plus get this," Lee added. "Morgan volunteered to stay at the mission if ever we were attacked. I knew Morgan would have stood toe-to-toe with me if the shit went down. It was good to know he was only a phone call away."

Rosie glanced at me, warmly. "Thanks, Morgan. Thanks for making that offer. It's appreciated."

"It wasn't just me. It was Dan, too. We'd both have come to Lee's aid if he needed us."

"That just reinforces the points I was making," Robert interjected. "You need more security here. More boots on the ground. Proper physical security measures would help, but the key thing is having solid, reliable guys on the ground."

Rosie nodded vigorously. "I get what you're saying. Don't worry, I'll get it all in hand. I'll be writing a full security survey of the Mission, and I'll ask for the extra funding, manpower, and equipment we need." She turned to me. "So, Morgan, you've instructed the guard force on everything as per contract? I'll be testing them and drilling them on everything they're supposed to know."

"Feel free," I confirmed. "Go ahead. They're ready."

"The guard force is really, really good now," Lee volunteered. "They're well up to speed."

"I'm only here for three more days, anyhow," I remarked, "but I'll help you all I can with the drills. Then I'm gone."

Rosie coughed, a little uncomfortably. "Well, you know, I wanted to talk about that." She turned to Robert. "Looking over Morgan's CV he's the kind of guy we need here to run security. We'd like him to stay, if that's at all possible."

Robert nodded. "Not a problem. Morgan's good to stay."

Was I? It was the first I'd heard of it. I felt like I'd been set up here, but after all the fine things that Lee had said about me, how could I refuse?

Rosie looked from Robert to me, and since I didn't object I guess she presumed we were all good. "Great. Good to have you on board." She smiled. "But I warn you, I'm a perfectionist where security's concerned and especially the paperwork. I need to be on top of everything and I'll need you likewise."

That first meeting was over pretty quickly. The new RSOs were jet-lagged, and they only had twenty-four hours before they'd be taking over for real, as Lee would be gone.

Robert and I left the meeting and took a stroll outside. "You good with that?" he asked.

"Yeah, I guess. I don't have a lot of choice, do I?"

He laughed. We both knew I'd been set up. Robert must have known they wanted me long-term, and I guessed he'd sprung it on me like that so I didn't have a chance to refuse. The plan now was for Dan and me to work back-to-back rotations. Shortly, Dan would be heading off on his break, leaving me to hold the fort.

Now that I was on the job long-term I did a proper walkabout of the compound with Robert. We mapped out where we needed powerful security lighting, so as to illuminate key areas at night.

Ideally it would be motion-sensitive, so the lights would come on only if there was movement in the compound. We worked out which CCTV cameras were operational and which needed replacing, and where we needed more. We checked out the three gates, all of which were supposed to be operable from the TOC—so that an emergency exit could be planned and executed from there. At present the rear and side gates weren't working.

Then I raised the one thing that was worrying me almost as much as the QRF. I pointed out a tall, towerlike building at the far end of the compound. It lay in the property opposite our own, but it was high enough so as to provide a vantage point offering visibility into just about every corner of the Mission.

"You see that?" I asked Robert.

He eyed the tower. "Couldn't miss it. It's bloody horrendous."

"We can't even erect a sniper screen, 'cause it's not on our land."

A sniper screen is a simple length of canvas or tarpaulin that blocks a potential sniper's view of his target.

Robert scanned the roof. "That's where I'd want to be if I was attacking this place. You could pick 'em all off from up there."

"Too right. You know what I do every time I get here? I walk in the front gate, see that place, and dogleg around Villa C. That way I'm not visible from that roof for the sixty seconds it takes you to walk up the main drive. I'm vulnerable for less than five seconds doing a dogleg like that."

"Yeah, but you can't exactly ask the diplomats and their guests to keep doglegging, to remain out of a sniper's line of fire!"

One of my best friends had been killed by a sniper perched on a high roof in Iraq. The gunman had put the bullet through his neck, and his head had nearly come off. He'd bled out, and there had been nothing any of us could do to save him. I'd been paranoid about snipers ever since, and I was going to do whatever it took to avoid that building.

That evening Robert, Dan, and I headed back to our villa— a place that had suddenly become much more of a permanent home for me. I'd sought out Lee to say a last goodbye, for he'd be gone by the following morning. Now that Rosie, Jim, and Adam were here Lee seemed to have let his guard down a little. I could see how utterly exhausted he was. He looked as if he was barely capable of crawling out of here. He'd been working all hours, and pretty much defenseless. But once a Marine, always a Marine: Lee wasn't bitching.

We shook hands. "You made it, mate. You're done. Travel safely. Semper fi."

"Semper fi, brother. If you're ever in the States, you look me up, y'hear. You got my details."

I was sad to see Lee go. He was ex–Marine Corps, and you don't get better than a Marine in terms of holding the line and putting down the rounds. But on balance, three RSOs should be a damn sight better than one.

That night Robert, Dan, and I had a simple supper of grilled chicken breast and salad. Over the past few days I'd taken on the role of doing the cooking, for Dan didn't seem to bother much about eating. We sat in the lounge having a TV dinner when a deafening burst of gunfire tore the night apart. It sounded as if some serious weaponry was being used, and it sounded real close.

Robert flicked his eyes across to me and Dan. "Fuck was that?"

Dan and I shook our heads. The possibilities were endless: drunken trigger-happy guards, warring militiamen, or maybe the Shariah Brigade coming with their orange jumpsuits.

"Right, get Tom over here now with the AK and some rounds," Robert grated. "I ain't sitting this out without a weapon."

I put a call through to Tom and he confirmed he was on his way. It was Robert's first night; he was a veteran of three top Special Forces units, yet still Benghazi had him rattled. And in truth, Robert's attitude was the right one. Maybe Dan and I had been here too long and we were getting lackadaisical.

The Benghazi night was often torn apart by gunfire—though

not such sustained or heavy bursts as were hammering through the skies around the villa right now. But that didn't mean we weren't under threat, and especially as we ourselves were ripe for a kidnapping.

Pzzzt-pzzzt-pzzzt-pzzzt! Rounds juddered through the air, as whoever was out there unleashed on automatic. It sounded as if we had something like a PKM—a 7.62mm Russian general-purpose machine gun—firing from right outside the villa, and rounds coming back our way on what was definitely a two-way range.

Within minutes Tom was with us and we bombed up the mags for the AK. With Robert and Dan providing cover, Tom and I ventured forth to try to find out what the hell was happening. Machine-gun fire was still being traded back and forth, fingers of fiery tracer probing through the night sky. They appeared to come in slow motion at first, but as they got closer they streaked by at killer speed.

We spoke to someone who was out on the street, and it turned out to be a typical messed-up Benghazi story. Ahmed, the guy who owned the villa, was running in the upcoming local elections. The rival candidate lived in a villa several blocks away. They'd clearly decided that rather than settling it via the ballot box, they'd each have a go at blasting the other away. Ahmed was unleashing fire from a position adjacent to our villa and his rival was returning it with gusto.

I went inside and explained things to Dan and Robert. Robert gave me a look, like he couldn't believe how screwed up this whole place was.

"Is it often like this?" he asked.

"Pretty much, yeah," I said.

"And we're paying this guy good money . . ."

"We are, and the worst of it is we don't have any proper weapons."

"Listen, guys, let's not mess around," Robert told us. "If it gets any worse, relocate to a hotel downtown. First time you really don't feel safe, get out, end of story."

After an uneasy night we took Robert to the airport to catch an early flight. It didn't escape my notice that had I not been persuaded to stay, I would have been catching my own flight out in a couple of days' time. Still, I'd made my bed. I was going to have to lie in it.

Dan and I headed for the Mission, and it was straight into an early meeting with Rosie. We got chatting over a coffee and she revealed that she was scheduled to be here only for a month, as were Adam and Jim. After that, she was off to work at the U.S. Mission in Nigeria on a yearlong contract.

"You seem to have worked in just about every bad place the world has to offer," Rosie remarked to me. "Any experience of Nigeria? Any idea what it's like?"

"Honestly, it's a shithole, and especially if you're going to be stationed in Lagos. It's a dangerous old place, particularly for a woman."

"When were you there?"

"On and off several times over the past few years, and mostly working antipiracy. They've got a problem with piracy off the coast, just like they have in Somalia."

"So Benghazi versus Lagos: which would you go for—not that I've got a choice?"

"On balance, Benghazi. By rights, as we helped topple Gaddafi the Libyans should be our friends."

Rosie nodded. "I guess so."

I didn't want to start moaning on about all the problems here— the 17th February Militia being the worst. I figured I needed to show willingness first, and once Rosie was fully up to speed I could give voice to some of my worst concerns.

"Okay, so the guard force," Rosie began. "So, I'm gonna drill them to death until they're exactly as we want them. I want to hit them with drills when they least expect it, so at all different times of the day. If I ask you, can you come at say ten at night or three in the morning, so we can really shake 'em up?"

"No problem. Tell me what time you need me and I'll get Tom to drop me over."

"I'm gonna hammer and hammer them to get them exactly right."

I smiled. "Great. Perfect. Let's do it."

"No time like the present, then, eh?" Rosie checked her watch. "Say we start the first drill at ten hundred hours, so an hour-thirty from now? I'll take the front gate, Jim can take the side gate, and I'll have Adam in the TOC."

"You got it."

At ten o'clock sharp Rosie rushed up to the guard supervisor, who happened to be Nasir, and yelled that the compound was under attack. For a long moment Nasir just stood there with his mouth hanging open. The guards carried walkie-talkie-type radios for communications between themselves and the TOC, but since most couldn't speak any English the alarm had to be raised in a way that all understood. Hence the drill that I'd banged into them: *hit the duck-and-cover alarm.*

For a moment I feared the guard force was going to fail dismally. But then Drizzi, one of the original guards who'd helped us recruit the new guys, hit the duck-and-cover alarm using the mobile fob that he carried on patrol.

A disembodied metallic voice started blaring out from the loudspeakers set all around the compound. "WHAAAH! WHAAAH! WHAAAH! DUCK-AND-COVER! DUCK-AND-COVER! DUCK-AND-COVER!"

The next part of the drill was for the guards to hit the deck, while they checked out the level of attack they were facing. If it was a serious force of armed men they were to run for it. Otherwise they were to muster at the canteen and wait for further instructions.

It was all a bit of a mess but eventually they made it to the muster point. Nasir radioed Adam in the TOC, telling him that the guard force was awaiting further instructions. It had been a bit slow and disorganized, but they'd got there in the end. I'd have given them a six out of ten, but this was Rosie's show and she was going to do the debrief.

Once we were stood down from the drill Rosie gathered the guards around her. I could hear them sniping at each other in Arabic, each trying to blame the other for why it hadn't been one hundred percent.

"You don't tell me what to do—that's my job!"

"If it's your job then do it properly, or don't bother."

"We had this foreign woman watching us and you messed things up . . ."

"Since when do we work under a woman anyway . . ."

Libyan men tend to treat their own women pretty abysmally. Working under a female boss was going to be very alien to them. Rosie was standing there ready to speak, but they were ignoring her. This promised to be very interesting.

"Right, stop right there!" Rosie ordered. "Shut it! This is when you get to hear from me."

The guards had gone completely and utterly silent. It wasn't so much what Rosie had said as how she'd said it. Rosie was totally fluent in Arabic, yet she'd not let on to a soul. Even I hadn't known. The faces of the guards were a picture. They were in shock. They now knew that Rosie had understood just about every word they'd been saying, and some of it had been pretty sexist stuff. Not only could Rosie speak fluent Arabic, she could write it as well, which blew me away.

Rosie's debrief was merciless, but that was only the start of it. Debrief done, she made them do the same drill all over. After that was done, she just yelled at them: "Again! Again! Again!" She made them do it eight times that first day, running like crazy and getting hammered through the boiling heat of the day. The guards were dropping by the end of it, but Rosie hardly seemed to have broken a sweat.

The next shift got hammered just as intensively, and the next after that—and so the guards learned the hard way to have the highest respect for their new, female boss. At the end of a forty-eight-hour period of such full-on drilling there wasn't a man among them who didn't think that Rosie was the business.

Rosie gathered Jim and Adam and we had a collective heads-up. "They're improving," she told me, happily. "But they still got some way to go."

"I totally agree. A lot of them are pretty much brand-new, fresh out of training, but at least we've got rid of the shit."

"I'd say they're eighty-five percent there. We're getting there."

The main issue was what the guards were to do if attacked by an armed force. All three RSOs were of a similar mind. Once they'd hit the duck-and-cover alarm, they were to make themselves scarce if it was safe to do so.

"They're to run, get out of here, and blend in with the crowd," Rosie concluded. "And from there they're to make their way to safety."

Rosie said she had an extra reason for wanting the guards gone if we hit trouble. It would be hard enough for three RSOs to secure the clients—the diplomatic staff—let alone having to look after a bunch of unarmed Libyan males.

The guards grew to love Rosie, just as much as they respected her. The fact that she spoke fluent Arabic got her halfway to winning their hearts and minds, but it was her iron control coupled with her kindly attentiveness that won them over. She was forever taking them chilled bottles of water, and checking if they were okay and that they understood what they were there for. She even started a daily English lesson for them, which was a big hit.

And no doubt about it, under Rosie's instruction the guards were getting good. If we'd been able to train them to use weapons and arm them properly, they'd have been a force to be reckoned with.

More was the pity then that all they carried were those flip-out metal batons.

CHAPTER SEVEN

From the get-go Rosie, Adam, and Jim worked insanely hard. They were up at 5:00 A.M. checking on the overnight security. They had to plan routes to get the clients—the diplomats—to meetings, plotting their A-to-Bs based on intelligence, known danger—"red"—areas, and prior reconnaissance of the meeting location. They would be working until close to midnight. Three RSOs were certainly better than one, but more were needed to handle the workload, and they needed to be stationed here for longer.

The turnover was a major issue, for as soon as an RSO got to know the ropes, they—like Lee—were burned-out and gone. That formed part of Rosie's earliest feedback that she sent to Washington, but I got the sense that Washington was proving to be something of a black hole: it sucked in every bit of information that she gave them, but nothing came back in return.

Thankfully, my local intel network was proving somewhat more responsive. I'd put out the word that I wanted maximum vigilance, and my guards were to report to me any information they might pick up on the streets. I wanted anything on the Shariah Brigade, plus other assorted bad guys. Snippets of intel started filtering in, and word was that people were getting "disappeared" almost daily.

The city's supposedly peaceful image was a mirage, behind

which dark forces were at work. There was a growing Al Qaeda presence in the area. Partly, it was lone-wolf-type extremist individuals, and partly the ranks of the Shariah Brigade. The Shariah Brigade hailed from the eastern provinces of Libya, an area long associated with Islamic extremism. They'd supposedly joined the liberation struggle to topple Gaddafi, but in reality they were a coalition of various extremist militias that had emerged after Gaddafi's downfall.

Their fighters were tolerated in Benghazi but hardly welcomed. Shortly after Gaddafi had fallen the disappearances had begun. It was an "open secret," according to my guards, that there was a long list of those who were to be "dealt with." It included top commanders from the Libyan Army and Air Force, government officials, bureaucrats, and businessmen, plus anyone else who could be remotely linked to the former regime.

These people were getting blown away on the streets of Benghazi. There was no rule of law to stop these extrajudicial executions, and it wasn't just the Shariah Brigade who were at it. All the militias—the 17th February included—were apparently putting bullets in people's heads as they worked through the "to-kill" list. It was cold-blooded murder and score-settling and it was rampant.

The fact that the militia who formed our QRF were out there killing on the streets made the situation at the Embassy seem all the more insane. There were even reports that 17th February militiamen were joining the ranks of the Shariah Brigade. The more I looked around me, the more I saw Shariah fighters lurking around the city. It was deeply ominous. I kept briefing the new RSOs on what my guards were telling me, and what I was seeing with my own eyes.

Jim, Adam, and Rosie thanked me for the warnings but said they were aware that there were "Al Qaeda elements" in the city. I didn't have a clue where they were getting their intel, for they didn't seem to be building up much of a local network of sources.

Whenever they left the Embassy compound they were driving their armored SUVs all tooled up with weaponry. In a sense they were better protected than me, for I drove around in a thin-skinned local vehicle, keeping a low profile. But they were still only three, and that didn't make the Embassy itself a great deal better protected. We'd had some small-scale attacks already, and I was worried that if the bad guys came in force they could seriously hurt us.

All three of the new RSOs put the obvious question to me: Did I think the bad guys could get into the Embassy compound?

"If they come at night with ten guys or more, they can take us," was my reply. "They'll hit the point of greatest weakness, the front gate, take that out, and kill the guards. No duck-and-cover alarm will be pressed, so you'll have no warning. You'll be in your beds, with no weapons or body armor. They'll be in among you and have the compound before you even know it."

They knew this was the truth but they hated having to hear it—for what more could they do to counter the threat? We were desperately in need of more manpower and resources, but for that they needed backing from Washington.

In my head I'd nicknamed the new lead RSO "Take-No-Shit Rosie." Already she'd caught our first guard sleeping on duty. She told me right away and made it clear that it was unacceptable. I told her that I was in complete and utter agreement with her. I drew up a sign in Arabic and posted it in the guardroom. It warned that anyone caught sleeping on duty would face immediate dismissal. All the guards would be forced to read it before starting their shift.

A week or so into Rosie's reign Tom was driving Dan and me to work when I spotted a familiar figure on the street. It was Alif, one of the first guards that I'd sacked and the first who'd threatened to kill me. I was getting reports that Alif was thirsting for revenge, and that he was trying to foment unrest among my guards. I figured now was as good a time as any to deal with it.

"Pull over, will you, mate," I remarked to Tom.

Being none the wiser Tom drew to a halt at the roadside.

I jumped out and walked up to Alif. "I hear you're still looking to kill me," I announced, in Arabic. "Here I am. Come on—you and me, man to man."

By now Tom had realized what I was up to. He came rushing over and tried grabbing me by the shoulder to pull me back. "You can't do this, Morgan, you can't do this!" he hissed, in English. "You can't just challenge him on the streets."

I shrugged him off. "I can. Just watch me." I repeated my challenge to Alif, in Arabic.

"I didn't threaten to kill *you*," Alif tried. "It's Dan I wanted to kill. He was the one who disrespected me."

"Well, that's even worse," I countered. "Dan's older than me, and he's old enough to be your father. You know, in the Koran it says you must respect your elders. You should be ashamed."

"But Dan disrespected me . . ." Alif tried again.

"Well, d'you want me to go fetch him? He's in the vehicle. You can have it out with him right here and now, if you fancy it."

"No, no . . . As you say, we should respect the elders."

"Look, let's cut the crap. I'm the one who sacked you. So either we get it on now or you can shut it. Period."

"Okay, I will shut up," Alif conceded.

"That's better. And don't ever disrespect Dan. He's seen more action in more wars than you've had hot dinners. Got it?"

Alif told me that he had.

"And if you keep trying to mess with my guard force, trust me, I'll come looking for you."

Alif assured me that he wouldn't dream of it. As far as he was concerned, we were all good.

I made my way back to the vehicle feeling it was a job well done. But I could tell that Tom was fuming. No sooner were we under way again than he started.

"Morgan, you cannot do this! Challenging people on the streets! You do not understand Muslim culture . . ."

That was it. Tom worked for us, we paid his wages, and for days now we'd had this twenty-year-old Libyan twerp giving us death threats and messing with our guards—and here was Tom trying to defend the guy. I'd had more than enough of this.

"Listen, mate, I've worked in Iraq, Somalia, Saudi Arabia, Afghanistan, and the list goes on. I've seen more Muslim culture and more Muslim wars than you'll ever see. Between us, Dan and I have twenty years' experience working in the most dangerous parts of the Islamic world, so don't ever think you can use your you-don't-understand-Muslim-culture bullshit on us. You need to sort out where your loyalties lie. Is it to us and the guards, or to Alif and his sort?"

Tom didn't reply. He knew he was out of order, not to mention out of his depth. I expected honorable, decent behavior from my guards, and especially from the guard force commander. If Tom's loyalties lay with Alif—a lazy, duplicitous ex-employee—then I'd get rid of him, too, and I think he more than knew that. I had challenges enough to deal with as far as the guards were concerned, without Tom's shit on top.

It was around this time that Dan rotated back to Britain, leaving me in the hot seat. I figured I needed to get myself seriously "local" now. I would be back at the villa every night, alone, and I wouldn't always manage to settle it so I had our shared AK-47 with me. I needed to get streetwise. I got Tom to take me into downtown Benghazi, but to drop me at different locations and to wait in the car as I moved around the streets running whatever errands needed doing.

The more time I spent alone on the streets, and the more I settled into the pace of life here, the less anyone seemed to notice me. I needed to be able to operate low-profile like this, for I had zero backup. At the best of times Tom was a drive away, and I wasn't sure I could really count on him. As for Rosie, Adam, and Jim, if I was hit in the villa it made sense that the bad guys might be coming for them, too, in which case they'd have to prioritize their clients—the Embassy staff.

In such circumstances the only person I could depend upon was myself. I didn't particularly like it. It hadn't been like this on previous jobs. The smallest team I'd ever been a part of was four, and that was when shepherding a ship through pirate seas. On a ground operation such as this one you'd never normally form a team of fewer than eight, all of whom would be well-experienced and battle-hardened Brits, Aussies, Kiwis, Canadians, or Americans.

In addition, you'd have a layer of good local security around you. In Helmand Province, Afghanistan, we'd had some immensely brave Pashtuns working for us, and I'd grown close to our local operators. I'd made friends for life there, literally. One guy used to guard our villa in the midst of Lashkar Gah, the capital of the province. It could hold up to sixteen men, and it was a safe house where we could run to if we'd been badly hit.

We'd nicknamed him "Crack Head," for he looked so wired from all the gunfights he'd been in, but he was one hundred percent reliable. He had a team of four under him, and he'd been there since day one of G4S—the security company—getting the contract. Nothing ever seemed too much for Crack Head. I'd have given anything to have a few guys like him on our security team here in Benghazi. If Crack Head and his boys had been parachuted in to replace the 17th February Militia, *then* we'd have had a QRF to be reckoned with.

Crack Head and his men had been our first line of defense, and we knew we were safe with them on duty. One night I'd had a major row with Kevin, one of my fellow white-eye operators. Each day we'd save some of our food to share with the guards. Kevin had started volunteering to take it out to the guys on sentry. At first I'd thought he had to be a real nice guy for doing so. Then I discovered he was taking the main course and mixing it into a mush with the dessert, so deliberately spoiling the food.

It was so utterly mindless and disrespectful, not to mention plain stupid. We depended on Crack Head and his boys for our lives, and over the months they'd become our friends. And now this. Kevin tried telling me they were "only a bunch of stupid rag-heads, so what did it matter." I went berserk. I was team leader, and I made it clear that one more transgression like that and he'd be gone.

A few days later we were heading through open countryside in a four-vehicle convoy. Kevin was driving and I was commanding, so sitting in the passenger seat. We were moving toward the villa when he spotted two young kids coming the other way on a little putt-putt moped. A moment later he'd spun the wheel around in an effort to force them off the road and into a ditch.

I reached over, wrenched it back my way, and just managed to save the kids from getting crushed by four tons of armored SUV. I went completely mental. I practically ripped the guy's head off and stuffed it down his throat. And when we got back to the villa I made it clear to the boss that I wanted rid of this joker, *now*. Or if not, I was out of there.

It wasn't just that he was a racist, cowardly, murderous bastard. He was also a total liability. His behavior with the food had threatened to turn Crack Head and the others against us. That was bad enough. But if he'd succeeded in killing those kids—for there was no doubt in my mind that they would have died—word would have gone around like wildfire, and the entire population of Lashkar Gah would have turned against us.

There was a strong sense of honor and duty among guys like Crack Head, and woe betide anyone who disrespected it. Had those kids been mowed down, we'd have been lucky to escape with our lives. And the key difference between our local security in Afghanistan and here in Benghazi was this: if any one of Crack Head's guys had proven himself incapable of handling his weapon, Crack Head would have been the first to get rid of him. It rested upon his honor to ensure that all his guys were utterly dedicated and shit-hot.

The guy I'd seen at the Embassy who'd lost the magazine off his AK-47 actually turned out to be Mutasim, the *leader* of the

17th February QRF—so there was a fat chance of Mutasim sacking himself. Crack Head and his boys were also some of the bravest of the brave. On several occasions I'd fought shoulder to shoulder with them, and I'd had absolute confidence they would have died for us. By contrast, my confidence levels in the 17th February Militia were at zero.

I already had Mutasim's measure by now and he knew it. He was in the midst of doing a tourism and leisure degree at Benghazi University, yet here he was acting as the leader of the American Embassy's QRF. The rest of his boys were equally inexperienced and unsuited to the task. One was a guy called Hamza. His favorite pastime seemed to be boasting about being a sniper during the revolution to topple Gaddafi.

"I have twenty kills to my name," he'd announced to me. "Twenty confirmed kills."

What a load of shit, I'd thought. "Really? Twenty kills. So what kind of range were you hitting them at?"

"Erm . . . Well, it varied."

"Okay, so what was the maximum kill range?"

"Oh, around a mile or more," Hamza blustered.

"A mile? Wow. Some shooting. So, what kind of weapon were you using—a Dragunov?"

The Russian Dragunov is the most common type of sniper rifle used by militaries and rebel forces the world over. It is ubiquitous and iconic. Every sniper and most soldiers in the world would know of it. It's a bit dated compared to more modern sniper weapons, but it's still a fine piece of equipment.

Hamza shrugged. "Dragunov? What is this?"

"It's more or less the sniper rifle version of the AK-47. It's also the most commonly used sniper rifle in the world."

"Oh, I have never heard of it."

Enough said. Hamza's twenty confirmed sniper kills were a figment of his imagination.

One morning I arrived at the Embassy to see Mutasim strutting around with his AK and ordering my guards about. He was trying to give them all kinds of shitty, menial tasks which had nothing to do with what they were here for. It wasn't the first time he'd tried to lord it over my guards, and I'd had more than enough of it.

I walked up to him and gave it to him straight. "The guards answer to me and the Americans only. You got anything you want to say, you say it to me, direct."

Mutasim's English was great—it had to be for him to be QRF leader—but he barely uttered a word in response. He couldn't even look me in the eye. Here was I, unarmed, but I was more than happy to call him out—for I knew he didn't have a clue how to use the weapon he was carrying. Mutasim was actually scared of his own gun. I knew it, and he knew that I knew, and that's why he so resented me.

Mutasim went off to find Rosie and he had a good moan. She called me in for a chat. She asked me if I had a problem with the QRF, and I guessed now was the time to go for it. I told her that I did, and if Mutasim continued to try to lord it over my guard force then I was out of here. She asked me what exactly was my issue.

"Put simply, when the shit hits the fan the QRF will not back you up," I told her.

She asked me how I could be so certain.

"I've worked with these kind of people all over the world—or rather, I've tried to avoid working with Mutasim's sort. Trust me, they'll take your money, but in the event of an attack at best they'll run, and at worst they'll help your attackers."

Rosie was visibly shocked. I told her that the QRF's weapons skills were atrocious. I told her if she doubted me, then she should get Jim and Adam to do some weapons drills with them. I told her about Hamza boasting to me about being a sniper with twenty kills to his name, something that had sent my bullshit detector off the scale. Of course, Rosie had heard of the Dragunov—not that she claimed to be an ace sniper at more than a mile of range.

Rosie was doubly shocked. The supposed role of the QRF was to repel any attackers once the duck-and-cover alarm had been sounded, so the RSOs could get the Embassy staff into a position where they could protect them. But I knew for sure the 17th February militiamen would never fight and die alongside the Americans they were supposedly charged to protect, and I told her as much.

I'd forged a close bond with many of my guards—first and foremost Nasir and Mustaffa, plus a new guy called Zahid. They were smart, loyal, and sharp, and with Rosie's help they were fully up to speed. None of them put the slightest faith in the QRF and their ability or willingness to stand and fight.

I'd just recruited two extra guards, Karim and Saladin, both of whom had fought big-time to topple Gaddafi. They even had videos on their mobile phones of themselves in action on the front lines. Saladin was still in need of an operation on his leg from where he'd been shot. They knew the 17th February guys employed as our QRF, and they knew that none had seen any combat—which helped explain their appalling lack of weapons-handling skills.

I explained all of this to Rosie. She pointed out that right now the QRF was the only force mandated by the State Department to carry weapons on the compound. Put simply, she didn't have anyone else. The QRF was it. She asked me to help her do some joint drills—the QRF along with my guard force—so we could get them working as one team. I told her that I'd help in any way that I could—but in my heart I knew it was hopeless.

We scheduled the first joint training session for the following morning. I arrived at the Embassy early and went and found Rosie. She looked as if she hadn't slept too well.

"I caught another of your guards sleeping on duty," she announced. "So, I guess that's one that's gotta go."

"Absolutely," I confirmed. "In the British Army if you're caught sleeping while on sentry you'll never live it down. The guy's history."

I asked who it was. She told me it was Suffian. I winced. I'd always seen Suffian as one of my best. I left it until an hour before the end of his shift before telling him he was done. I gave him half the outstanding wages he was owed and told him he'd only get the remainder once he returned his spare uniform and ID card.

Suffian begged me to give him a second chance. "Anyway, I wasn't sleeping. Not really. I was dropping off, but not asleep."

Rosie was a smart lady and she'd taken a photo of him on her cell phone. I showed Suffian the image.

"That you?" I asked.

He peered at the screen and nodded morosely. "Yes, it is."

"Tell me, do you look wide awake or fast asleep?"

Suffian had to admit that he had been sleeping. Still, he was desperate for the work and begged me to reconsider.

"Suffian, you've read the sign. You know the score. I've got no option but to get rid of you."

I told him he was sacked, but I'd try to see if we could bring him back in. Maybe there was a way he could reapply for his job after a suitable lapse of time.

I went and talked it through with Rosie. "Suffian's gone, but he was one of our best. What about if we let him go on a standby list to reapply?"

"Good idea. He'll never do it again, that's for sure. Offer him the option to reapply, but we don't ease up the pressure. We keep showing the guard force real tough love."

I agreed with Rosie on all of this absolutely. But there was also a part of me that was baffled by this focus on my guards. On the one hand it was fine: I was glad Rosie was kicking them into shape. But who was getting on top of the god-awful QRF—the only guys with the weaponry to mount a proper defense of the compound?

Maybe all of that was about to change. We'd scheduled the first combined drill—QRF and guard force—for directly after lunch. I got in position at the front gate so I could check how my guys performed. Rosie headed over to the QRF Villa, rousted Mutasim, and made the announcement.

"Quick! Quick! The compound is under attack!"

No sooner had she uttered those words than one of my guys hit the duck-and-cover alarm, and the horrible metallic wailing began. I saw Mutasim disappear into the QRF Villa, presumably to get his gun. The first to emerge after him was Hamza, the guy who'd boasted about being the world's greatest sniper. I watched in utter amazement as he tripped over his own bootlaces, which were undone, and went crashing to the ground, his AK-47 scooting off into the bushes.

Mutasim came next. He leapt over Hamza, making no effort to help him up, and as he did so two magazines went flying out of his chest rig, spinning through the air, then hit the driveway, spilling rounds all over the place. He didn't stop to pick them up but made for a sandbagged bunker in front of the VIP Villa.

From there Mutasim's supposed role was to put down fire onto the main gateway to prevent the bad guys coming through, while the RSOs got the Mission staff to safety. But right now all he had was one thirty-round magazine for his AK to fight off the hordes of gunmen who were supposedly attacking us. The rest of the ammunition was scattered over the driveway.

The QRF were then supposed to grab their armored SUV, which was parked outside their villa, and slam it in front of the main gate to stop any hostiles driving through. A third member was supposed to get into a second armored SUV and bring it to the VIP Villa, ready to evacuate the Embassy staff. It wasn't a bad drill in theory, but right now it was proving a total fiasco.

By the time Mutasim had made it halfway to his sandbagged position Rosie had decided to give voice to her disquiet, and boy did she let rip.

"START THE DRILL ALL OVER AGAIN!"

Rosie began to drill the QRF day and night. They never knew when the next was coming. She'd seen with her own eyes how my damning assessment of them was at least partly accurate. In terms of tactics and weapons-handling skills, they were hopeless. But she still didn't seem to believe that they would turn and run when the bullets started to fly. Of course, I didn't want to be proven right on that. The last thing I ever wanted was for the Embassy to be attacked and for the QRF to run, leaving the Americans to face the fire alone.

But I feared very much that that was what was coming.

CHAPTER EIGHT

Rosie's awakening about the appalling state of the QRF seemed to draw us closer together. I think she knew by now that I wasn't a whinging Brit, a glass-half-empty kind of guy. I think she understood that my only concern was for the safety of the Embassy, and the American operators and diplomatic staff stationed there.

Rosie cleared it with Rick, the IT guy, that if I was around at mealtimes I was on the canteen roster. The heart of such an operation is always the canteen, and it was over lunch that we all got to know each other better. There were two Egyptian chefs in the kitchen, plus a Bangladeshi waiter, called Asaf, who doubled as the canteen's cleaner. I'd worked a lot with Bangladeshis on the ships, and Asaf and I hit it off right away.

Maybe it's the colonial legacy—Bangladesh being part of the former British Empire—but Bangladeshis certainly can swear. Their favorite everyday curses are the Hindi words *gandu* and *benshoot*—neither of which I am willing to translate. Despite the fact that they are thoroughly obscene, Bangladeshis use them as an informal way to greet each other. Asaf and I took up that time-honored tradition, combining it with our intense rivalry over cricket.

"Gandu!" I'd greet him with, as soon as I saw him.

"Benshoot!" he'd fire back.

We'd crack up laughing.

"England no good," Asaf would continue. "No good cricket."

"We don't even need eleven guys to beat you lot: five would do it! Even Pakistan is better than you . . ."

Bangladesh was getting hammered at cricket and Asaf hated it. The RSOs didn't really get the bond that countries of the former empire have over cricket, and they certainly didn't get Asaf and me firing Hindi curses at each other. At the same time they could see that Asaf loved it: he was always the first to start. But when they asked me what the Hindi insults actually meant, they were dumbfounded.

"Gee, I mean, you can actually *say* that?" Rosie asked, laughing a little nervously. "Doesn't he get upset?"

"Asaf? No, he loves it. He knows he's a gandu. Anyway, he's calling me a lot worse."

I got Asaf talking, and he explained how his six-hundred-dollar monthly wage was sent home to his family in Bangladesh. It paid for his mother and father's upkeep, and for his brother and two sisters to go to school. He kept twenty dollars a month for his welfare, and at night he'd sleep in a gangmaster's room crammed with dozens of other migrant workers. I took to slipping Asaf the odd twenty-dollar note. He was reluctant to take it, but he needed the money.

What made Asaf and my cussing all the more amusing was the smart waiter's uniform he wore—white shirt, black tie and trousers, plus highly polished black shoes. There he was supposed to be all formal and polite, and yet he was cursing like a trooper. It was so incongruous.

We took to watching cricket matches on the plasma TV, and I'd try my best to explain the rules to Rosie, Adam, and Jim. I tried explaining how it was like a giant game of chess. With every ball you moved your fielders into different positions, so that if the batsman did hit the ball you could still catch him out.

"So, the cricket ball, like it's rock hard, right?" Adam would ask.

"Hard as. Way harder than a baseball. If it hits you in the face it can kill you."

Jim would shake his head. "No way."

"Yes way. The ball can come at you close on a hundred miles an hour, and it's rock hard. Sure it can kill you."

Jim shook his head again. "But the guys just look so freakin' gay."

It was the pristine white cricket dress, complete with sharp creases in the trousers, that Jim found so unmacho.

"Hey, gandu, Jim reckons your guys playing cricket look gay!" I'd yell over to Asaf.

The three RSOs would be choking in their soups.

"No, benshoot, English cricket players gay!"

Jim would be grinning from ear to ear. "Like I said—gay as fuck."

That was my cue to have a dig at baseball. "Least it's not a load of fat blokes running around in circles dressed in Lycra tights and chewing tobacco."

Everyone would be killing themselves laughing by now—Americans, Welshman, and Bangladeshi included.

One lunchtime Adam started telling me all these stories about how the QRF had fought heroically in the revolution to topple Gaddafi.

I threw him a look. "Really? Is that so? Big revolutionaries, are they?"

Adam nodded. "Man, yeah, they got some stories."

"Yeah, and that's all they are—*stories. None* of them fought in the revolution."

"Why d'you say that?" He sounded a bit nonplussed.

"'Cause two of my guards did fight, and they have the footage on their cell phones to prove it. And they know the QRF boys, and they know they are full of shit."

Adam looked doubtful.

"Tell you what, mate, take them out on some weapons-handling tests," I suggested. "Then you'll see just how good they are."

"Oh, right." I could tell that Adam didn't believe me. He just thought I was bitching and being awkward.

Rosie was still drilling the QRF like crazy, so I figured she at least had to be getting their measure by now. The truth was no amount of drill would help when the guys didn't even know the basics—how to assemble, load, and operate their weapons. Whenever I saw one of the QRF around with a loaded gun I would get well out of the way. I didn't want to be accidentally shot by someone who thought he was a U.S. Navy SEAL but in reality didn't know one end of an assault rifle from another.

I came in one morning and there were four guys in the compound whom I'd never seen before. They were dressed in the same casual "uniform" as the RSOs, and for a moment I thought that all our prayers had been answered and Washington had finally agreed to send out some more RSOs.

I bumped into Rosie on her way to the TOC. "Jesus, Rosie, result! Four new RSOs! How the hell did you manage that?"

She shook her head. "Sadly, no. It's four guys down from Tripoli to teach the QRF some tactics."

I laughed. "It's worth a try, I guess. But how long have they got? A couple of years?"

Rosie grinned. "Stop it, Morgan, stop it!" She was getting used to my sense of humor by now.

At least this meant that my complaints about the QRF had to be hitting home. But in truth there was only one way to deal with the QRF—and that was to sack the whole lot of them and get a dozen U.S. Marines in their place. Even if it *was* possible to teach them all they needed to know, that wouldn't for one moment put the necessary moral fiber or loyalty into their souls that the job demanded.

Rosie and Adam gathered with the four arrivals as they prepared to do their stuff with the QRF. I could tell by their body language that they didn't want me around, so I moved off to a place where I could watch unobserved. Jim joined me. He was a straight-talking ex-Army guy, and he and I got along real well. In a firefight, he was the kind of soldier I'd want by my side every time.

I nodded in the direction of the four new guys. "You seen that lot?"

Jim spat tobacco juice. "I seen 'em."

"Not SF, obviously," I remarked. "You wouldn't waste Delta or SEALs on that shower of shit."

Jim laughed. "No way. Green Berets, maybe. Or Marines."

We watched as the four guys tried to teach the QRF some basic room clearance techniques. They started by doing a demo. They had their M4 carbines at the shoulder, as they bunched up tight at a doorway, kicked it in, and stormed inside. They were awesome. Their drills were perfection. But the trouble was, room clearance was way above the QRF. They needed to start by learning to strip and reassemble an AK-47, and by doing some live firing out on the ranges.

In room clearance you have to keep your formation tight before going in, but without putting a bullet in the head of the guy in front of you. In spite of what the instructors kept telling them, Mutasim kept holding the muzzle of his AK-47 against the head of Hamza as they massed to go in.

The instructors were going mental: "*Stop* putting your gun on the back of his head, brother! One slip and he's dead!"

The QRF boys kept blaming each other when they got it wrong, and Mutasim typically went into a big sulk. He had Americans yelling and bawling at him, and he was too much of a man to take any of that. He chose now to use the "I don't speak English" excuse. Mutasim was the QRF leader for the simple fact that his

English was great. Claiming that he didn't understand was total bullshit.

I shook my head, despairingly. "This is just lost on 'em."

Jim grunted in agreement. "You can't teach those motherfuckers nothin'."

Jim would say things to me in private that he wouldn't in front of his fellow RSOs. He'd completed two tours of Iraq and been in some major firefights. In my eyes he'd more than earned the right to voice such thoughts.

"Get those pieces of shit in a firefight, they'll run. Plain as." Jim spat into his bottle, as if that was the gospel on the QRF, and in my view it pretty much was.

We had to laugh as we watched, but it was a laughter born out of desperation—not of any sense of high spirits. After all, this was the force tasked to defend the American Embassy in Benghazi. We headed to the canteen for lunch and the four instructors came in. The leader was a fiery-looking redhead.

"Morgan, right?" he remarked, as he took a seat. "You're the security guy, right?"

"That's me."

"I'm Sam, from Vegas," he continued. "And this here's Ivan."

Ivan nodded a greeting. "Good to meet you, Morgan."

Ivan spoke with a thick accent that had to be Russian. "Ivan? Where the hell are you from, Moscow?"

"Somewhere in Russia, yes. But now I am serving in the U.S. military."

"Fuck me, if they let the Russians in there's hope for me yet," I joked.

Being a typical Russian, Ivan got the humor right away. He was a small, wiry, tough-looking operator. I told him how he was the second Russian I'd met who'd gone over to the Americans. Janos was an ex-Spetsnaz—the Russian Special Forces—guy who'd been on my team for the U.S. ACE contract in Iraq. He was a crack operator and we'd become great friends—a friendship we'd maintained when Janos subsequently went to live in the United States.

"So, Morgan, what d'you think of security at the mission?" Sam ventured.

"Lacking in many areas."

"Such as?" he probed.

"Not enough RSOs, obviously. Physical security. Visual barriers. There's all sorts you could do. Put up signs saying 'electrified fencing.' Electrify the fencing. Hell, just complete the fence so there's no gaps in it. You could put up dummy cameras everywhere. You could put up signs saying 'guard dogs on patrol.' You could get some dogs. Muslims hate dogs. They're shit scared of them. There are kennels out the back there and the former occupants had dogs. That way at least my guards would have some dogs to bite the bad guys on the ass."

Sam couldn't help but laugh. "Yeah, yeah, buddy, I hear you. So, what about your guard force?"

I fixed him with a look. "What about them?"

He shrugged. "Like, are they up to the job?"

"What job is that, exactly? Guarding a U.S. diplomatic mission armed only with batons? If we get hit in a sustained attack we've trained them to sound the alarm and run. So are they up to that job? Yeah. Running away—I figure they can manage that."

"Agreed, buddy." Sam shook his head. "Five unarmed guards against armed attackers . . ."

"You'd run and all," I finished the sentence for him.

"So, what do you think of the QRF?"

I put down my knife and fork. "You want the truth? Or d'you want it dumbed down a little, so it's all good and politically correct?"

By now Rosie and Adam had joined us and were listening in. I could see them cringing.

"No, no, buddy—give it to us straight," said Sam.

"All right. The QRF are totally out of their depth. You could spend a year instructing them and you'd still not get them up to speed. Plus they're not to be trusted. They won't stand and fight for Americans or the Mission. You could spend a lifetime training them and that won't change."

Someone choked on their food. People were looking at me horrified. Ivan was staring hard at his plate, trying not to laugh. I figured the guys had realized this during their abortive training session, but no one wanted to be the one to say it.

Sam whistled. "Jesus, buddy, you don't hold back."

"You asked. You got."

At that moment the cricket came on the TV. I threw an insult at Asaf, just to lighten things up a little.

"Hey, gandu, so who you losing to today?"

"Hey, benshoot, England no good!"

I knew I was sounding like a stuck record as far as the QRF were concerned. Rosie and Adam were probably thinking, *Jesus, does he ever stop.* But I had this horrible suspicion I was going to be proven right, and if they kept asking I'd keep telling the truth. I did not want to be proven right. I really liked the Americans here, and I felt we'd gelled as a tight team. They were good-natured, hardworking professionals, and the last thing they deserved was to get saddled with the 17th February Militia as their QRF. No one deserved that.

I was expecting someone to say something to me afterward, maybe Rosie to pull me aside and have words. But not a bit of it. It was like there was an emperor-has-no-clothes syndrome going on here. Everyone knew. No one wanted to say anything. So they left it up to the grumpy Brit to give voice to the unspeakable.

Mutasim became even more unbearable once he was issued an old M16 assault rifle. It didn't make any sense for him to have one, for now he was armed with a weapon that fires 5.56mm ammo, whereas the other three had AKs that use a 7.62mm round. If Mutasim ran out of ammo, he couldn't use that of his fellow

QRF—not that I believed they would ever stand and fight. But still Mutasim with his M16 clearly felt vastly superior to the others with their AKs.

Mutasim had a somewhat schizophrenic attitude toward me. On the one hand he knew I saw right through his bluster and bullshit, and he hated it. On the other, he kept trying to ask me to tell him my "war stories." I was a good deal older than Adam and Jim and I guess Mutasim knew I must have seen some action. I didn't tell him or any of the other QRF boys anything. I didn't trust them, and as far as they were concerned I was more than happy to remain the gray man.

But truth be told, all this crap with the QRF was getting to me. I'd never known anything like it, not in ten years working as a private military operator. It was so obvious what needed to be done here: 17th February Militia out, Marine Corps in. With 250,000 U.S. Marines to choose from, I couldn't believe Washington couldn't spare us a dozen. I decided I needed to go find me a proper gym. I needed to work out some of my anger and frustration pumping iron.

I'd noticed this place in downtown Benghazi that looked like a members-only gym. It was a white building with a mural of a bodybuilder painted on the front. I got Tom to drive me there and ask if there were any other Westerners using the place. He came out and told me there were. I offered him a deal. I'd pay for his membership if he'd train with me, just so I had someone to watch my back.

Tom knew well he could do with losing some weight, and so we started to train there every day. We'd alternate timings, either before or after work, so as not to set too regular a pattern. It was a well-equipped place, and there were at least three hard-core bodybuilders working out there. I didn't see any other Westerners, but the locals couldn't have done more to make me feel welcome and secure.

From the get-go the owner gave me a great deal of reassurance.

"Don't worry about being here," he told me. "If anyone tries to come in who I don't know and trust, I'll warn you—then you can get out the rear."

He showed me where the back exit was, and how to make a getaway from there. The other regulars gave me similar reassurances. These were the decent, honest Libyans whom I hoped the revolution would favor, not the likes of the Shariah Brigade—but sadly, I wasn't too sure these educated, liberal types would come out on top. Still, I had myself a gym and a training partner in Tom, and I was able to work off some of my worst frustrations, which was a blessing.

I was at the Embassy a few days after the abortive training of the QRF when something struck me as being really odd. My guard force, the QRF, and the RSOs shared the one radio net. They carried these small Motorola radios, which were fine for communications in and around the compound.

But I'd noticed that the RSOs had an extra radio, and every now and then I'd seen them take a call on it. They'd do their best to make themselves scarce whenever they got a buzz on this second net, but today there was going to be no hiding it. We were at lunch in the canteen when all three of the RSOs' radios hummed into life. They reached as one to turn the volume down, but still I caught most of the message.

"Bulldog, Eagle One, wheels up in five minutes. Wheels up in five . . ."

Rosie got up from the table, and I knew she was going to take the call somewhere private. The caller's accent had been very American, and I knew Rosie had to be communicating with some other "agency," one that couldn't be so far away. Even with a repeater station—a gizmo that would sit on a rooftop somewhere between the two transmitters, to increase the reach of the radios—they wouldn't have a range of more than a few kilometers.

With Rosie gone there was a bit of an uncomfortable silence, because both Adam and Jim knew that I'd heard. "Wheels-up" is generally code for a vehicle or aircraft leaving a base, "wheels-down" meaning the opposite. A few moments later Rosie was back, trying her best to act as if nothing had happened.

I stopped eating and glanced at the three of them. "Okay, guys, listen, I'm not stupid. You've clearly got another call sign somewhere in Benghazi. I don't know where or who they are, but I don't need you to keep running outside every time they come up on the net. I've worked alongside your CIA and SOF for eight years or more, so I know how it works. When they come up on the net I'll walk outside, for the less I know the better."

There was a moment's silence after my little speech, before all three of them burst out laughing.

"Fair enough," Rosie remarked. "From now on, we'll do it your way."

I meant what I had said. The less you know about a secret, black outfit—one that's operating under the radar—the less you can give away to an enemy if you're captured and interrogated. Whoever this other call sign was, it was clearly a need-to-know operation, and I didn't need to know anything about them in order to do my job properly.

As matters transpired there was a second American base in Benghazi situated about ten minutes' drive away from us. It was called simply "the Annex." The mixed CIA/Special Operations Forces team located there served a dual purpose. Their primary role was to hunt down any MANPADS—man-portable surface-to-air missiles—and sophisticated antitank rockets that had fallen into militia (and hence possibly Al Qaeda) hands.

Over the years Colonel Gaddafi's regime had sourced thousands of antiaircraft missiles, the most sophisticated being the Russian Igla-S. The Igla-S is known as "the Grinch" to NATO forces, and it is a state-of-the-art missile system. It boasts a six-kilometer range, a two-color infrared seeker system that is all but impossible for an aircraft's defenses to defeat, plus a 2.5-kg high-explosive warhead with a proximity fuse, meaning it can explode simply when close to a target (in other words, it doesn't actually have to hit it).

There were also worrying reports that the French had air-dropped MANPADS to the militias, as part of the process of arming them to bring down Gaddafi's regime. If that was true, then the French had doled out MANPADS to the rebels only for the Americans to have to try to hunt them down and get them back again. I guess this all made sense to someone, somewhere—just not to me.

If any Igla-S had fallen into Shariah Brigade or Al Qaeda hands, airliners were very likely going to start getting shot down, hence the need to track them down. Trouble was, the MANPADS in Libya had gone underground: they'd fallen into militia hands and very quickly been squirreled away. Likewise, many of the Libyan Army's sophisticated ATGMs—antitank guided missiles—had gone the same way. The MANPADS and ATGMs had been cached by the militias, awaiting future conflicts—or, with the more extremist groups, terrorist applications.

Hence the Annex.

Officially, the Annex didn't exist, but there were those in Benghazi who knew about it, and now I was one of them. It was what people in the know call a "Velvet Hammer Operation"—a deep black project, one hidden behind layers of "deniability," denoting a soft approach to getting something hard done. I figured there would be a mixture of CIA, Delta Force, and SEAL operators based there, plus ex–Special Forces private contractors. The secrecy surrounding the Annex had to be real tight, for my guards had never mentioned it, and they knew pretty much everything that went down in Benghazi.

Apart from hunting for surface-to-air missiles, the other role of the Annex was to act as an extra layer of backup for the Embassy. While I didn't know exactly where they were located, it was good to know the boys from the Annex were around somewhere, as an added layer of security.

Once I had learned of the Annex's existence several things fell into place. I understood now why we were billeted off compound, and why there had been sensitivity over us using the Internet and the canteen. No one wanted us hanging around too much and witnessing the liaison between the Embassy and the Annex, and the night visits that were very likely going down. That was all part of the deniability. I also had a good sense now from where Rosie, Adam, and Jim were getting their intel.

Shortly after learning of the Annex's presence I was in the canteen eating lunch when a guy walked in whom I'd never seen before. He glanced in my direction, uttered a quiet "hello," then went to the hot plate and loaded up some food. He came and joined me. He had U.S. Special Forces written all over him. When you have worked with these types before you start to be able to recognize certain traits. He was around six feet tall, lean and muscular, but quiet.

"You must be Morgan," he volunteered. "I'm Frank."

"Yeah, nice to meet you, mate," I replied.

We ate the rest of our food pretty much in silence. I knew the protocol. No outside agency was supposed to be privy even to the existence of the Annex, let alone its function, and to all intents and purposes I was an outside agency. I finished my meal, got up to leave, and wished the guy a pleasant day.

"You too, buddy," he replied.

I never saw him again, but I did see other teams coming through now and again. I made a point of making myself scarce whenever they were around. I didn't want to embarrass any of the RSOs, or the Annex guys, by forcing them into a situation where they'd have to ask me to leave. It was better I got out of the way of whatever cloak-and-dagger stuff was going down at the Embassy.

All seemed to be going well at the downtown Benghazi gym, and it offered a good refuge whenever I had to make myself scarce at the Mission. Tom was acting a bit like Arnie throwing the weights around, but otherwise all seemed to be good. One afternoon we were working out and one of the regulars, a thickset Libyan, took his position at the bench press next to me and struck up a conversation.

"All right, mate? I'm Sulli, how you doing?" I was surprised to find he had a thick northern England accent.

"Yeah, I'm good."

Sulli told me he was Libyan by birth, but he'd lived in Manchester—a city in the northwest of England—for decades. He spent a few weeks in Benghazi every year, visiting his parents, which was what he was doing now, and the rest of the time he lived and worked in the United Kingdom.

"You working in town?" he asked me.

"Yeah, I'm a paramedic."

He stared at me for a long moment. "Is that right? Not what your mate there's been telling everyone."

He proceeded to relate to me everything that Tom had been saying at the gym. Apparently, he'd been going around telling anyone who would listen that I was the head of security at the U.S. Embassy and that he was my personal bodyguard.

"Everyone in here knows, mate," Sulli added. "No one in here gives a damn, but if the wrong people find out, that guy and his mouth are going to get you killed."

I was speechless. "Everyone knows?"

"Everyone knows. Get rid of him or he'll get you killed."

"Everyone knows?" I still couldn't believe it. This was my worst-ever security nightmare.

"Yes, mate, because he keeps telling them—all the time. He goes on about being your BG *all the time*. I don't care where you work, mate. That's your affair. I'm just trying to watch your back."

"Thanks," I told him.

"Get rid of the idiot with the mouth, then you'll be okay."

"No, mate, that's it—I can't come here again."

"No, no—you can still come," Sulli remonstrated. "Just get rid of him."

I shook my head. "It doesn't work that way."

I got my stuff, got hold of Tom, and we left. I was never going to set foot in that place again. Our security had been spectacularly blown. I marched Tom to the vehicle and once we were safely on the move I related to him all that Sulli had told me.

His face was ashen. "No, no—he's lying. I never said—"

"Tom, cut the crap. Am I supposed to believe the guy somehow guessed from out of nowhere that I run security at the U.S. Embassy? Tom, you are a liar and a liability. Fact."

I got him to drive me direct to the villa and I sent him home. There was no point in my unloading on him. He knew how badly he'd messed up. He'd put my life and his own in danger and all in an effort to make himself look big. But my real worry was this: If this is what Tom was saying to the guys in the gym, what was he telling everyone else in Benghazi? I shuddered to think.

Another thing was crystal clear to me now: the threat level just kept escalating. Even a guy like Sulli—someone who spent most of his life in England—knew how real the danger was to an American, or anyone perceived to be an American, on the streets of Benghazi. His warning had been specific and very direct.

If the wrong people find out, that guy and his mouth are going to get you killed.

CHAPTER NINE

I briefed the RSOs on the basics of what had happened. I figured they needed to know due to the specific threat to Americans. But before we could take any action, we had our next crisis at the Embassy. Perhaps he was trying to make amends for his galactic security breach at the gym, but Tom went in early to check on the guard shift, after which he intended to roll by the villa and collect me.

Tom reached the Embassy's main gate and there was Mutasim waiting for him. Mutasim announced he was going to search Tom and all my guards, before any were allowed to start their shifts. Tom told him to get lost. None of the QRF had ever asked to search anyone before, and it wasn't their job. It was a guard force role. Mutasim reacted to Tom's words by blowing a fuse.

Tom went into the guardroom to start work and Mutasim stormed off to the QRF Villa. He came charging back with his weapon, yelling at Tom: "I'm going to kill you! I'm going to kill you!" Seeing Mutasim brandishing his AK, Tom had taken off, driving away in his Chrysler at top speed. He'd made his way to me, which meant I was fully briefed by the time we made it back to the Embassy.

I told Tom to drop me fifty yards from the main gate so I could walk in and get a sense of things. I told him to stay in the vehicle until we had it sorted, just in case Mutasim was still spoiling for a scrap. I got to the gate, my guards let me in, and there was no sign that anything was particularly amiss. But I knew the RSOs would be on the case and I made my way directly to the TOC.

Sure enough, Rosie, Adam, and Jim were in there, watching the tapes of the incident on CCTV replay.

"D'you know what's just happened?" Rosie asked me, worriedly. "Watch this."

They rewound the tape, and played it. There was no sound, but it didn't really need any. I saw Mutasim tearing out of his villa in what for him amounted to killer mode. I could see him pointing an AK-47 at Tom and yelling something about his intention to kill my guard force commander. But by the end the whole thing had me in fits of laughter. It was like a sketch from a bad B movie, only worse.

The RSOs didn't seem to share my amusement. "So, Morgan, mind telling me what exactly is so funny?" Rosie demanded.

"If Mutasim can't handle a verbal confrontation with one unarmed man, how d'you think he'll react when faced with an armed force?" I replied. "But that's not the funny part." I reached forward and pointed out something on the screen. "How does he think he's going to shoot Tom when there's no magazine on his weapon?"

It was true. Mutasim had come rushing out of the QRF Villa screaming that he was going to kill Tom, but with no magazine on his assault rifle, which meant he had no bullets to fire.

"More to the point, how do you think he's going to defend the Embassy when he can't even arm his weapon? Rosie, you need to get rid of this idiot before he causes some real damage and kills someone—that's providing he can remember to load his gun. Let's face it: the QRF need to go. They need replacing with some proper, professional soldiers—like U.S. Marine Corps."

I knew I was overstepping the line here, for in a sense this wasn't my business. My role was to manage the guard force. But hell, it needed to be said.

Rosie radioed Mutasim and ordered him into the TOC. He turned up a minute later with Hamza, his fellow QRF groupie. Mutasim was actually in tears, and Hamza had his arm around him.

Hamza glared at us, reproachfully. "Mutasim, he is really upset."

I could not believe what I was seeing and hearing.

"Mutasim, why did you pull a weapon on Tom?" Rosie asked.

Mutasim half sobbed out a reply. "He called me a motherfucker."

"You pulled a weapon on someone for that?" I asked, incredulously. "You know what—you're a total bloody liability."

Rosie turned to me and asked me to leave the TOC. She would sort it out from here, she explained.

I did as I'd been asked. I actually walked across to my guardroom with a new spring in my step. At the very least this had to mean that Mutasim was gone, and maybe this spelled the end of the 17th February Militia working at the Mission. God knows, it was long overdue. I could sniff the winds of change blowing through the compound. *Yee-ha, let's get the Marine Corps in.*

An hour later I was called back to the TOC, I presumed to hear the good news. I arrived and all three RSOs were in there, but the atmosphere wasn't quite as positive and upbeat as I had been expecting.

"I'm afraid Tom is no longer allowed on the compound," Rosie announced. "So, you'll need to find a new guard force commander."

I narrowed my eyes. "I take it Mutasim's also got the boot then?"

Rosie gave a quick shake of her head. "No, I'm afraid we need to keep him."

I forced myself to count to three. "Right, just so I've got this clear, 'cause I'm having some trouble understanding: you're sacking my guard force commander, who didn't pull a weapon on anyone, but you're retaining the leader of the QRF—someone who did pull a weapon on someone who was innocent, and then started crying afterward—and all because *you need him*? Yeah, he sounds really stable. So, to be clear—is that it? Am I understanding things correctly here?"

"Yes, Morgan, I'm afraid you are, but—"

"Fuck this," I cut in. "I'm out of here. I cannot work with this pathetic, tree-hugging attitude. You give the QRF far too much credit and one day you'll see what they are made of. Christ's sake—he doesn't even know how to load his own weapon! When the shit hits the fan, trust me, they will be found wanting. Anyhow, it won't be my problem. I'm resigning. I'm out of here."

Rosie, Adam, and even Jim were shocked into silence. I turned and left. I made my way to Tom's vehicle and gave him the news that he was sacked. For a moment he didn't know what to say. It was the last thing he'd ever been expecting.

"But sacked for what?" he asked, disbelievingly. "I didn't pull a gun on anyone!"

"No, you didn't. Did you call Mutasim a motherfucker?"

"Yeah, but he called me it, too."

"Well, whatever, you're sacked. And I'm out of here, too. I'm resigning. I've had more than enough of this shit."

Tom dropped me at the villa and I set about packing my gear. It was early evening by now and still I was fuming. I logged on to the Internet to search for a flight. Once I found one I'd phone Robert and give him the news. He wouldn't be happy. He'd need to find a new security manager and at short notice. But on paper this read like a cushy little posting, so it shouldn't be too difficult to find one. In any case, once I told him what I'd been put through I figured he'd understand.

My phone rang. I answered. "Morgan here."

A moment's silence, then: "It's Rosie. Listen, will you come in, in the morning, so we can talk? Will you do that for me?"

I respected Rosie hugely and I owed her that much. And because of that I said I'd be in at 0800 hours as usual.

That night I stewed on what had happened. I wasn't falling on my sword because of Tom, although I sensed he appreciated the gesture of solidarity. Tom had his faults, as do we all. I am hardly the most diplomatic of individuals and my blunt outspokenness rubs people the wrong way. I was resigning because I could not work in this kind of environment anymore, and especially alongside the QRF.

The RSOs thought they needed the QRF, because they had so little firepower and backup. But we'd be far better off getting rid of them and bringing things to a head. If the QRF were sacked for being the incompetent and dangerous liabilities that they were, surely that would force Washington's hand.

The following morning Rosie and I met in the TOC, just the two of us. There was zero hostility in the air, just a sense of sadness that things had come to this. We'd been pulling together as one team and making real progress. It sucked that a guy like Mutasim had come between us. Rosie made me a coffee. I was half hoping that she would have come to her senses overnight and sacked Mutasim.

"Morgan, whether you stay or go, you've got to understand one thing," she began. "With Mutasim I have no choice but to keep him on. He knows too much about the inner workings of the Mission, and I can't afford to replace him. Plus he's the only one of the QRF who speaks decent English."

"So, you sacrificed my guard force commander in order to keep Mutasim?"

"Pretty much, yeah. But I want us all—you, your guards, the QRF—to work as one, tight team." Rosie paused. She looked me in the eye. "Morgan, will you stay on? Will you stay and help me get there with all of that?"

I thought about it for a moment. I tried putting myself in Rosie's shoes. From her perspective, it was easier for me to replace

Tom than it was for her to replace Mutasim. But that made sense only if you believed the 17th February lot were worth keeping on. After all that Rosie had seen of them she had to have their measure by now, so I could only presume that Washington had forced her hand.

Maybe they'd told her outright that no other force was available? The more I thought about it, the more that was the only scenario that made any sense: *she didn't have anyone else.* If that was the case then Rosie had been placed in an impossible situation. She'd made the only call she could make—*to retain the only armed force on offer to her*—and my resigning would only serve to make matters worse.

"Yeah, okay, I'll stay," I conceded, "but only on one condition: I cannot have Mutasim and his lot ordering my guards around. You have to understand, Rosie, my guards have seen more combat and action than Mutasim and his lot have had hot dinners. If the QRF can order them about, my guys will be a laughingstock and we'll lose the lot."

Rosie said she was good with that. The QRF would have no role overseeing my guards. But even so, it was obvious that Mutasim had got one over on us, and now I had to recruit a new guard force commander. In spite of his faults guys like Tom were as rare as rocking-horse shit here in Benghazi. The only consolation was that my stint here was almost done. In a few days' time I would be going on leave, and in truth I couldn't wait.

I phoned Robert and told him the news: I was stand-in guard force commander until I could find a replacement for Tom. Robert had some news from his side, too. Dan wasn't coming back. He'd declined the offer to return for his second stint in Benghazi. Robert had a handful of guys he was looking at as a replacement, but I didn't think any of them would cut it. I told Robert I knew of a guy I'd worked with before on the circuit who would be perfect.

Bob Raymond had spent ten years working as an undercover policeman in some of the United Kingdom's toughest urban environments, busting drugs gangs. There were six British cities that he could never return to, or his life would be in danger. He had the ideal background and skill sets for the Benghazi job. I shared his credentials with Robert and Rosie and we agreed that Bob was the one.

Bob flew in two days prior to the start of my leave, so I had time to do a proper handover. By now I'd managed to recruit a new guard force commander, a guy called Omar. He was an older, skinny waif, but at least he spoke reasonable English. Most important, the guards had recommended him and seemed to trust him. Omar was harmless, if a little sycophantic, especially where the Americans were concerned. He was also incapable of shutting up. He could talk the proverbial glass eye to sleep.

Bob seemed more than happy with his role—managing the guards—but he was visibly shocked at the lack of any American forces standing security at the Embassy. He was a cool, calm, unshakable kind of a guy. You'd have to be to do the kind of undercover work that he'd done with the drug gangs. Yet the same security failing that had so unsettled Robert and me had Bob ill at ease. I told him the obvious: we could only work with what we had.

At the same time that I was leaving Rosie, Adam and Jim were on their way out, which meant it was all change at the Embassy. Rosie knew she was leaving the job half done and she was troubled. She confessed to me that she'd happily have served twelve months here, if that was what it took to get things in shape. I told her it was due to her "take-no-shit" attitude that they were as good as they were.

Under Rosie's watch my guard force had been transformed. They were smart, alert, and slick with their drills. Each of my guards was equipped with a fob, via which they could activate the duck-and-cover alarm from anywhere in the compound. Construction on the security fence was done. All three gates could be opened and closed from the TOC, and the CCTV cameras were working. This was serious progress compared to how things had been, and it was all down to Rosie.

Rosie was one of the best security professionals I'd ever had the pleasure to work with, and I told her as much. She would be sorely missed at the Embassy . . . and especially as it was about to get hit big-time.

It was 0330 hours when a massive blast tore apart the peace of the night. Luckily, just a few minutes earlier the guard force had spotted trouble. They'd seen a man in traditional Islamic robes crouched by the front gate fiddling with something on the ground. His dress alone had roused their suspicions: Libyan men tend to wear Western clothing. It was only the Shariah Brigade and their ilk who dressed in turbans and robes, and as tonight's attack would indicate, their ranks were very often filled with foreign fighters.

Moments before the figure had dashed off into the night, yelling "Allahu akbar! Allahu akbar!"—*God is great*—my guards had hit the duck-and-cover alarm. Luckily that night's guard force supervisor was Nasir, one of my best. He'd radioed for an RSO, and from the guardroom window they could hear a hissing noise and detected the acrid smell of burning. The RSO had ordered an immediate evacuation, and as they'd sprinted from the guardroom the device had detonated.

The explosion was powerful enough to blast a hole eight feet wide and twelve high through the Embassy's outer wall, tearing apart the inner security fence and hurling debris far and wide. A cloud of pulverized concrete and thick smoke had engulfed the front gate, and it was only the fact that they were running away from the attack point that saved my guards and the RSO. They were no more than twenty-five yards from the gate when the device exploded, and by anyone's reckoning the fact that no one was killed or injured was a miracle.

It was highly unusual to see a guy dressed in traditional turban and robes in Benghazi. I'd only noticed a handful myself, and I was out on the streets more or less every day. That alone suggested this was an attack by foreign elements, as opposed to a homegrown affair. More to the point, the explosion was caused by an IED, and seldom had IEDs been used in the war to topple Gaddafi. That made this a first for Libya.

IEDs are a very deliberate, premeditated form of attack. If someone had hit the Embassy with a grenade, or even an RPG, we could have put it down to opportunism. But not an IED. An IED needs to be manufactured by a competent bomb maker, someone with the tools, the knowledge, and the raw materials. Such skills do not come easily. British soldiers aren't taught them. Neither are Americans, and neither were Gaddafi's armed forces. In short, IEDs are the domain of professional insurgents and terrorists.

In order to blast a hole that large in the Embassy wall, this IED had to have been a significant one. It was still a "one-man carry"— we categorized IEDs in Iraq and Afghanistan by how many it took to carry them—as evidenced by the lone guy who had planted it. A larger device would have needed two people or even a vehicle to deliver it. But we suspected the real target of the bomber was the Embassy's front gate. The attacker had been spooked by the guards' vigilance, and stopped short with the device, setting it instead against the wall.

If he had hit the gate it would have been blasted off its hinges. Even as it was, the IED had still punched a massive hole through the perimeter wall. Had the bad guys been mustered in strength to attack, they would have been able to pour through and they'd have been inside the compound within seconds. At that point my guards would have run, and the QRF would very likely have taken to their heels—leaving Rosie, Adam, and Jim to face the enemy. It didn't bear thinking about.

While working on the U.S. ACE contract in Iraq I'd been hit nine times in IED strikes. IEDs are only ever planted so as to hit a specific target with a specific intention. That had proven the case every single time we were hit in Iraq, and I figured it would prove likewise here in Benghazi.

Route Tampa was the main supply road leading to our base in northern Iraq. It quickly earned the nickname "IED Alley." One day we'd been on a four-vehicle move, with a gun truck—an armored Ford Excursion 550, with a 7.62mm M240 machine gun mounted in a roof turret—taking up the front and rear positions. In the two central vehicles were the HVTs—State Department officials—plus myself as team leader and various operators from the security team.

We were fourteen security guys in all, and we each carried a Colt Diemaco assault rifle or a squad automatic weapon (SAW) light machine gun, with one thousand rounds of ammo per person. That was the right size of force and weaponry for such a vehicle move—or for securing a setup like the Benghazi Embassy, for that matter.

We were barreling along Route Tampa when an IED detonated at the roadside, taking out the lead vehicle—the gun truck. It was highly unusual for the bad guys to hit the gun truck. They would always try to smash one of the two central vehicles, for they knew the HVTs rode in those. The triggerman must have hit the detonation button just a fraction early, but still it wasn't good news: Danny, the turret gunner, had had his head and shoulders exposed to the blast.

The gun truck had been blasted side-on to the road, and it was a wreck. We had no idea how many casualties we'd taken, plus we were forty miles from the nearest friendly base. The second vehicle—mine—pulled alongside the stricken truck, so we could open our doors and cross-deck the injured from theirs into ours. At the same time I radioed in our location and status to operational headquarters. As team leader it was my responsibility to get us out of this one without losing anyone, and in particular the clients.

Because we had high-level U.S. government officials on board we knew we'd get priority in terms of air cover. We were told air support was on its way, although we had no idea what assets were coming. Amazingly, Danny wasn't seriously injured, and the four guys inside the armored wagon were pretty much okay. But before we could get them moved across into our vehicle, stage two of the attack was sprung. A murderous barrage of fire started hammering into us from positions set to either side of the road.

This was now a complex attack, the IED being the trigger. We knew we needed to keep our vehicles together and put down some serious return fire, but we had to do so without making ourselves an easy target. If we pulled in too close, they could put one RPG into the heart of us and cause some serious carnage. Having got the HVTs' heads down in the armored SUVs, the other gun truck pulled in parallel to us. We'd now formed a firebase from which to repel the attack.

We dismounted the vehicles and got into cover behind the engine blocks, and started returning fire. Danny was back in the turret of the stricken gun truck blasting out the rounds on the M240, and the other turret gunner roared into action. Against us we had dozens of shooters who were in good cover in the farmland to either side of the road. They were hosing us down with AK-47s and PKM light machine guns, and we were exposed here out on the road.

At the same time as getting the rounds down I scanned for an inbound vehicle. If they were smart they'd have planned a third stage to the ambush: some kind of truck laden with explosives—a VBIED, or vehicle-borne IED. If they could slam one of those into our position, they could really make us fry. The only way to stop a speeding truck is to hit it a good three hundred yards out from your position—hence the need to keep one eye scanning the highway.

Luckily, the enemy's fire discipline wasn't up to much. They were hitting us with typical "spray and pray" tactics. There were a massive amount of rounds going down and a lot of noise and smoke, but much of it was wide of the target. Even so, we were five long minutes into the firefight by now, and even with a thousand rounds per man our ammo supplies were fast dwindling.

We got fifteen minutes into the fight and I was sure we'd killed some of the bad guys, but there was no sign of them backing off. More to the point, we were running out of ammo. It was then that we heard the most welcome sound of all—the *thud-thud-thud* of incoming Apache helicopter gunships. We knew the Apache pilots well. We used to drink coffee with them and have a laugh back at the base canteen in Mosul. There were none better than those guys.

Danny and his fellow turret gunner had lasers, with which they could paint the enemy positions. The Apache crews homed in on the hot point of those lasers—where they struck the ground—and opened fire with their 30mm cannons. *Brrrzzzzzzzzzzzzt!* With the pair of gunships hammering the enemy positions the fire dropped off almost to nothing.

Finally we managed to transfer the last of the guys from the stricken gun truck into the other vehicles. We torched the gun truck by throwing a white phosphorus incendiary grenade inside it, then got the hell out of there, leaving the Apaches to finish off the enemy.

That time, we all survived the IED strike and follow-up attack. But we'd been lucky. We were fourteen crack operators with some serious firepower to hand. Even so, via a well-planned IED strike the bad guys had had us pinned down and running short of ammo. It was only the superlative air cover that had got us out of there. And the key point with relation to the Benghazi IED strike was this: *no one ever wasted an IED.* No one ever planted one without proper planning, a specific target, and a bigger-picture strategy.

The big-picture plan on Route Tampa had been simple: hit our convoy, disable a vehicle, prevent our escape, and tear us to pieces in the follow-up ambush. Their intention had been to kill us all.

They hadn't managed it that time, but during another period we lost five men in the space of three days. Such well-planned, multi-stage attacks could prove extremely debilitating and deadly.

Likewise, no one had planted the IED at the Benghazi Embassy simply to blow up some concrete blocks. After all, the wall could be easily repaired, as indeed it was. It didn't take a rocket scientist to work out what the IED must have been for. It was to test the Embassy's defenses, and to see how easy it would be for a follow-up force to gain access to the compound.

But in a sense it wasn't my problem anymore, nor that of Rosie or the other RSOs. I got myself out of Benghazi on leave, and Rosie, Jim, and Adam were likewise gone—Rosie reassigned to Nigeria, and Jim and Adam rotating back to the United States.

For now, at least, the IED and its aftermath were someone else's worry.

CHAPTER TEN

I arrived back in Benghazi on July 24, 2012, but I hardly felt as if I'd been away. Bob was desperate to get out of there and I could understand why. While there had been no further attacks on the Embassy itself, the security situation in the city appeared to have gone into free fall.

In the worst attack yet, the British ambassador's convoy had been ambushed as it drove through the city streets. It had been raked with fire, one RPG punching through the rear windshield of a vehicle and passing out the front window, but miraculously without detonating. The RPG had been unleashed at such close range that it hadn't had time to arm itself properly—hence it hadn't exploded. Had it detonated, everyone in that vehicle very likely would have been killed.

As it was, the RPG round had torn apart one of the security operator's shoulders. He was a fellow Welshman who worked on the British Embassy's close protection team and was a good friend of mine. I'd been emailed the photos of the wreck of the RPG-struck vehicle: no doubt about it, the guys had had a miraculous escape. So while I'd been away from Benghazi physically, news like that had kept dragging me back again, at least in my head.

The six guys riding security on that convoy were battle-hardened operators who loved a fight. But by the time they'd de-bussed from the vehicles and got their weapons in the aim, the bad guys had melted away into the crowd, the attack had been so slick. This acted as a powerful wake-up call, at least to the British. Two days after the attack they shut down their mission and pulled out of Benghazi.

I wasn't surprised the Brits had pulled out. Having worked on Foreign and Commonwealth Office contracts, I knew how the system worked. The FCO's Overseas Security Manager would have reviewed the security situation on the ground, the likelihood of a repeat attack, manpower, and how critical the mission was, and concluded that the only option was to withdraw. Yet they had *double* the number of close protection operators—the equivalent of RSOs—as the American Mission had.

I'd watched the events unfold from afar, fully expecting the Americans to follow suit. But not a thing of it: the Mission had carried on, business as usual. It didn't make any sense, and to me it was doubly worrying. My friends working on the British security team would have come to our aid had the U.S. Mission got hit. Now even that promise of backup was gone, yet still the Americans had chosen to stay.

I just didn't get it.

Attacks had skyrocketed across the city. The Tunisian Consulate in Benghazi was stormed by "protesters." A consul vehicle was carjacked and the driver savagely beaten. The Red Cross building was hit in RPG strikes—and surely by anyone's reckoning the Red Cross are the good guys. As with the British Mission, the Red Cross pulled out of Benghazi. A United Nations convoy was hit in a grenade attack, and it was only the armor of the vehicles that saved those inside. A Spanish-American dual national was kidnapped. The Egyptian Embassy was bombed.

The city was like a pressure cooker, and as far as I could see, the U.S. Embassy was a target going begging.

While the security situation had been imploding, Bob had noticed an upsurge in black-flag vehicles on the streets. The Shariah Brigade gun trucks seemed both more numerous, and to be crammed full of more of your archetypal Al Qaeda fighters—non-Libyans dressed in flowing black robes and headgear. Bob had seen them cruising around the Garden City neighborhood at night, when he was alone as usual in the villa.

As a result he'd moved into downtown Benghazi's Tibesti Hotel, where he figured there were lower odds of him getting targeted. The Tibesti seemed to be the main hangout for those foreigners left in Benghazi. Bob had managed to get a room overlooking the European Commission's office, one of the few foreign missions still operating in the city. The EC had their own guard force, and Bob figured that offered us an extra layer of security.

The Tibesti also had its own security people, but they looked about as five-star as the hotel itself: it claimed to be a five-star establishment, but you wouldn't have given it one star had it been situated in Europe or the States.

Upon my arrival back in Benghazi, Bob showed me around the hotel. I could see immediately why he hated the place. It was full of oil workers, construction contractors, plus a smattering of aid types and the media—but no one was there by choice, that was for sure. Like us, they'd been forced into the Tibesti by the supposed security it offered. Other than that, the hotel was dirty and dingy, the staff were rude, and the service was nonexistent.

That first evening Bob and I tried to grab a meal together, but the food was stone cold and the chef hung out at the buffet smoking and flicking ash. Over inedible food Bob did his best to warn me of what was coming at the Embassy. Apparently, Rosie's replacement as head RSO was intent on having our guard force searched by the QRF whenever they came to work. It was the same old same-old. I told Bob it wasn't happening, but boy did I have a sinking feeling.

There was more bad news. After the IED strike on the Embassy, Tom had decided he wanted out completely. We'd kept him on as our driver, but he had a wife and young kids to provide for and he figured the risk of working at the U.S. Mission had just gone to unacceptable levels. Bob had had no option but to let him go.

The one upside was that he'd managed to recruit a fine replacement. Via Stuart—my private-security buddy who'd warned me about carrying the thirty thousand dollars through Tripoli airport—Bob had got in touch with Massoud, an ex–Libyan Army guy based in Benghazi. While Massoud's faction of the military had fought against Gaddafi in the revolution, he wasn't from one of the militias, which was the crucial point as far as we were concerned.

What distinguished Massoud was his military discipline, his excellent timekeeping, plus the fact that he was a genuinely decent, honorable kind of a guy. As a bonus he was hugely well-connected in Benghazi, having excellent contacts at the airports among his Libyan Army buddies. Massoud truly had his finger on the pulse of this troubled city and he'd proven to be a gold mine of intelligence.

I'd met Massoud briefly when he and Bob had picked me up from the airport. He was around my height, of slim build, with typical dark Libyan good looks. He had to be in his late thirties, was married with two children, and was still serving as a sergeant in the Libyan Army. He seemed to be on some kind of sabbatical from the military, which enabled him to work as our driver. Most important, he was as honest as the day is long, and bulletproof reliable. Right away I liked him, and I let Bob know what a fine choice he'd made in Massoud.

After a dismal evening in the Tibesti's one restaurant Bob and I retired to our rooms. The best I managed that night in terms of my own personal security was a chair propped under the handle of the door to my hotel room. I knew already that I hated this place, and I didn't figure I'd be staying here long. As soon as I found a way to get out I was most definitely going to be checking out of the Tibesti.

Bob left early the following morning for the airport—like he couldn't wait to leave. Massoud picked me up for the drive to the Embassy . . . and I was back on the job again. Of course, the guards were pleased as punch to see me. By contrast, just as soon as Mutasim laid eyes on me he had a look on his face like a dog taking a shit.

As I headed for the TOC I had no illusions as to what was coming. I tried to comfort myself with the thought that the three RSOs only had a few days left to run on their rotation and they'd be gone. I met Justin Connor, the head RSO, in the TOC. He struck me as being a cool customer—the kind of guy who never raises his voice or gets rattled. With him were his fellow RSOs, Peter and Paul. Of the three of them it was Paul whom I warmed to most. He was a giant of a guy from Miami, and he had this easy, laid-back air about him that I liked.

But it didn't take long for the nonsense to begin. "Okay, so the new policy we're gonna implement is that every guard shift gets searched by the QRF," Justin announced. "Just as an added layer of security."

I tried to stay calm and keep a lid on things. "No problem. One question: who's searching the QRF?"

Justin looked a little taken aback. "The QRF? What d'you mean, who's searching the QRF?"

Despite my best efforts, my fuse was going to blow. "I mean exactly what I say: who is searching those useless bastards the QRF?"

Justin hesitated for an instant. Pete and Paul were staring at me mouths agape.

"Well, no one's searching the QRF," Justin ventured. "I mean, they're not getting searched. What's the problem here?"

That was it: I blew. "I'll tell you what I've told every RSO before you—the QRF cannot be trusted, and they are not searching my guards. You let them search my guards and the guard force will leave. We've taken months getting them up to scratch, and we will not be able to replace them. And while you're at it, you can get a new security manager. You just don't get it, do you? The Seventeenth February Militia is no better than any other militia in this city. One day you guys are gonna find out just how much moral fiber those bastards have—and they will be found wanting.

And I will stand by those words." I got to my feet. "Right, I am out of here."

I had made up my mind already that this was my last rotation at the U.S. Embassy in Benghazi. I could handle the deteriorating security situation. After all, that's what private security operators like me are paid for—to provide security in challenging circumstances. What I couldn't handle was that no one at the Embassy seemed to be listening, and I was damned if I was going to allow that to spoil the top team of guards that Rosie and I had built up.

I left the TOC and went to hang out for an hour or so with my guards. It was really good to see them alive and well, and doing what they'd been trained to do. I'd bonded with these guys and I counted many of them—Nasir, Mustaffa, and Zahid, among others—as my friends. These were guys we could rely on, of that I was certain, and more the damn pity that none of them were armed.

I spent an uncomfortable night at the Tibesti, and returned to the Embassy the following morning fully expecting to get the sack. I was waiting for Justin to say: *listen, buddy, you're a troublemaker and we don't want you around*. Instead, and in the true mark of the man, he couldn't have been more reasonable. He got me into the TOC so he and I could have a chat one-on-one.

"Thanks for being so candid yesterday," he began. "I've thought about what you said, and we talked about it among the three of us. We respect the fact you've been here longer than us and you know the setup and the different people coming in and out of here, so we need to listen to what you have to say."

"Listen, mate, all I'm trying to do is make sure you guys are safe," I told him. "That's all I'm trying to do. The only control I have is over my guards. I cannot do a thing about the QRF. I do not want to sound like a stuck record—but trust me, you need to go and investigate them for yourself."

Justin nodded. "I hear what you're saying."

"I'm happy for you guys to search my guards. But if you get the QRF to search them, my guards will leave. And if they walk off the job, I'll never replace them. I've gone through eighty guards to get twenty good ones. They're irreplaceable."

"I hear what you're saying," Justin repeated. "Feel free to decide how and when your guards are searched."

I thanked him for that. I left the meeting knowing that I couldn't fault the guy's professionalism. Like Rosie and Lee before her, this guy was a class act. The trouble was all the RSOs were falling victim to a top-down system that seemed designed somehow to make the security setup here fail disastrously.

I killed the morning doing the usual, then headed to the canteen for some lunch. After trying to survive on the inedible garbage that the Tibesti restaurant was serving up I was ravenous.

"Gandu!" I called out to Asaf.

He broke into an enormous grin. "Benshoot! My friend, you are back!"

"Still losing at cricket I see . . ."

The hulking great form of Paul, the Miami RSO, sat at one of the tables. I grabbed some food and joined him. I noticed his shoulders had started shaking, like he was trying not to laugh.

"What's so funny?" I asked.

He let out a chuckle. "Bob had warned us you were a straight talker, but holy shit! We couldn't believe it when you just went right off and unloaded with both barrels. But hell, it sure was refreshing to hear it straight."

I laughed. "Yeah, I guess I could have been a bit more diplomatic. Never my strong point. Anyhow, I've tried that already and it hasn't got me anywhere."

Paul gave me a look. "Buddy, trust me, you said exactly what you thought and you handled it just right."

We were joined by another American, one who was noticeably more smartly dressed than any of us military types. It turned out this was Silvio Miotto, a guy who I figured had to be the new Deputy Chief of Mission. I greeted him with a handshake and explained that I was taking over from Bob.

Silvio smiled. "Great. Heard all about you. Thanks for all the hard work and good to see you back again."

Silvio was five feet seven, slim, with black hair graying around the edges, and he was your typical snappily dressed Italian-American. He was superintelligent and I figured he had to be well on track to being a full ambassador, but at the same time he proved to be totally down-to-earth, with a wicked sense of humor.

Asaf had the cricket playing on the TV, and I could tell that Silvio loved the banter that was pinging back and forth between our Bangladeshi waiter and me. Silvio started going on about baseball. He told me he was a die-hard Philadelphia Phillies fan. With a sly grin he explained how baseball was a far superior sport to cricket, a game that didn't make any sense to anyone outside of the Commonwealth. He told me I needed to start following a real man's sport, like baseball.

He gestured at the TV screen. "I mean, you don't take that crap seriously, do you? Cricket is a sport played by poofy English gentlemen."

"Yeah, I guess that's why you Americans can't play it," I shot back at him, "'cause you're not qualified to be gentlemen."

Silvio cracked up. A moment later he was serious. "You live downtown, at the Tibesti, right? How is it there right now?"

"It's getting a little bit tasty. A bit hairy, if you know what I mean. Not a lot of foreigners left, that's for sure."

Silvio shook his head, exasperatedly. "Right now, I don't know what we're here for. Ramadan's started and everything's grinding to a halt. We won't be doing anything useful for a month: no one's available, no meetings will be had, nothing, and it'll be like this all through Ramadan. You know, even the QRF are refusing to go out now due to Ramadan. They say they're too tired."

I did my best to bite my tongue. I didn't think Silvio wanted me going into one of my rants about the QRF. "Funny that, 'cause my guard force seem okay," I remarked. "Not a word from them about Ramadan, not a sniff of it, and they're all Libyan Muslims."

Silvio snorted. "You know what, I've got zero confidence in this QRF. I mean what kind of QRF guys refuse to go out on missions? That's what they're paid to do. They're paid to ride shotgun and tell the RSOs where it's safe to go, 'cause they're supposed to know the ground here. Instead, they're refusing to go out 'cause it's Ramadan."

"Sounds like a load of horseshit to me."

Silvio laughed. "You got it!" He paused. "You know, we need some real proper security around here. Either that, or we need to pull out—like the British did. You know they pulled out completely, right?"

"I do. A couple of my mates were on the security team when they got hit." I glanced at him. "Still, you've got the Annex. Bit of extra backup there maybe."

Silvio didn't miss a beat. "It's still a total waste of time us being here during Ramadan, when nothing happens, and especially if we're not safe 'cause we don't have any proper security."

I was getting the sense that Silvio and I were of the same mind.

"You know, I sure am glad I'm fasting," Silvio added, as he poked at the fish that was on the serving platter. I'd noticed that he hadn't been eating much. "Seriously, I'm fasting with the locals out of respect. And what do I get in return?" He poked at the fish. "Fish, fish, and more fish, and then some fish again."

I grinned. Silvio was a seriously funny guy. "Rather you than me—fasting. Best I can go is a couple of hours without snacking on something."

He pushed the fish platter my way. "Well, you know, have some more fish—heads and all!" Silvio glanced over at the kitchen. "Next person I see cooking fish I will sack! I am sick of seeing fish! And why always with the goddamn heads on!"

It was so funny he had me cracked up. As for Asaf, he was all doubled over from the effort of trying to stop laughing.

Asaf sidled up to me once Silvio was gone. "That one—he is very funny man. But is he Muslim? He is fasting?"

"Nah, he's just doing it as an excuse to avoid the fish. You blame him?"

Beneath the humor there was a serious subtext here. Silvio was clearly a high achiever, and he was bored out of his brain being stuck here for the entire month of Ramadan. During Ramadan Muslims are supposed to fast from dawn to dusk. It's supposed to enable them to experience the suffering of those less fortunate than themselves who may not have enough to eat. In Libya the entire country shuts down during daytime and absolutely nothing seems to get done.

But over and above his frustration I could tell that Silvio was seriously worried. He'd worked at U.S. missions all over the world and he would know how security should be done, and he could see that wasn't how it was being done here. Silvio was "the principal"—the main man whom all were charged with protecting. It was somehow shocking to have my concerns echoed by the top guy at the Embassy, but at least I didn't feel quite so much like a broken record anymore.

There was just the one bright light on the horizon now that I was back. With the British Embassy having been shut down, we'd managed to get our hands on the majority of their gym equipment and weight-training gear. I busied myself installing it in the make-shift gym that my guards and I had established, in the outhouse adjacent to the side gate. I started a regular weight-training session for my guards, and I let the RSOs know they were free to train there if they wanted.

One thing I noticed about our makeshift gym was how easy a stepping-stone it would make, if ever anyone wanted to get into the Embassy from outside. There was some road maintenance taking place on the far side of the wall, and they'd left a pile of construction materials there. That would provide the leg up onto the wall, from where you could leap the razor wire security fence and land on the gym's roof. From there it was a drop into the thick cover of an orchard that lay to the front of the TOC.

I killed the daylight hours with my guard duties and sessions in the makeshift gym, but the nights were long and dismal at the Tibesti—and with each passing hour the place just seemed to keep emptying. I was a few days in when I sat down to yet another morose breakfast and there was only one other person in the restaurant—a German businessman. Everyone else was gone.

I did my day's stint at the Mission, after which Massoud ran me back to the Tibesti for another evening's fun and games. We were halfway to the hotel when he gave me the news.

"So, Morgan, they have found an IED in the basement of the Tibesti."

"What? So why the hell're we going back there then?"

"No, no—it was there last night."

"You mean, I slept there last night with an IED in the basement? Why didn't you warn me?"

"But I only found this out today. But it's okay, it's gone now."

"What kind of IED?"

"Sixty kilograms. A sixty-kilo IED."

"But fuck me, that's massive. That's a two-man lift. How the hell did they manage to smuggle that past security and into the basement of the hotel?"

Massoud shrugged. "Morgan, this I do not know."

"Massoud, if that's sixty kilos of plastic explosives and they'd detonated it in the basement, that would have brought the entire hotel down with me lying in my bed. That's hotel gone and me with it."

"Yes, my friend, I know. I am glad they did not detonate it."

We reached the hotel and it was utterly deserted. Even the lone German businessman was gone. Trouble was, I had nowhere else to stay right now. I figured no one was going to bother blowing up an empty hotel, so I could probably last just the one more night. But I told Massoud I needed out of there by tomorrow, and I asked him to try to find me some kind of alternative.

I didn't bother with supper. I was in my room watching an endless stream of TV news reports when my phone rang. It was Stuart, my buddy doing security in Tripoli.

"Where are you, mate?" he asked. "Tell me you're not in the Tibesti."

I told him that I was.

"Mate, haven't you heard? You need to get the hell out of there. There was a massive IED—"

"Yeah, I know. I've got nowhere else to go. I'll move tomorrow. Best I can do—"

"No, it's not," Stuart cut in, angrily. "You're getting complacent, and complacency gets you killed."

"I'm trying, but it's not that easy."

"It *is* easy. You get out now and you sleep on the bloody beach if you have to. You get me?"

Stuart was fuming. He wasn't angry at me, so much as angry for me. He was scared that I was getting lackadaisical, and that I was going to get myself blown up. The truth was, it was hard to stay on top of good routines and proper security when everything at the U.S. Mission seemed so disconnected. Security was in free fall in Benghazi, yet there had been zero changes at the Mission. It was like living in a parallel universe, and I suppose I'd been affected by it.

Stuart's call was the kick in the ass that I needed. I packed my stuff, sanitized my room, and got myself good to go. I called Robert and briefed him: I didn't know where I was going, but no more Tibesti. I called Massoud and told him that whatever it took, I needed out. And that's how Massoud found me my beachside villa: I was going to hide in plain sight in a little slice of paradise.

The villa was Massoud's genius. During Ramadan, Libyans tend to sleep all day and party all night. Most reasonably well-off Benghazians had decamped to the beach complexes that line the city's shoreline. Libya being a North African country, its coastline forms part of the southern shores of the Mediterranean. Less than two hundred miles across that semitropical sea lie the sunwashed Greek Islands and the Italian Riviera, and the beaches here in Benghazi were stretches of dreamy, palm-fronded white sand running into aquamarine waters.

The villa Massoud found me came complete with bedroom, lounge, bathroom, and kitchen, and you walked off the front doorstep onto gleaming white sand. There were similar villas all around full of families celebrating Ramadan: the entire resort was one big party town. Then there was me—the Blue Mountain security manager, and the U.S. Embassy guard force guy, right in their midst.

On one level I had zero security here whatsoever: no walls, no alarms, no fences, no guards. All someone had to do was move in along the beach and come through my flimsy front door, and they'd have me. But on the other hand, who from the Shariah Brigade or Al Qaeda would ever think of looking for someone like me here? There certainly weren't any black-flag gun trucks cruising around the neighborhood, as there had been at our previous villa.

I liked Massoud's way of doing things. He was happy to think well outside the box, and for sure this beachside villa beat the cursed Tibesti. To left and right were the kind of easygoing, liberal Libyans who were our natural allies. There were so many kids around, it made me think of my family back home—of Lewis and Laura. In another time and place I could have seen the three of us here on holiday.

But not now.

Now, after the abortive attempt to blow up the Tibesti several things had crystallized for me. One: Whoever the IED team was that was working the city, they had the capacity to build sixty-kilo IEDs. *Monsters.* Word was that the IED had been a viable device— it was just that the trigger guys hadn't detonated it. The kind of bomb makers who build sixty-kilo IEDs are real professionals. Two: The target was clear. It was the kind of foreigners who frequented the Tibesti. Three: The message was clear—Westerners, get the hell out of Libya. Well, instead of leaving I'd got me a beachside villa in among the Ramadan party crowd.

That first morning I went for a long run on the beach, then looped back through the peace of the villa complex, which was all partied out. I decided I'd make this an early morning ritual. I spotted a sign for a gym, so hopefully I could start using that as well, plus there was a shop and a restaurant. So far, Massoud's choice of alternative accommodation was coming up trumps. The only drawback seemed to be that with all the music, fireworks, and high spirits of the neighbors' partying, I was going to have to sleep with earplugs!

I'd barely made my move to Paradise Villa when Justin, Paul, and Pete had to leave, their time being done. We'd bonded well, considering that we'd worked together only a matter of days and in light of my appalling skills at diplomacy. The evening before he flew out Justin took me aside for a last private word.

"I've made some inquiries about the QRF, using all the sources I can tap," he told me. "Everyone is in total agreement with you and your assessment. I've recommended to State that the QRF are replaced with immediate effect." He shrugged. "What effect that will have I really can't say though."

"Great. And thanks." I was genuinely grateful for the effort he'd made and I wanted him to know that. "That's real progress from where we were before."

"I will hand over that recommendation to my replacement RSO," he continued. "It will say that the QRF are not fit for purpose and need to be removed. Hopefully, you'll get some movement on this pretty soon now."

I thanked Justin again for all his efforts. At last the truth about the QRF had been documented to the State Department. I didn't see how they could ignore it anymore, so maybe we were about to see some changes around here. If only we could get a proper QRF in, then we'd stand a reasonable chance of holding this place and safeguarding Silvio and his staff in the event of an attack. Twelve U.S. Marines. That's all we needed. That's all we were seeking.

Surely, that wasn't too much to ask of Washington?

CHAPTER ELEVEN

During my time at the Mission we'd been through Lee the lone RSO, then take-no-shit Rosie and her team, and now Justin and his guys. As soon as one group learned the ropes they were gone and all seemed forgotten. I was convinced these short rotations contributed massively to the painfully slow pace of change. What the Embassy needed was some real permanence, but it wasn't about to get it: the new team was scheduled to be yet another month rotation.

I was fully expecting matters to be the same again—that we'd have to relearn all the lessons from scratch—but I was going to be pleasantly surprised. The lead RSO was a guy called Jeff Palmers. He looked to be in his mid-thirties, he had a completely shaved head, and in appearance and attitude he reminded me of a cool, laid-back surfer dude. He wasn't ex-military, but he'd worked as an RSO in Yemen and just about every other hellhole you could imagine, and Jeff really knew his shit.

He also had a very dry and wicked sense of humor. "So, I hear you're a big fan of the QRF?" Those were practically his opening words to me. "I hear you've taught them everything they know?"

I smiled. "Yeah, I'm their greatest fan. The Seventeenth February Mutant Ninja Turtles Militia—coming to a shopping mall near you soon."

"Seriously, though, I've been made aware you do not trust them?" Jeff probed.

"That's right. It's best you make up your own mind and use your own judgment. But like I've been saying to all the RSOs before you—we need shot of the militia boys, and in their place we need a proper bunch of kick-ass Marines. A dozen would be about right."

Jeff nodded. "One thing's for sure, we need more security guys around here. Nothing else will do it."

From the get-go I liked the cut of this guy's jib.

Jeff introduced me to his team—David Ubben and Scott Wickland. Dave was a six-feet-four monster of a guy, with broad shoulders and a swimmer's physique. He spoke in a relaxed and slow southern drawl and I could tell right away that he was a quiet type. He struck me as being the intelligent guy who thought carefully before he spoke—unlike me, who tends to speak before thinking.

With his crew-cut dark hair and contemplative manner I figured Dave was maybe an ex–Army officer, but it turned out that he was, like me, a sergeant. Not only that, he'd served for nine years and completed multiple tours of Iraq and Afghanistan, and he absolutely knew his stuff. From the get-go I liked Dave, but it was clear that he didn't seem to know what to make of me. It was fair enough, really: I was the Brit with the bad attitude that they'd all been warned about.

Scotty was a whole lot different from Dave. He was six feet tall and of a lithe build, with brown spiky hair. He was an ex–Army sergeant of six years' service, with several tours behind him, but he was far more voluble and chatty. As with Dave, I figured Scotty was the kind of guy who'd be absolutely unshakable when the bullets started to fly. In fact, with Jeff, Scotty, and Dave I figured we'd landed ourselves the A-Team here at the Benghazi Mission.

The QRF were still refusing to do any form of work "due to

Ramadan," and I warned Jeff there was some three weeks of this to go. Jeff was visibly shocked at their attitude, and as for Silvio, the top diplomat at the Benghazi Mission, he was spitting blood. In fact, Silvio only had a couple more weeks to work here, and I could tell he was counting down the days until he could get himself gone.

Jeff, Dave, and Scotty had been on the ground just a matter of days when there was yet another security incident in Benghazi. A seven-man delegation from the Red Crescent (the Islamic counterpart of the Red Cross) was kidnapped, right outside the place where they were staying—the Tibesti Hotel. The Red Crescent guys were all Iranians, and their convoy was hit as it returned to the hotel. They were forced into the bad guys' vehicles and driven away, and nothing was heard of them. To all intents and purposes they had disappeared.

Massoud was driving me to work and I made a passing comment. "You heard about the Iranian Red Crescent guys? Poor fuckers."

He nodded to a compound that we happened to be passing—an old Libyan Army camp. "Morgan, they are in there."

"They're in there? What, so they're all okay?"

"Yes. They are getting fed; they have their own beds even. They are fine."

"How the hell do you know?"

"I was in there yesterday on my own business. I saw them—all seven of them."

"So who's holding 'em and why?"

Massoud shrugged. "Same old same-old. It is a Shia–Sunni thing. There are some who think those Iranian Shias are not welcome here. But they are all perfectly okay."

I was in the canteen having lunch later that day when Jeff, Dave, and Scotty came in. Jeff made some passing comment about the kidnapping, and how frustrating it was that no one could get any leads on who was holding the Red Crescent guys.

I popped my head up. "The seven Iranians? They're in the old Libyan Army camp on the Tripoli Road. That's where they're being held."

The three of them stopped eating and just stared at me. "You fucking serious? You know where they are?"

"Yeah, I just told you where they are."

Jeff went outside to make a radio call. It was obviously to the Annex. Moments later he was back.

"You absolutely sure about this?" he asked.

"Yeah, Massoud told me this morning. He was in there yesterday and had eyes on them."

"It's reliable," Jeff confirmed into his radio, as he stepped outside again.

He was back a few minutes later. He sat down laughing. "Fucking unbelievable. Everyone's been looking for those guys—and the goddamned Brit here knew where they were all along. What the fuck?"

Scotty piped up with a wiseass remark in an awful imitation English gentleman's accent. "I say, old chap, the name's Bond. James Bond . . . Jolly good show, y'all."

"You know your problem, Scotty—you've been watching too many Hugh Grant movies," I shot back. "Anyway, what point are you trying to make exactly? Like I told you, I'm Welsh. James Bond is English. It's about as different as Americans and Canadians . . . But then again, what would you know about it? English: we invented the language—you just buggered it up. I mean 'y'all.' *Y'all.* What kind of word is that?"

Scotty and Jeff were laughing fit to burst. Dave was shaking his head and smiling. He didn't join in that kind of back-and-forth much, but in his own laid-back way he loved it.

We quieted down a bit as Dave and Scotty said a short grace over their meals. Once they were done praying, I threw a question at Scotty.

"What did he say? God. Did he say anything about me?"

The team that I led on the U.S. Army Corps of Engineers (U.S. ACE) security contract in northern Iraq, where I first learned to deal with threats posed by terrorists and insurgents. I am standing right on the nose cone of the Black Hawk helicopter. *Morgan Jones*

Briefing my team of twelve private operators, providing security on the U.S. ACE contract, in northern Iraq. This was such a dangerous posting that we would only ever move VIP clients in a four-vehicle convoy, sporting roof-mounted M240 7.62mm machine guns. *Morgan Jones*

Remains of one of our armored Ford Excursion SUVs after an IED strike on Route Tampa in Iraq. *Morgan Jones*

Ready for anything. The author is second from the left, with fellow private security operators in Iraq. The Iraq tasking was so dangerous that every man in our team was very heavily armed, carrying two thousand rounds of ammo each. Even so, we lost five men in one three-day period. *Morgan Jones*

Our Iraq security team zero in their weapons on the ranges. This number of well-armed and experienced operators would have saved the Benghazi Mission on the night of the attack. *Morgan Jones*

A pressure-pad-activated IED—an improvised explosive device—in war-torn Helmand Province, Afghanistan, where the author learned to deal with such threats during repeated attacks. When the Benghazi Mission was hit by an IED, it blasted a hole through the perimeter wall large enough for an army of attackers to surge through. *Morgan Jones*

On security operations in Helmand Province, Afghanistan. For three years I ran a close protection team in Afghanistan for both the United States Marine Corps and the British Foreign and Commonwealth Office. *Morgan Jones*

Battle damage. IED strikes in Afghanistan and Iraq—remotely detonated roadside bombs—nearly always heralded a multistage attack, with further hidden IEDs and gunmen hitting our convoys. It was the ideal training ground for the kinds of threats we faced in Benghazi, if only we'd had the right defenses to repel the enemy. *Morgan Jones*

Blood trail left by an Afghan suicide bomber, one of the hardest of all threats to defend against. Yet at least in Afghanistan we had the weaponry, the right operators, and the means with which to do so. In Benghazi, sadly, we did not. *Morgan Jones*

The mangled remains of an armored SUV hit by an IED. In Iraq our team survived nine such IED strikes and we never lost a VIP client. My friend and fellow operator, Nick, walked away from this with a head injury, but is okay now. *Morgan Jones*

Chinook heavy-lift helicopters flying across Afghanistan—the ideal way to move without being vulnerable to attacks on the ground. Sadly, as the security situation in Benghazi deteriorated, forcing most other foreigners to leave, the U.S. Mission in Benghazi remained. *Morgan Jones*

Suspects held in Helmand Province, Afghanistan. As with Libya, the bad guys—Al Qaeda and affiliates—tended to dress and look pretty much like any other locals, which meant our weaponry, defenses, and teams had to be the very best. *Morgan Jones*

In spite of the recent civil war to topple Colonel Gaddafi's regime, much of Libya showed little sign of war damage. The plush Corinthia Hotel, where I stayed in Tripoli, en route to Benghazi, had just the odd bullet hole in the outer walls. *Morgan Jones*

Benghazi airport, my entry point into the strife-torn city. It was a place of chaos and insecurity post-Gaddafi, and it would be the one exit point for all Americans who survived the attack on the U.S. Mission on September 11, 2012.

Security at Libya's airports post–Colonel Gaddafi was run by rebel militias like the Zintan Brigade. I had to carry $30,000 in cash through the airport as wages for our guard force at the Benghazi Mission, and predictably the Zintan mob tried to beat me up and steal it. *Morgan Jones*

A Gaddafi-era downtown Benghazi monument, now daubed in anti-Gaddafi graffiti courtesy of the rebels who toppled his regime. *Morgan Jones*

At the foot of that monument. The rebels claimed that Gaddafi's mother was a Jew, hence the star of David on the left side of his chin. *Morgan Jones*

Downtown Benghazi's Tibesti Hotel. This was where I had to billet myself once our villa became too dangerous to live in. Then the Tibesti had a sixty-kilogram IED driven into the basement one night I was sleeping there. *Morgan Jones*

The only security I had at the Tibesti was a chair shoved under the hotel door. As the Blue Mountain guard force manager for the Benghazi Mission, I was not allowed to carry any weapons, and unbelievable as it may seem, my guard force was *unarmed*. *Morgan Jones*

The 17th February Militia, one of the rebel outfits that fought to topple Gaddafi's regime in Libya, but one that was sympathetic to Al Qaeda. For some unknowable reason, 17th February militiamen were employed as the main armed guard force at the U.S. Mission in Benghazi. I and the Americans stationed there feared they were the enemy within. *Morgan Jones*

The villa and compound of the Benghazi Mission. Photo is taken from the roof of the VIP Villa—from where Dave, Scotty, and all mounted their defense the night of the attack—showing just how far it was from the main gate. *Morgan Jones*

The front gate of the Benghazi Mission. As with much of the security, this was inadequate: a non-armored metal gate. The roll of barbed wire was added only *after* the attack, to deter looters. *Morgan Jones*

Swimming pool and chill-out area at the Benghazi Mission. This was where the Mission's Regional Security Officers—Dave, Scotty, and Jeff—and I would drink a (non-alcoholic) beer on the rare evening when we got downtime. *Morgan Jones*

The security fence at the Mission. It should have been topped off with coils of razor wire and it should have been *complete*: there were places where it stopped for no apparent reason. *Morgan Jones*

The outhouse near the side gate of the Mission, which we turned into a makeshift gym. On the night of the attack I scaled the wall and climbed onto the roof of this building, to fight my way into the Mission and try to find and rescue the trapped Americans. *Morgan Jones*

The rear gate of the Mission. This was where I first tried to enter the Embassy compound the night of the attack, but was fought off by a Shariah Brigade gunner. *Morgan Jones*

Left: British private security company Blue Mountain was contracted to provide a local Libyan guard force for the Benghazi Mission. I served for six months as their Security Manager prior to the attack, training up a force of twenty-plus Libyan guards. *Andy Chittock Right:* Blue Mountain trainees rehearsing an armed patrol. We trained the guard force to deal with medical trauma, to search vehicles and persons, and in attack drills and unarmed combat. Sadly, they were not allowed to carry any weapons at the Mission. In the event of an attack, orders were to raise the alarm, then save themselves. *Andy Chittock*

One of my Libyan guards posing as a terrorist sympathizer managed to get inside the Benghazi Mission the night of the attack to take these photos: this shows one of the Embassy's armored SUVs having been torched by the attackers. The gunmen burned them so the Americans couldn't get away. *Zahid Arman*

Embassy grounds the night of the attack, with the guardroom where my Libyan guards were captured in flames. *Zahid Arman*

One of the Shariah Brigade attackers "celebrates" the seizing, destruction, and firebombing of the Embassy complex on the night of the attacks. *Zahid Arman*

The Quick Reaction Force villa in flames, having been torched by attackers who surged into the Mission in heavily armed numbers. *Zahid Arman*

Terrorist gunman brandishing an AK-47 assault rifle silhouetted against the burning remains of the Mission. Four Americans would die during the attack, with more injured. *Zahid Arman*

The interior of the Embassy villa in the midst of the attack, showing the kind of conditions in which IT specialist Sean Smith and Ambassador J. Christopher Stevens lost their lives. *Zahid Arman*

The Mission swimming pool during the attack. Smoke rises from the main building behind and debris is floating in the pool. *Zahid Arman*

The Benghazi Mission main compound gets fire-bombed. The attackers used diesel fuel and petrol to set the buildings alight. *Zahid Arman*

The Benghazi Medical Center, better known as the 1200 Bed Hospital, where I would discover the body of Ambassador Stevens the night of the attack. I found him lying dead and unidentified on a hospital trolley. I sent out a photo and message to alert the powers that be that the American Ambassador to Libya had been killed. *Morgan Jones*

Burned-out remains of the Mission's Tactical Operations Center (TOC), where all sensitive documents were stored. The morning after the attack I went back to photograph the crime scene and search for the bodies of any of my dead American friends. *Morgan Jones*

Firebombed and smashed–up front entrance to the VIP Villa, the building in which the ambassador and Sean Smith died. *Morgan Jones*

Burned-out front entrance to the TOC. Graffiti to the left side of the doorway reads "Mohammed is the Prophet of Allah" and that on the right reads "Allahu Akbar—God is great!" *Morgan Jones*

Wrecked and burned-out interior of the Mission canteen, where I used to share meals and jokes with Scotty, Dave, Jeff, and the others. *Morgan Jones*

A Navy SEAL operator in action overseas. On the night of the attack, a force of six ex-SEALs and other elite operators on contract to the CIA launched a heroic mission to rescue those trapped. *U.S. Navy SEALS*

Navy SEALs in action overseas. Two former SEALs—Tyrone Woods and Glen Doherty—would lose their lives that fateful night in Benghazi. *U.S. Navy*

An MQ1 Predator unmanned aerial vehicle or drone of the type flown over the Mission and Annex the night of the attack. However, this one is armed, and the one over Benghazi was not. *U.S. Air Force*

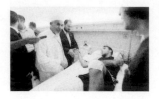

Mansour, one of my Libyan guards who was captured and shot in the legs by the Shariah Brigade gunmen. The attackers let the captured guards live, because they had attacked with one intent only—to "kill the Americans." *Zahid Arman*

Glen Anthony Doherty, former U.S. Navy SEAL from SEAL Team 3, who was killed the night of the Embassy attack. *Michael Shannon*

Tyrone "Ty" Woods, former U.S. Navy SEAL, who led the heroic six-man team to rescue Americans trapped at the Embassy. He was killed later that night by the Shariah Brigade. *Credit unknown*

Sean Smith, the IT specialist at the Mission, who died during the attack. He had been at the Mission only a matter of days when the attack came. *Morgan Jones*

American Ambassador to Libya J. Christopher Stevens, who was killed the night of the attack. He spoke fluent Arabic and was a consummate diplomat and a real gentleman. He—like many other U.S. personnel—had repeatedly asked Washington for more guards and security, but little, if anything, was provided. *U.S. Dept. of State*

Scotty was trying not to laugh. "You're an asshole, man."

As for Dave, he was staring at me like he couldn't believe what I'd said. I'd dug my grave already, so I figured I might as well dig it real deep.

"Did he say Morgan says hello?"

Jeff spluttered into his food. He'd been trying to keep the laughter in but he'd lost it completely. Jeff didn't pray before his meals, so I guessed he like me was a searcher. In truth, I loved seeing those guys saying their grace, for it gave me a strange sense of peace in the chaos and crap that was Benghazi. I had no faith in my life, but I often wished I had. I just couldn't ever seem to get my head around it.

The following morning Jeff told me that a force was readying itself to go rescue the Iranian Red Crescent guys. I guessed the boys from the Annex were poised to go in. Great news. I told Massoud that evening during the drive to my beachside villa that there was going to be a rescue mission.

He glanced at me, a faint smile playing across his lips. "It is too late, my friend. They left yesterday."

"What?"

"The Iranians. They left Benghazi and flew to Tripoli en route to Tehran."

The first thing I did when I got to the villa was call Jeff. "Mate, cancel the cavalry. Whoever is going in to get the Iranians—stand 'em down. They left yesterday on a flight to Tehran."

There was a moment's silence. "Buddy, tell me you are shitting me."

"No. No messing—they're on their way home."

"Are you sure?"

"Yep. Massoud's cousin works at the airport. He saw all seven of 'em fly out of here."

"You are one hundred percent?"

"Yeah. He just told me. Massoud doesn't lie. They are definitely gone."

"Okay."

I went in the next morning and as soon as Jeff saw me a smile split his face from ear to ear.

"What is it?" I demanded. *"What?"*

"You know, you were right. About the Iranians. They had left. And those who were going in to get them—they got stood down."

"So what's so funny?"

"The word that came back to me was: *Where the hell does that goddamned Brit get his int? Who the hell is he talking to? He knows stuff before we do!"*

Jeff left the rest unsaid, but I knew what he was driving at. I wasn't the Annex, but sometimes I knew more than the Annex—thanks to Massoud and the wider network. Someone somewhere had to be thinking: *Does that Brit know more than he's letting on? Is he playing both sides? Or is he just doing whatever he has to do to keep himself safe out there?*

From all their perspectives—of the RSOs and those at the Annex—I was feral. I was living on the streets and mixing in with the locals. I was billeted in the heart of Ramadan party town, now I was in my beachside chalet, and I was often out walking the streets doing my various chores. And after five months working the Embassy contract I'd grown the kind of beard that would make any jihadist proud. Some of them had to be thinking, *just who the hell is that guy?*

Jeff was constantly asking me for guidance on how to make a road move, whenever they had to drive Silvio or some of the other Embassy staff anywhere. He'd ask which areas in particular to avoid and I'd advise. I told him to remove the red diplomatic plates from their vehicles, for they were recognizable a mile away, and it was because of the red plates that the British Embassy's convoy had been identified and hit. But once again the word came back from Jeff that they couldn't, because it was against the rules.

We were maybe ten days into Jeff and his team's time here when

Dave and I were having a quiet chat. Gradually Dave was opening up to me, and he chose today to pop the million-dollar question.

"Say, the only time I see you animated is when we're talking the QRF. So what exactly is the root of the problem? What happened?"

"Nothing specific. But I'm convinced they will not protect you when the shit goes down. They don't even have the skills: their weapons-handling skills and tactical knowledge are zero. Mate, they are gonna really let you down one day," I added. "That's my biggest fear of all."

I could see Dave's mind whirring as he processed what I'd just said. The more I got to know him, the more I realized that when Dave spoke, people listened. He didn't say much, but what he did say was well thought through and pertinent. He was a still-waters-run-deep kind of guy with very much his own mind.

"Okay, buddy, then this is what we'll do," Dave announced, quietly. "After lunch, me and Scotty will go up and test them on basic weapons handling and drills."

"Fine—that's if you can get them out of bed." I wasn't joking. From all that I'd seen of the QRF during Ramadan they seemed to be sleeping 24/7.

Dave leveled his gaze at me. "No, we'll get 'em out of bed all right."

I didn't doubt that he would. "Make sure you wear your body armor when you go over to test 'em."

Dave grinned.

"No, mate, don't laugh. I am serious. If they've going to be handling live rounds anywhere near you when you go up there, put your body armor on."

A while later I saw Dave and Scotty heading over to the QRF Villa, and sure enough they were both wearing their body armor. I guessed my warnings had hit home.

Jeff sidled up to me to have a word. He nodded in Dave and Scotty's direction. "So what d'you reckon?"

"I don't reckon anything. I know what will happen."

"What happens if they both come back saying they're like ninjas?"

I snorted, derisively. "Yeah, mate, whatever."

A couple of hours later Dave and Scotty were back, and their faces said it all. In fact Scotty was so angry he couldn't talk.

"That bad, huh?" Jeff asked.

"Morgan is one hundred percent right," Dave replied, evenly. "They are totally fuckin' inept and should not be allowed to carry a weapon, whether in the compound or the vehicles. They can't even strip down an AK properly."

Jeff was ashen with shock. He had his head in his hands. "Oh Jesus . . . Is it that bad?"

Dave nodded. "Yeah. It's fuckin' scary. In fact, it's unbelievable they've been around the clients this long and have not been found out. It's a miracle no one's been injured or worse."

Scotty still hadn't said a word, but it was clear from his face that he was boiling. Dave nodded in his direction. "Mutasim got upset 'cause his drills were so shit. He shoved Scotty really aggressively in the chest. He said Scotty had no experience and couldn't tell him what to do."

"That's Mutasim," I remarked. "He's always right and hates being questioned on anything. The guy's a worm."

"He said he'd been trained by U.S. Special Operations forces," Dave continued, "so who were we to teach him anything."

Scotty had served as an RSO at the U.S. Embassy in Burma. He was fluent in Mandarin, and it took a real towering intellect to grasp that language. I'd worked several security contracts with the Chinese, and I'd never managed to learn more than a few words. But aside from Scotty's intellect, I could tell that he was hard as nails. To take that kind of crap off a fool like Mutasim must have rankled.

Jeff glanced at me. "Morgan, I owe you an apology. I'm only sorry we didn't take what you said at face value and sooner."

I shrugged. "No worries. No harm done. I'm just happy you've proved it for yourselves and before any Americans got hurt. But it needs to be rectified. Let's get the QRF out and the Marines in. Then we're laughing."

Jeff ran his hand over his scalp. "It's August, so the vacation season . . . I dunno how quickly I can get anything done. But you're right—we need rid of those clowns and pronto. I'll start drafting the email to go to Washington."

Considering what he was tasked with here, Jeff was one of the coolest customers I'd ever met. He was also terrific at his job. But he knew now what an absolutely shit situation we were in. Apart from those in the Annex, we were basically the last good guys in Benghazi. And now the brutal truth had hit home: *this mouthy, grumpy Welsh idiot is right—the QRF are worse than useless.* Until now the QRF had at least offered some kind of reassurance: they were a visible presence carrying weapons. But now Jeff knew the truth about them: *they did not know how to fire their guns.*

For two days Jeff practically disappeared. He was in his office crafting an urgent email to Washington, alerting State to all that he now knew. He worked on it ceaselessly, sharing drafts with Silvio and getting advice and input. Jeff knew the score. He knew that this was his gig, and if the bad guys came for us we were all going to end up either dead or in orange jumpsuits. He was carrying some heavy responsibility on his shoulders.

Jeff was deep in the email-drafting process when he came to have words with me. "Tell me, again, buddy, what can we do to sort this place out?" There was none of the normal joking now. "What are your recommendations?"

"Well, every RSO before you has asked for more manpower and we've been denied. So presumably that's not going to change. If you can't get more men, your only alternative is more firepower. So, imagine you site a .50-caliber on top of Villa C, mounted on a tripod. From there you can hit the front gate, but also swivel it around to hit the rear. A .50-cal will make even your most die-hard jihadi stop and think twice about trying to get in. A round from one of those can kill you even if it doesn't hit, simply by the pressure wave thrown off." I paused. "Get one of those on the roof of Villa C. At least it'll buy you enough time to get the principal into one of the armored SUVs and out of here."

"It's a great idea, but I'm not convinced we'll get one. They'll say it'll look too aggressive."

"Trust me, mate, it's nowhere near as aggressive as a bunch of Shariah Brigade gun trucks storming into the compound. Anyhow, you can lay it down covered by a tarpaulin. No one will ever know it's there. You pull it up and unleash it only when required. And it needs an RSO—Dave or Scotty—on it, *not the QRF.*"

Jeff shook his head, worriedly. "They'll never go for it. It'll look too aggressive. A heavy machine gun on a tripod . . . we'll just never get it through. How do we stop a large body of men getting in the gate without it?"

I shrugged. "Like I said, you need more men or a .50-cal. Without one or the other you're buggered."

Jeff rubbed his hands worriedly across his face. It was well out of character to see him this apprehensive. "There's nothing else we can do?" he queried. "No alternatives?"

"No. It's either more men with guns or more firepower." I paused. "You heard anything specific? Any specific threat?"

"No. Why?"

"You seem different. Nervous." I wondered whether it was just the realization of how utterly shitty the QRF were that had got to Jeff. "You know, mate, I'll fight with you. I'll be here, shoulder to shoulder with you guys. You know that, don't you."

"I know," Jeff confirmed. "But still, the four of us . . . Tell me honestly: a full frontal attack—what'll happen?"

"Honestly, you will get fucked. Or rather we will. The guard force are unarmed. The QRF are useless. There's three of you and one of me. Say you've got two of you securing the clients, and two of us putting down the rounds with a couple of M4s. It doesn't add up, does it? If you're gonna get hit it'll be the main entrance. That's where I'd come in. A guy with an RPG on his shoulder hits that, they're in."

"So, there's nothing else we can do?"

"Guard dogs. They'd give you an early, early warning, buy you some extra time. Plus Arabs hate dogs. Would it put them off? Would it stop them? It might do. But not like a dozen Marines and a .50-cal."

"I'll draft an email to my bosses in Washington," Jeff told me. "I'll tell them what we need, and I'll warn them that if the compound comes under a sustained, organized attack it will be overrun." Jeff shrugged. "That's the best I can do . . ."

Dave, Scotty, and I started to drill the guard force now, to double-check they were totally up to speed. They were all the backup we'd got. The RSOs started standing a 24/7 sentry rotation, so one of them was always awake and on watch. But the long hours and the constant stress were taking their toll. The guys looked as if they were getting precious little sleep, and they were wired.

It was partly because of that that I figured we needed a DVD Night. I purchased a load of nonalcoholic beers—all I could get—at the beachside complex shop, and put it in Massoud's car. I added a bunch of war movies on DVD and headed over to the Embassy. The guys had said they didn't like the idea of me being out in the city on my own at night, and that I was always welcome at the Mission—so tonight was time for some poolside beers and a clutch of movies.

I'd also scored a bunch of sticky, honey-filled Ramadan cakes. They were tonight's big temptation, and I was keen to see which of the Americans would crack. Dave was big into fitness and I didn't figure it would be him. With my early morning beach runs and my weights regime I was in peak physical condition. There wasn't an inch of fat on me. But I also have an incurable sweet tooth, so I

knew for sure I'd munch the cakes. Jeff had a ripped surfer's physique, and he'd even talked about trying to ride some of the waves
out on Benghazi's coastline. It was Scotty who was the wild card.

As I doled out the beers and cakes I kept going on about fitness
and diet and nutrition, and warning how bad all of that sugar was
going to be for us.

Scotty just grabbed the nearest Ramadan cake and started
munching. "Yeah, yeah, I agree—diet, it's crucial, blah, blah,
blah . . . But these cakes—man, they taste good . . ."

"You look like you're gonna scoff the bloody lot," I told him.
"Better get munching, guys, or they'll all be in fat Scotty's gut . . ."

"Indeed, old chap, but you see—I'm Hank Marvin," Scotty re-
torted, trying to put on a posh English accent.

"You are *what*?"

"Hank marvin. It's Cockney rhyming slang for 'starving.'
You know: apples and pears—stairs; Scooby Doo—clue; Hank
Marvin—starving."

I just stared at him. "Where do you guys find all this crap?"

Scotty laughed. "Google. I googled 'Cockney rhyming slang.'
Hell, man, this is the way you guys speak, so why don't you know
this stuff?"

"Do you have any idea where Cockneys are from? They're
from the East End of London. That's about as far from the Welsh
mountains as Texas is to New York. And like I told you before—
I'm Welsh, not English."

"Yeah, okay, but you gotta know some of this stuff," Scotty
insisted. "Come on, tell us some."

It was happy times all around.

As the evening wore on, Dave got to reminiscing about his family back home. He showed me the photos of him with his wife and
baby, and he sure looked like one very happy and contented dad.
I reciprocated, showing the guys the snaps of Laura and Lewis,
plus me posing as proud pappy. We live up the end of a long dirt
track on top of a Welsh mountain—so absolutely in the middle

of nowhere. The guys loved the wild look of the place, and I told them—not for the first time—that they were more than welcome to come pay a visit.

Scotty likewise had a young family. It was clear that he and Dave missed their lady partners and their kids just as much as I missed mine. Time away on overseas missions was time away from our families, and especially with young kids you could never get those days back again. Kids grow up so quickly, and as part-absent dads we missed out on so much of the early days and the magic.

I really liked and respected these guys, and the very idea of the risks they were being forced to take here, including getting wasted by a load of Benghazi militiamen, made my blood boil. They clearly felt something similar with regards to me. Dave, Scotty, and Jeff were in their early thirties and I was pushing ten years their senior, so I was something of the old hand. In spite of my grouchy, mouthy, rude ways, I guess there was a part of them that looked up to me a little.

When it came time for me to leave—I couldn't keep Massoud waiting the entire night—Jeff voiced the thought that I guessed was on each of their minds.

"Morgan—you know we've got your back, right? Just 'cause you're down there on your own, don't think we haven't."

"After all those cakes and beers—man, you gotta know that we're there for you," added Scotty.

"No, guys, I'm all right," I told them. "It's not your job to come and help me, plus you'll get into a shit storm if you do. You look after what you got to look after, which is here."

Jeff fixed me with this look. "No. Understand: You live out there in Benghazi on your own with no support. So, understand—if anything happens to you we will be en route to help immediately."

"Jeff's right," Dave added. "If the shit goes down at your villa you only have to call and we'll be there. We got your back, buddy."

I didn't doubt for one moment that they had. These kind of

guys would fight through hell and back for one of their own, and that was how I reckoned they saw me now—*as one of their own*. I found their words and their brotherhood both uplifting and hugely humbling.

Scotty brought over the last of the beers. "Here you go, man, break a leg. And say, listen, if you ever manage to get to the States, you know you gotta come visit."

"Sure thing, buddy, come visit," Dave added. "You're always welcome in the Ubben family household. I'll even take you to my church," he joked. "That'd be awesome."

In a strange way Dave's invite was the one that really touched me. I was forever kidding Dave about his beliefs, and he'd never once let it get to him or taken it badly, though he'd have had every right to do so. One lunch I'd listened to him reciting his prayers over his meal—just the sound of it giving me this odd sense of peace—and when he'd finished I'd fired one of my regular digs at him.

"Say, Dave, tell me—just how did Noah manage to cram all those animals into that one ark? It must have been some kind of massive boat."

Dave had stared at me for a long second, shaking his head in disbelief. Then he'd cracked up laughing. "Come on, man, they dug it up. They dug it up for Chrissakes."

Around that poolside the four of us agreed on an informal protocol via which we would provide mutual support to one another. If the bad guys hit the Embassy, one of the first things they were to do was call me on my cell phone, so I could head on over. Likewise, I would get their help at the villa if I called for it. And unbeknownst to the four of us, one of us was just about to make such a call.

Massoud had a Libyan Army VHF radio bolted to the dash of his car, which was a crappy old Nissan sedan. The radio sat above the gear lever, and he used to keep it on so he could monitor the radio traffic. A day or so after our poolside party we were driving along and I heard some shouting and screaming over the radio. I asked him what was going on.

"A bomb has just gone off at the Tibesti," he told me.

Apparently, a car bomb had exploded right outside the hotel, and the roadside scene was chaos right now. As I listened in I heard the sound of a second explosion blasting over the radio. A second car bomb had just gone off, again right outside the Tibesti. I felt sick at the sound of it, for I knew that Scotty and Dave were out on a job with Silvio somewhere near that very location.

I dialed Scotty's cell phone. I wasn't surprised when he didn't answer. It would be against their protocol to take a private call from my number when out on a close protection job, but little did they know I was trying to phone through a warning. I tried Dave.

He answered. "Can't speak. On a job . . ."

"I know, mate, but listen: two car bombs have just gone off at the Tibesti. Unless you're in a secure location pull your mission and return to base."

"Are you sure?" Dave queried.

"I am listening to a live feed on VHF as it's happening."

"Thanks." Dave cut the line.

An hour or so later I got a call from Dave at my beachside villa. "Thanks for the heads-up, buddy. We had no idea. We weren't far away and we were heading right through that route."

I told him it was no problem. That's what brother warriors were for.

I went and sat on my veranda. As I gazed out over the moonlit ocean I could hear the Ramadan partying going on either side of me. Jeff, Scotty, and Dave: they were an awesome bunch of guys. More was the pity I couldn't invite them down to my place for a good old-fashioned barbecue and beers on the sand, plus maybe some beach volleyball. Lord knows they could do with the downtime.

The following day I was having lunch in the canteen when Silvio came to see me. "I wanted to say thanks for the warning yesterday. You gotta know it's great having you out there in Benghazi keeping the info coming through, 'cause we're pretty much going out on those streets blind."

I shrugged. "It's the least I can do for you guys. Anyhow, I need to know about this kind of stuff. They're the kind of dangers I have to avoid as well."

"I just want you to know from me that sharing that kind of stuff with us—it's appreciated."

"Like I said, no problem. A lot of people believe in guarding their intel. Keeping it close. I'm not one of them. Intelligence has to be disseminated if it's to protect and inform the good guys. That way we can try to avoid the kind of thing that happened yesterday—those bombings—hurting our people."

Silvio nodded. "Couldn't agree with you more. Yesterday's call—it was one hell of a timely warning, so thanks."

I smiled. "You earned it. After all, I get to eat in your canteen— and especially when there's fish on the menu!"

Silvio burst out laughing. "With the goddamn heads on 'n' all!"

It was later that day when Jeff came up to me at the guardroom. I could tell immediately that something was wrong. The poor bastard looked as if someone had died. He proceeded to tell me the response he'd got to his urgent email to Washington. The reply he'd received was that we were to "keep working with what we'd got." Come December the security situation would be reassessed, with a view to whether they'd continue with the Mission. Basically, in spite of all the warnings Jeff—and Silvio—had raised, we'd been told to carry on as usual.

Jeff shook his head, despairingly. "It's no change, buddy. No fucking change at all." He spat out those last words. He was furious. He was entombed within a dark cloud of anger and I could tell he was at his wits' end.

He and Silvio had been battling daily to get what we needed

in terms of security, yet they'd been given nothing. In fact, they'd been point-blank denied. Jeff had kept trying and trying, and yet he'd been denied, and that rejection and failure as he saw it had broken him. He was a true professional and a perfectionist. He knew that if anything happened it was due in part to his failure to prevent it. Like Rosie before him, he was beating himself up over it.

"Listen, mate, you tried your best," I told him. "No one could be expected to do any more than you've done. Every RSO before you has tried and failed. They keep getting denied. So, it's not as if it's a new thing."

Jeff seemed to take little comfort from what I'd said. He wasn't the type to take the easy road. He knew the Embassy was horribly vulnerable, and he knew he'd failed to change that. He'd tried his very best and done all he could, but he'd been denied.

The Benghazi Embassy was a disaster waiting to happen, and Washington seemed happy for it to stay that way.

CHAPTER TWELVE

It was the first week of September by now and Jeff was scheduled to leave shortly, his month done. Scotty's and Dave's contracts had been extended for two weeks, and they were well aware that all the pressure was going to be on them now. They'd be leaving around September 15, when my present stint would also be done. Sleep deprivation was kicking in, on top of the stress, and they looked about as burned-out and finished as Lee had done at the end of his lonely month here.

A couple of days before Jeff's departure Massoud delivered another intel bombshell. He picked me up from the villa and just as soon as we were under way he started talking.

"So, Morgan, you need to ensure no Embassy staff fly into or out of Benghazi today."

I asked him why.

"A bad guy was caught at the airport, about to unleash a surface-to-air missile against a passenger aircraft."

"Fuck me, a SAM? How d'you know?"

"A good friend of mine from the Army works at the airport. He is the one who caught him."

"You sure it was a SAM? I mean, it's a big piece of kit. It's not as if you can stuff it in your pocket."

"Yes, I am sure."

"Any idea what type it was?"

"Shoulder-launched. An Igla-S we think."

I phoned a warning through to Jeff, knowing that it would get relayed direct to the Annex. With the Annex boys being tasked to hunt for MANPADS—"SAM" being the generic acronym for surface-to-air missiles—this was sure to be of top interest to them. One of the bad guys had been caught red-handed trying to shoot down an airliner, which was just what the Americans feared would happen—hence the Annex being here, to try to stop them.

Along with the thanks I got from Jeff for the intel, the word that came back from the Annex was this: *Where the HELL is that Brit getting all this stuff?* If I hadn't needed Massoud as much as I did—he was a lifeline for a lone white-eye operator like me living out in Benghazi—I would have suggested he go on the Annex's payroll. But right now I was determined to keep Massoud real close, or at least until I was finished with my time here.

Jeff left on September 3. I really did not want that guy to go. We shook hands, then did a man-hug. He thanked me for doing a great job with the guards, and for all the int and the warnings I'd given. He told me that I was welcome to visit him in the States anytime, and I reciprocated, extending an invitation to the Welsh hills. But the goodbye was short and sweet. I couldn't look Jeff in the eye, and he didn't want to make eye contact with me, either.

I turned away as fast as I could, because in truth I was all choked up at his leaving. The pool parties had become a regular thing by now, and we'd grown close. More important, we knew we had the skills and the experience to sort this place out, if only we'd had backing from Washington. I didn't doubt the capabilities of Jeff's replacement, but I was going to be gone in a couple of weeks myself, and I didn't think that anything would change in the interim. Jeff and I couldn't look each other in the eye because we knew that we'd failed.

Jeff's replacement, Alex James, was a short, wiry, and quiet kind of guy. Jeff had briefed me that Alex had been stationed at the Tripoli Embassy for almost a year, so he was sure to know his stuff. But I was tired now of the RSO rotations, and all I really wanted was to go out on a high with Scotty and with Dave. I had no desire to return to this utterly messed-up situation and I was counting down the days until my leaving.

Along with Alex came a new IT guy, Sean Smith. Rosie had been the first to clear it with IT that I could eat in the canteen, but I needed to check in with Sean to make sure I was good to continue doing so. I went and sought him out in his IT room, in the rear of the TOC.

"Hi, I'm Morgan from Blue Mountain. When I'm in is it okay for me to eat at the canteen?"

Sean gave me this look, like it wasn't a question I should even have to ask. "Fuck, one hundred percent yeah. Far as I'm concerned you work here to protect guys like me, so you're one of us. Damn right you can eat here."

Over lunch I noticed that Alex was wearing an Arsenal cap. Arsenal is one of the top soccer teams in Britain, but being a rugby man I'm no great fan of soccer.

I nodded at his cap. "What's that piece of shit you've got on your head?"

He removed the hat and glanced at it, as Dave and Scotty dissolved into laughter. "This? It's a gift from a British friend."

"Well, all I can say is your friend must hate you. That's one horrific soccer team."

In truth, it could have been any soccer team on that hat and I'd have ripped into Alex. I just hated soccer. But more to the point I was pissed about the fact that we had lost Jeff as our chief RSO, and I guess I was taking it out on the new guy. But at least it broke the ice a bit, and Alex took it in very good spirits.

Once everyone had finished lunch, Sean the new IT guy and I got to chat for a good hour over coffee. He was a smiley, shaven-headed dude who was based at a diplomatic mission in The Hague, in Holland. He told me the Hague job was a great contract to be working, especially as he was there with his wife and kids. He'd been posted out to Benghazi for a twenty-eight-day duration only, after which he'd be straight back to The Hague.

"I'm at The Hague on a three-year contract," he added. "It's fantastic. I love it. What a great place to live."

I told Sean how I'd served with the British Army for a year or so on the Dutch-German border, so not far from The Hague. We'd paid a lot of visits to Holland, and we'd loved the country and it's people. Sean talked a bit about some of his previous postings— about being in the Baghdad Mission and getting hammered by mortars on a daily basis. He'd been in the job for a good ten years and he was more than used to having incoming.

"But you know, this is gonna be my last hostile environment," Sean remarked. "It's just not fair on the wife and kids—this kind of shit. Anyway, I've done my share of hostile deployments: time for others to take the strain. I won't be forced to do any more, that's for sure—'cause I've done so many." He paused. "So anyways, what d'you think of the security here?"

I needed to choose my words carefully. I didn't want to scare the guy too much. "Well, my guards are good, that's for sure. They're shit-hot. But they can only do so much since they don't carry weapons."

"They sure look the part. They look really good. So what do you think of the QRF?"

I sighed. "Don't get me started." I didn't want to say what I was thinking: *If the bad guys attack you're all dead.* I restricted myself to this: "Let's just hope if anything happens the QRF perform."

"Would people be able to get in—the bad guys, I mean?"

"Yeah, as I've told all RSOs before—if there's a substantial amount of the bad guys they're gonna get in. But the RSOs will look after you. I can't see it happening, anyway. Nothing like that has happened so far."

"Okay, well, we should be fine then. Seems quiet enough, eh?"

Sean was used to working at embassies that were heavily forti-
fied and with U.S. Marines as guards. We had none of that here.
I was trying to be nice to him and give him some kind of reassurance. But I will regret saying those words for the rest of my days.

Things settled into a kind of a rhythm now. Ramadan was
over and Dave and Scotty were out doing missions on the ground.
Alex kept himself pretty much to himself, for he was busy manning communications in the TOC. I ran on the beach in the early
mornings, kept on top of my guard force during the day, and every
night I ticked off another day until I would be gone.

September 8 came around and Dave, Scotty, and I had less than
a week to go now—but the boys seemed really on edge. They kept
pacing the compound, making sure the guards were in place, and
checking the barriers, the gates, and the fencing. I knew something was up, I just didn't know what. Scotty was my linkman over
the guard force and he came over to talk.

"Buddy, the guards are doing a fine job, but you know—can
you really make sure they're on the ball for the next four to five
days? Make sure all vehicles get an extra-thorough search—same
as usual, only better. I really need your boys to be one hundred
percent."

"No problem. You want me to bolster the guard force with
some guys from the standby shift?"

As Scotty knew, I had loads of extra guys trained and vetted
and ready to go. They all wanted the work.

"No, no—just keep on top of them for the next four to five
days."

I didn't ask why, but I guessed from what he'd said that we had
a VIP visit coming up. In the world of security you treat such
visits on a need-to-know basis: only those who absolutely need to
know will be aware who is coming and when. In Afghanistan we
never used to know who a VIP visitor might be until the moment
they arrived—and that included the British prime minister and
the commander of the U.S. Marine Corps.

I went and relayed Scotty's instructions to Omar, my newish Guard Force Commander.

"Listen, I need the guards to stay extra vigilant for the coming week. If a visitor doesn't have proper documents—if they don't have a valid visitor's pass—you do not let them in. Even if the person has a U.S. passport, you do not let them in. You radio the RSOs, so they can come check."

"Yes, yes, of course, Mr. Michael, no problem. But what is the cause for so much concern? Have the guards been doing anything wrong? I have been rigorously checking—"

"Nope, the guards are doing great," I said, cutting him off. If anything, Omar had a tendency to be too much of a worrier. He was certainly too much of a talker, that was for sure. But at least his heart was in the right place.

For the next twenty-four hours the guards were at their very best. I went back to my beachside villa on the evening of the tenth knowing we were well on top of things. I had five days left to go, and the nearer my homecoming came the more my mind kept drifting to the Welsh mountains, and a beautiful woman and a feisty little boy who couldn't wait for me to get home.

Massoud drove me into work the following morning, and he had no new intelligence to report. All seemed well until I arrived at the Embassy gates, whereupon a very worried-looking Omar came running out to me.

"Mr. Michael! Mr. Michael! Very worrying news! This morning! A Libyan policeman—he was taking photos of the Embassy gates!"

Omar was firing words at me like a machine gun. I got him to calm down and explain things properly. A couple of hours earlier the guards had spotted a man in a Libyan policeman's uniform in the building directly opposite the Mission. He was on the roof of that three-story property taking photographs. There was no mistaking what he was taking photos of: his lens was pointed at the front gate and the interior of the Mission. This was heavy shit.

From up on that roof you could see into the entire compound and get shots of just about everything.

"So did you challenge him?" I asked. "Did you ask what the hell he was doing?"

"Yes, yes, we did! But he told us to get lost, it was none of our business."

"Did you report it to the RSOs?"

"No, Mr. Michael, I was waiting to discuss it with you first."

I told Omar he'd done well and that I'd take it from here. As I hurried over to the TOC my mind was racing. If he was a genuine Libyan policeman he'd have been armed, so my guards were right not to have pushed it. In any case, they had no jurisdiction over the Libyan police. More important, the Libyan police were renowned for being corrupt as hell, so who knew the real reason why he was taking photographs. If it had been official police business why hadn't they phoned and asked the Embassy for permission? It just didn't add up.

I entered the TOC and it was a buzz of activity. It all stopped when I told them the news. "Guys, my guards just caught a Libyan policeman taking photos of the front of the Mission. Or at least, a guy wearing a Libyan policeman's uniform."

Dave spun around. "You are fucking joking!"

"No, mate, I am not."

"Did they hold him?"

"No, they didn't. They figured he was armed. Anyway, there's no way my guards can claim to have jurisdiction over the Libyan police—not unless they're on Mission property."

Dave shook his head in disbelief. "This is not good. We need to chase this up with the Benghazi chief of police pronto. See if he's a real policeman here on official business, and if so, what do they want with the photos."

"And if he's not?" I prompted.

Dave's eyes met mine. "Then it's some kind of a recce . . .

Buddy, I gotta get moving. Tell your guards to keep their fuckin' eyes peeled!"

He grabbed the phone and started making calls. I could hear him giving updates and briefings to all on what had just happened. I left the TOC feeling deeply unsettled. I figured we had about as much chance of getting any answers out of the Benghazi chief of police as we had of hell freezing over.

I went around my guard force praising them for what they'd done and urging them to keep vigilant and on the ball. "Guys, keep bloody switched on, okay. You do the job I've trained you to do, but even better today."

"Yep, yep, no problem."

I spoke to Omar and congratulated him again. It was Omar himself who'd approached and challenged the supposed policeman. In Libya, it took a lot to do that. In a place like Benghazi the police would know who you were and where you lived, or they'd be able to find it out pretty damn quickly. If you crossed a policeman you were very likely to have him come knocking on the door of your family home. The guards were unarmed. They'd challenged a supposed Libyan cop who very likely had a gun. Hats off to them for doing so—it was a ballsy move.

I made my way to the canteen for a coffee but ran into Dave on the way. He told me the State Department was seeking answers from the Benghazi chief of police as to who had been taking the photographs. I figured we had about a zero chance of getting any answers, but I didn't say that to Dave. He'd done all that he could, and I didn't want to bring the guy down. He was looking hyperstressed as it was.

We left it at that and I headed into the canteen. As soon as I entered I noticed two black guys sitting at one of the tables. They were dressed in the same kind of clothing as the RSOs—our de facto uniform—but these guys had pistols slung on their belts. I figured we had two extra American security guys at the Mission right now, but I didn't know exactly why. I grabbed a coffee and asked them if they minded me joining them. They told me to pull up a chair.

"I'm Morgan. I run the guard force here."

"Hey, nice to meet you, Morgan," one of them replied.

"Your guards sure seem up to speed," remarked the other.

I took a sip of the coffee, spotted Asaf, and yelled over a greeting: "Gandu!"

"Benshoot! England no good!"

"Bloody *Bangladesh* . . . We're gonna ban you from cricket these days your team's so shitty . . ."

The two black dudes were laughing at the exchange, especially since they could see that Asaf loved it. I glanced outside, absentmindedly, and my eyes came to rest upon a gray-haired figure moving past the window. I recognized him instantly, mostly from having seen the guy in the newspapers and on the TV news. It was J. Christopher Stevens, U.S. Ambassador to Libya.

The penny dropped instantly. I now knew why the place was so busy and so tense, and who the couple of guys were that I was sharing a coffee with. They had to be part of his close protection (CP) team. I presumed there had to be at least four other CP guys here at the Mission, for the British political officer in Benghazi never had less than six, and he was one below ambassador level.

No one who'd worked here for any amount of time could fail to have learned of Ambassador Stevens's reputation as a friend of the Libyan people, and a real mover and shaker in the post-Gaddafi landscape. Over the years he'd had a close involvement with Benghazi in particular, this being where the revolution had started. Benghazi was where the first weapons had been shipped in to arm the rebels, and where Libya's Transitional National Council—the interim government—had been founded.

Ambassador Stevens's greatest renown was that he'd sailed into Benghazi at the height of the revolution on a Greek cargo ship carrying supplies to the rebels. From Benghazi, Stevens and his team had coordinated further shipments of "nonlethal aid." They'd had nowhere to stay in the rebel stronghold, so they'd based themselves at the Tibesti, until a car bomb had gone off in the parking lot. *Sounds familiar.* Stevens had stood by the rebels as Gaddafi's forces closed in on the city, which was saved only at the last minute by NATO air strikes.

Stevens had earned a legendary reputation by standing by the rebels in their hour of need, and facing the risks alongside them. He'd bought into their struggle, and especially their fight for basic freedoms and rights—ones that we in the West pretty much take for granted. Once the Transitional National Council had been recognized as the legitimate power in Libya, Stevens had been made its U.S. Special Advisor, and he'd been the obvious choice for U.S. Ambassador to Libya thereafter.

For the Ambassador, Benghazi was almost a home away from home and I was surprised we hadn't seen him here earlier. But as I turned back to my coffee a thought struck me most powerfully. The U.S. Ambassador had flown in, and this very morning we'd had someone posing as a Libyan policeman taking photos of the Embassy. I made the connection almost instantly: *Shit—the Ambo's here and we've just had some dodgy bastard doing a recce.* It was either the mother of all coincidences, or it was hugely ominous and menacing.

Scotty walked into the canteen, saw me, and came right over. "There you are, buddy. Been looking for you everywhere. Sorry, I couldn't tell you earlier but—"

I cut him off with a laugh. "No worries, mate. Don't sweat it. I know how it works."

"Yeah, well, sorry, you know, but we really couldn't let on."

"Not a problem. I'll make sure the guards are on top form."

Scotty smiled. "Cheers, buddy, I really appreciate it."

I made as if to finish my coffee. "Right, I won't hang around for long, as I don't want to get in anyone's way. You all seem busy and I don't want to get under anyone's feet. I'll be with the guards for a couple of hours, then shoot. But if you need me, phone me. You know where I'll be, and I'll be right back."

"Great. But wait five, 'cause he wants to have a quick word with you first."

By "he" it was clear that Scotty meant the Ambassador. "No problem. I'm around."

As if on cue Ambassador Stevens walked in. He grabbed himself a coffee, then came right over. I stood up to greet him, to show proper respect, and we shook hands.

"You're Morgan, right? Great to meet you. Thanks for the job you've been doing here. The RSOs tell me the guard force is working real well."

"Thanks very much, sir. It's taken a good while to get them into proper shape, but yes, they're an effective force right now."

We took our seats. My first impression of the Ambassador was of a warm, decent, down-to-earth kind of guy. Instinctively I liked him. I'd met a lot of diplomats in my time, and there were some at least who chose to treat private security guys like me as scum. They figured we were uneducated brutes who only knew how to hurt and kill.

I'd once had some snotty Englishwoman working for the British Foreign and Commonwealth Office say this to me and my men: "You lot—you're just thugs with guns!" Needless to say we'd canned the mission and driven her directly back to base, whereupon our boss had made her apologize, publicly, before we would take her on any further tasks. There we were supposedly prepared to take a bullet to protect her ass, and she'd said that to us. The gall of it.

"So, tell me, what d'you think of the security here?" the Ambassador asked. "You've been here longer than just about anyone, so I'd appreciate your take on things."

Oh fuck, I thought to myself, *here we go again—the Ambo's been told to get the lowdown from the mouthy Brit.* I reminded myself not to swear and to be polite and not to go overboard about the QRF.

"Put it this way, sir—more could be done." I was choosing my words carefully. "There need to be more physical barriers. We could do with doubling or even tripling the numbers of RSOs— that's what is needed to cover the workload. Plus the Quick Reaction Force—which is made up of four men from the Seventeenth February Militia—is not up to the task you require of them."

"Interesting. Very interesting. Please, go on."

"Well, I'm sure the RSOs have briefed you on all of this, sir, but in short we need a lot more manpower. Either that, sir, or we need more firepower. Preferably a bit of both, but if not, then one or the other would sure help."

"Anything else?" he prompted.

"Sir, there's a whole lot more. But I've briefed the RSOs repeatedly on what I see as the security deficiencies here, and I'm sure they've briefed you. I don't want to talk out of line here or go over what's already been said."

The Ambassador gave me this very direct look. His eyes were a gentle gray-blue, and there was a lot of honesty and decency in them. "Understood, Morgan, but you're the guy on the ground with the continuity, hence that's why it's good to hear it from you direct. What changes would you recommend as a priority?"

I met the Ambassador's gaze. "Sir, number-one priority: get rid of the QRF. Get shot of them, and get a force of U.S. Marines or similar in their place, a dozen or more. I'd also double the number of RSOs, and it wouldn't hurt to get a couple of heavy machine guns up on the roof of Villa C, as your firepower. That's exactly what I'd do, sir."

The Ambassador smiled. "Thanks, Morgan, that's exactly what I needed to hear. Is there anything else?"

This was a guy who struck me as being open and accessible, and ready to take feedback from whoever was best positioned to give it. The fact that this wasn't, strictly speaking, any of my business didn't seem to matter in the slightest with him. He hadn't challenged a word of what I'd said. In fact, I got the very strong impression he agreed with most of it. I figured there was no point in my not saying it all.

"Well, there's one more thing, sir. I'm sure you've heard, but we had a Libyan policeman—or someone posing as a Libyan policeman—taking photos of the Mission this very morning. Sir, that worries me greatly, and for reasons I am sure you understand."

The Ambassador nodded. "I had heard, and I understand your concern. Thanks for raising it."

We stood up and shook hands. Again the Ambassador thanked me for having the guard force in such good shape. He didn't need to. I was just doing my job, what I was paid to do, and what Blue Mountain was contracted to do by the State Department. The fact that he bothered to say all this reflected what a thoroughly fair and caring individual the Ambassador was. He may have achieved high office, but that didn't mean for one moment that he had forgotten the little people.

The Ambassador left, leaving me in the company of his two CP guys.

"Thanks, buddy, for speaking up," one of them remarked. "You said what needed to be said, and you got the credibility to say it, you bein' here so long."

I asked them what their procedure was for extracting the Ambassador if we got hit. They said they'd bundle him into an armored Land Cruiser and make a convoy move for the Egyptian border. That I knew was a good eight-hour drive away through numerous checkpoints controlled by various Libyan militias. I told them it was unworkable: they'd be a load of Americans armed to the teeth driving very recognizable armored 4x4s, and they were bound to be seen.

They asked me what my evacuation plan was. I said I'd call Massoud, my Libyan driver, and we'd sneak away in his battered Nissan sedan making like locals. They looked at me like I was insane, but frankly I'd have rather done things my way than take my chances with the Ambo in a convoy of highly distinctive armored

SUVs—ones from which the red diplomatic plates still hadn't been removed.

Before leaving for the day I watched the Ambassador do the rounds of my guards. This was a guy who somehow found time for everyone. Just as important, the guy was fluent in Arabic, and I could tell by the way he greeted my guards and how he related to them that he was a massive fan of their culture and their ways.

Just before I left, Omar grabbed me. "Who is that guy—the American? He is totally fluent in Arabic. He speaks like one of us."

I told him that I had no idea who he was. But I repeated the need for the guard force to be extra vigilant with such visitors around.

I headed to my villa and the regular-as-clockwork takeout-chicken guy who delivered my evening meal. We'd settled into a routine. Unless I told him otherwise, he'd deliver barbecued chicken, rice, and salad to my door at eight every evening. The fact that I felt secure enough to eat it on my veranda overlooking the sea really spoke volumes. Most of the Ramadan party crowd was gone by now, but it wasn't as if any of the bad guys had taken up residence in their place.

The next morning I went for a long run on the beach, followed by a major session in the villa complex gym. I didn't plan to get in to the Embassy before lunchtime. It would be a busy old morning with Ambassador Stevens in town and I figured I was better out of the way.

Silvio Miotto—the top diplomat here at the Benghazi Mission—had slipped away quietly the evening before, Ambassador Stevens flying in to replace him. Silvio had become deeply unsettled about the lack of security at the Embassy, and he'd shared a lot of that with me. I knew how desperate he'd been to get away, and I could just imagine how happy he was to be en route back to the United States. I had grown to like Silvio a great deal and I was glad he'd managed to get himself gone.

Massoud drove me to the Embassy at one o'clock. All was good with my guards, so I headed for the TOC. I'd got into a habit of checking in with Sean every day, for the new IT guy was such a dude. We chatted about this and that, and then he asked a favor of me.

"Can you change fifty euros? I need some Libyan dinar so I can buy my wife one of those silk scarves the locals sell around here. You know the things I mean? She'll look great wearing one of those around The Hague."

"Yeah, I've been meaning to get Laura one," I replied. "No worries. I'll get it changed for you."

I stuffed his fifty-euro note—the equivalent of sixty-five U.S. dollars—into my wallet, then headed for the canteen. En route I ran into Alex, the new head RSO. There was a flagpole right out front of the canteen block, and I noticed the flag was flying at half-mast.

I shaded my eyes. "Why's the flag down? Why at half-mast?"

Alex glanced at it. "It's Nine-Eleven."

God, so it was. "Sorry, of course it is, mate. I'm sorry. I forgot."

Alex grinned a little sheepishly. "Tell the truth, so did I."

Dave and Scotty were in the canteen, but they were mad busy.

"I'll be around for the next few hours then back at the villa," I told them. "If you need me call me and I'll be over. How're my guards?"

"More than happy," Dave replied. "They're doing great work. Gotta go, buddy. Laters."

Ambassador Stevens had a packed schedule for the day, but he wasn't going to take any meetings outside of the Embassy. It being the eleventh anniversary of the 9/11 terror attacks on America, the RSOs figured there was a heightened threat level right now. As a result, the Ambassador would take all of today's meetings here in the compound.

I ate lunch, after which I checked the guards and hung around with them for a few hours, by which time it was the boiling heat of late afternoon. I got Massoud to take me back to the villa. I went for a dip in the sea to cool down, then settled down to do some paperwork—checking the guard roster, when their next wages were due, that kind of thing. I got my evening barbecued chicken delivery and settled down to eat it in front of the TV.

It was half past nine when my cell phone rang. I checked the caller ID. It was Omar, my guard force commander.

"Morgan here. Anything to report?"

"Morgan, we are under attack! We need help!"

Omar sounded extremely distressed, but I was used to him being a bit high-strung. I figured it was probably a hand grenade over the wall or maybe another IED.

"Calm down," I told him. "We've been attacked before. Tell me exactly what happened."

"Morgan, you don't understand! There are armed men attacking the compound!"

"What d'you mean, *armed men*? Who are they? How many?"

As I said those words I detected the sharp crack of gunfire in the background to Omar's call. With a horrible feeling in the pit of my stomach I recognized it as the distinctive sound of AK-47s firing off long bursts on automatic. I could hear Omar panting now, as clearly he had started to run.

"I said—*Who is it and how many?*"

I could hear real fear in Omar's voice as he gasped out a reply. "Maybe one hundred! Maybe more!" Omar's voice was shaking. "Bad men, Morgan, really bad men."

I was on my feet now, yelling into my cell phone. "Omar, listen to me: make sure the duck-and-cover alarm has been pressed! Hit the alarm, okay! Then gather the guard force and get them the hell out of there!"

I didn't hear a reply. The phone clicked dead.

I was left staring at the handset, my heart thumping like a machine gun, and wondering what the fuck I was to do next.

CHAPTER THIRTEEN

In the seconds after Omar's call I tried to keep a grip on things, to force my mind to think logically. Omar exaggerated all the time. One hundred bad guys probably meant half that number. It was more likely fifty, but even that was too many. I'd seen no other CP guys with the Ambassador other than the two black dudes. That plus Dave, Scotty, and Alex meant we had five guys total. The CP guys would be with the Ambo, and Alex would be on the comms calling for help.

That left two guys—Dave and Scotty—on the guns.

Two against fifty: those kind of odds were pretty close to hopeless.

The next thought that struck me was this: Ambassador Stevens had been here less than forty-eight hours; we'd had a recce done of the front gate of the Mission; it was the anniversary of 9/11—and the Embassy had been hit big-time. It was too many coincidences. *Who the hell were the guys who'd hit us? How long had they been watching us? And for how long had this been in the planning?*

Such thoughts rushed through my head in a matter of instants. In the next moment I was overcome by the fear I felt for my American brothers—Scotty, Dave, Sean, and the others. Even at this moment my guards would be running for their lives—just as they'd been trained to do. But the Americans—they would stand firm. From everything I knew about Dave and Scotty they'd remain resolute, and fight until the very last round.

What I had dreaded for so long was now upon us: the U.S. Embassy in Benghazi was being hit by a massive force of gunmen . . . What chance did five stand against fifty? A voice was screaming in my head: *Get over there, Morgan, and help! Get over there now!* But what could I do? I was alone, I was unarmed, and I had no vehicle.

Then I knew what I had to do: *fucking call Massoud.*

I dialed his number and thank God he answered. "Massoud, get over here now! As soon as you can! Bring your AK and as many mags as you can get your hands on."

"Yes, I will be there. But what—"

"Just get over here!"

I cut the line. As soon as I stopped talking horrific images flooded into my mind. I'd bonded with Dave and Scotty over war stories from Iraq, plus all the kidding around and the shared joy of fatherhood. I sensed the fear they had to be feeling right now as the enemy surged through the gates, and I had visions of them getting captured alive and paraded around the city by their captors. I'd promised to stand shoulder to shoulder with those guys, if ever the shit went down.

I had to get in there and help.

But how?

I'd been in countless firefights before—against the Taliban, Iraqi insurgents, and Al Qaeda. I'd always been happy to lead from the front and make decisions on the fly. War demands it. Difference was, back then I'd had my team around me. I'd had guys with me with whom to throw ideas about before making any decisions. Now I was one hundred percent on my own. My head was spinning out of control. I was sick with worry for Scotty, Dave, and the others, but at the same time I couldn't think how I could get in there to the guys' aid.

I could hardly charge through the front gate: I knew from what

Omar had said that it had been surged. With fifty-plus bad guys flooding the compound, the side and rear gates were also very likely to have been taken. I couldn't scale the wall, for the simple reason that I had no ladder. Then I hit upon something: *the gym*.

How many times had I gazed absentmindedly at our make-shift gym's flat room, which abutted the fence and the wall, and thought: *If the bad guys ever want to slip over the perimeter and into this place, that's their easiest way in.* I'd never once thought: *If I need to slip unseen into the Embassy, that's my route in.* But that was exactly the thought that struck me all of a sudden, right now.

Last time I'd bothered to check, the construction materials were still piled against the outside of the perimeter wall. In fact, I'd made a mental note to add that to the long list of security improvements to be made at the Embassy: *Get rid of that heap of building materials.* Of course, it was way down on the list of priorities when compared to getting rid of the QRF, and right now I was glad I'd never managed to get it actioned—*for that was going to be my way in.*

I started tearing around the villa snatching up my gear. I gathered the essentials I always carry with me on a private security job that's likely to go bad: six hundred dollars in cash, for paying my way out of trouble; British passport, in case I had to run for the border; my out-of-date British Embassy ID card, in case I needed to bluff anyone; knife—because it was the only weapon I had right now; plus my cell phone, for comms between Massoud and me.

As I stared at my phone for an instant, a thought struck me: *I hadn't tried calling Scotty or Dave.* The protocol was that they'd phone me if ever they were in trouble. Well, tonight trouble had come in bucket loads, and I guessed the guys hadn't had the chance to make the call—and most likely because they were up to their eyeballs in the shit and getting down the fire on their attackers.

I tried calling Dave's cell phone. It wasn't as hopeless a gesture as it might sound. If Dave and Scotty had moved fast, they could have bundled the Ambassador out the rear of the Embassy as the attackers came in the front. We had the armored escape vehicle parked by the rear gate, for just such an emergency. Even now they might be tearing through the streets of Benghazi, making for the Annex, the nearest place of sanctuary.

I heard Dave's ringtone. I willed him to answer. *Come on.* No reply.

I tried Scotty. *No reply.*

I guessed both were busy under fire. I knew neither would take a step back in protecting the small slice of America that was the Embassy, or Ambassador Stevens for that matter. Scotty was the more hotheaded and gung-ho of the two, but Dave was solid as a rock and unshakable, and they'd both be smashing out the rounds.

Yet sometimes it was exactly that which got you killed. When you were as outnumbered as this—ten to one, for God's sake— sometimes you had to simply evacuate while you still had the chance. But would they know the numbers they were up against in the confusion and the darkness? It was a massive compound, after all.

I tried calling every number I had for guys at the mission: Sean's, Alex's, Dave and Scotty again, but still no answers. Time seemed to stand still. *I had to get in there and help.*

I phoned Massoud. "Where the fuck are you?" I screamed. "FUCKING HURRY UP AND GET HERE!"

Massoud told me to calm down. "I have only been five minutes. I am being as quick as I can. I am on my way."

He knew that something had to be badly wrong. He'd worked with me for long enough now to realize that this wasn't me. I'd never been like this before. Never once had I raised my voice at him. I didn't get like this without good reason.

The voices were back in my head now, almost as if there were two of me arguing with each other. One voice was going: *You're out of your depth! What can you do? You're one bloke alone, Morgan, that's all.* But at the same time the other voice—*my* voice—was raging: *How dare they try to take the compound? Who the hell do they think they are?*

I paced the villa. At one moment I realized I was yelling at myself in Welsh: "Come on, Morgan, pull yourself together! You've got to get up there and help!"

Christ, I was losing it.

I tried phoning Dave again. To my utter amazement a voice answered. I could hear fierce gunfire crackling in the background, half drowning out whatever words he was saying.

"Dave? Fuck! What's going on, mate? Are you okay?"

"We're under attack. They've penetrated the perimeter. They're all over the compound."

I couldn't believe how calm and collected he sounded. I had images in my head of him crouched in some cover as he took my call, Scotty beside him hammering out the fire with his M4.

"Where are you, mate, and how many are they?"

"There's fucking loads of 'em. Too many. They're everywhere. We're surrounded. We ain't gonna make it, buddy."

I told him to hold on. "Keep fighting, mate. *Keep fighting*. Just keep fighting. I'm on my way."

"Okay, buddy, I hear ya." He cut the call.

Dave had sounded so incredibly cool, just like he always was. It reminded me of when we'd been eating lunch in the canteen and I'd been jabbing him with the outrageous comments, and he'd be cool as the Fonz. Yet here was I close to losing it. It was almost as if Dave had accepted his fate already—that he wasn't getting out of there and would go down fighting—and he was at peace with it.

But I didn't want him—or any of them—to die. I wanted us to win this one, and at least now I had a good idea of where they were. They had to be mounting their defense from the roof of the VIP Villa, which was the agreed fallback option if the perimeter was breached. If they could hold off the bad guys for long enough, maybe there was still just a chance.

From the roof they'd be able to see nearly all of the compound, which was how I guessed they'd realized the numbers they were up against. I'd never seen Americans back down from a fight, not ever. With their prior experience from Iraq, I knew neither Dave nor Scotty would ever give ground. They'd fight to protect the clients—Ambassador Stevens and the others—at all costs. Anything else was anathema.

In a way, Dave's ultimate coolness during that phone call was only what I'd expected of him. I had absolute respect for these guys. I knew they would not falter or bend. They might hail from different walks of life but they were united under their patriotism—their love of America—and their beliefs. They took their duties to God, flag, and country very seriously, and right now I feared it would get them killed. But for guys like them there was no other way.

My mind flipped to thoughts of my one-year-old son, Lewis. Having grown up without a father, I'd always promised Lewis that he'd never be without me—that he'd never have to be the same as I was as a kid: *fatherless*. But I told myself if that was what happened tonight, then so be it. Dave, Scotty, and Sean all had young kids. Fatherhood: it was a big part of what had united us.

The one thing I was not willing to let happen was to get taken alive. During the years I'd served on the U.S. ACE contract, two Americans, Jack Hensley and Eugene Armstrong, plus the Brit Ken Bigley had been kidnapped by Abu Musab al-Zarqawi, then leader of Al Qaeda in Iraq. All three were engineers working on Iraqi reconstruction projects, but that hadn't stopped Zarqawi from beheading them and parading their sick killings on the Internet. The videos of the orange-jumpsuited victims' executions were chilling, sickening, and vile.

We'd made a pact among all the operators on that U.S. ACE contract that none of us was ever going out like that. "I ain't going out in a boiler suit begging for Blair and Bush to save me," was how the guys put it. If one of us was so badly injured as to not be able to shoot himself, and about to fall into enemy hands, one of his fellow operators would shoot him. That was the deal we had struck.

Having made my promise to Dave, I now had to get up there and get to them. I was going over the wall at the makeshift gym, and I'd link up with the guys at Villa C, whereupon we'd stand shoulder to shoulder and take the fight to the bad guys. Having a plan of action gave me focus, and I started trying to scope out the risk factors.

I had to presume the guys had got a call through to the Annex, asking for their help. It's a maxim of the Navy SEALs that they never leave a man behind, and I knew there were several ex-SEALs at the Annex. I had to presume that some kind of rescue mission was going to be launched from there, in which case I'd need to watch out for those guys as much as I did the enemy. I'd be one lone individual with a beard and a suntan going over the wall: to the Annex boys I'd most definitely resemble one of the bad guys.

In fact, Dave and Scotty might see the silhouette of my AK-47 in the darkness and they might try to shoot me, too. By now I had a good seven weeks' growth of beard and I really did blend in. The way things would be in there right now no one was about to say: *hang on a minute, don't fire—isn't that Morgan?*

I'd need to keep my eyes peeled for any rescue force from the Annex, and I'd need to somehow signal to Dave and Scotty that I was coming in. Easiest way would be to phone Dave and tell him from what direction to expect me. I didn't know exactly what I would do if that failed, but I'd cross that bridge when I came to it.

I decided to wear whatever I could to make myself more recognizable to the friendlies. Then I countermanded that. The greatest danger had to come from the enemy, and the one factor I had in my favor was that I could pass as a local when out and about in Benghazi. I needed to use that to the max now. I'd need to flit through the streets sneaking past the bad guys, and to do that I needed to look as much as possible like one of their own.

I pulled on my blue Chicago Cubs baseball cap, one that I'd picked up on a recent visit to the United States. It was sun-bleached and faded, and as most Libyan men wore such baseball caps it should help me blend in. They'd see that and the bushy beard and hopefully they'd think I was a fellow bad guy. I'd been lounging around the villa in flip-flops, but I pulled on my worn desert boots so I had something solid to climb, jump, and run in.

I was good to go. *Come on, Massoud, come on.*

My phone rang and I snatched it up. "Where the fuck are you? You're taking fucking forever."

I was venting on Massoud and he didn't deserve it.

"Morgan, I am waiting for you outside."

I took one last look around the villa, then closed the door. I wondered if I'd ever be back here. Fuck it, I was going anyway. I scanned the area, saw Massoud's beat-up old Nissan, and checked that there was no one else around menacing the place. I hurried over. Massoud jumped out and stepped forward to meet me, hands held out as if to stop me from getting into the vehicle.

"Calm down," he urged me. "Calm down, Morgan. Don't even think about it. We are not going up there."

"Fuck are you talking about?" I snarled.

"I fucking heard it all on the radio," Massoud fired back at me. He rarely swore, so to hear such expletives on his lips had to mean that this was bad. "I have heard all the chatter from the soldiers who are up there, trying to get some help to the Mission. There is no way, Morgan. There are two hundred Shariah Brigade fighters at the Mission. We can't get anywhere near. No one will know who we are and we won't get through. And even if we do, it will be suicide."

"Bullshit!" I countered. "Give me the car keys and I'll go on my own." I knew all the routes, as we'd driven them for weeks and weeks together. Massoud handed me the car keys. "Where's the AK?" I demanded.

"On the backseat with two hundred rounds."

"Right, I'm off. See you later."

"Fucking hell! This is bullshit, Morgan! All you will do is die!"

"I don't give a fuck. I'm going anyway."

Massoud turned away from me and started cursing in Arabic, his fist slamming onto the roof of the car. "Fuck it! All right, I will come with you! But I have two children at home and I do not want to get killed up there."

"Mate, I'm not hanging around. Jump in or stay here. You've got ten seconds."

Massoud told me to move over to the passenger seat. His face was set in a rigid death mask as he slid in behind the wheel. He held out his hand. "Keys."

I passed them back to him. He fired up the Nissan, floored the accelerator, and we were on our way.

I could hear an unbroken stream of yelling and screaming in Arabic coming over his VHF radio. Massoud started to give me a running commentary as he drove.

"Okay, so they are reporting a major firefight is in progress up there. They say RPGs, Dushkas, and PKMs are all being used."

Jesus, all of that kind of hardware had been brought to bear! That was rocket-propelled grenades, Dushka heavy machine guns, plus PKM 7.62mm belt-fed general-purpose machine guns. The Embassy was getting hosed down by a serious amount of firepower, and against all of that Dave, Scotty, and the others had a handful of M4 assault rifles. If only the State Department desk jockeys had listened to us, and given us the .50-cals we'd asked for, plus a QRF of Marines . . .

But it was too late for all of that now.

It was normally a fifteen-minute night drive to the Embassy. As we tore through the streets I kept yelling at Massoud to get a move on, but it was clear he was going as fast as he could. I was running through my plan of attack over and over, wondering if there was any better way of doing this. I tried calling Robert. With his wealth of Special Forces experience maybe he'd think of a better way of going in. But I couldn't get the call through.

With two hundred bad guys on the ground up there I figured I stood just about zero chance of avoiding them. If I blundered into a mass of the enemy I'd simply let rip with the AK and keep unloading mags into them until either I was killed or wounded or down to my final rounds. I'd save the last few for when I turned the AK on myself and put a bullet in my head. Keep it simple, stupid: that was the plan.

My phone rang. It was Omar, my guard force commander. I snatched it up, demanding of him how many of the guards had escaped. He told me two. I asked where the three others were. He told me the attackers had got them.

"What the fuck d'you mean, *got them*?"

"The attackers, they captured three, Mr. Michael. They made them kneel and shot them. In the head. They shot them in the head. With guns right up to their heads . . ."

Omar was close to tears. He'd escaped the attack by the skin of his teeth, dashing into the cover of the nearby orchard. From there he'd watched as the bad guys had forced the three captured guards to kneel. Yelling and screaming obscenities they'd put guns to the guards' foreheads and pulled triggers, at which moment Omar had made a run for it and got out of there.

I was seething with rage now. Burning up. I'd known many of my guards for six months. I'd trained them and nurtured them and shaped them into an impressive force. In the process any number had become my friends. My brothers. I told Omar to take the surviving guards home and lie low.

"Do not go back there," I told him. "There's nothing more you can do. Go home to the safety of your family. And do not go back to that place until you hear from me."

"Okay, I go home. But where are you, Mr. Michael?"

"On my way to the Mission."

"*No!*" he yelled. "*No, no, no!* Mr. Michael, you mustn't go there! They will kill you! There are hundreds of them! There is nothing you can do!"

"I don't care. I'm on my way."

We were two miles out from the Embassy. The sky over the compound was awash with a halo of flame. Fiery tracer rounds arced high into the sky, like a fearsome fireworks display. Any doubts I had about the ferocity of the battle were gone now. I'd been in numerous firefights before—the most ferocious ones being in northern Iraq and in Helmand Province, Afghanistan—but I'd never seen anything like this before in terms of the sheer concentrated volume of fire.

There were scores of Libyan Army vehicles heading in the same direction as us, plus dozens of Toyota gun trucks with armed men in the rear.

"Who the fuck're they?" I asked Massoud. "Are they the Seventeenth February lot?"

He hunched over the wheel. "Yeah, probably. But I'm not sure. It is dark. It might be people going to help the Americans."

"That militia—will they give it everything?" I asked him. "Will they fight tooth and nail to get the Americans out? Will they shoot the fucking attackers?"

Massoud shook his head. "Truthfully, Morgan, shoot their Muslim brothers . . . No, I do not think they will."

Just as I'd suspected—the 17th February Militia would never engage in a full-on firefight with the Shariah Brigade, who were only one step removed from Al Qaeda, to rescue the Americans, who were guests in their country. All of these 17th February Militia gun trucks—they were here just for show.

We were less than a mile out when Massoud slowed. More and more vehicles were ahead of us, part blocking the way. I asked him what was going on. He told me that the Shariah Brigade had placed blocking groups—roadblocks—on all the approach roads to the Embassy. They'd done so to stop any forces going to the Americans' aid, and the blocking groups would likely prevent any QRF from the Annex from getting to the Embassy.

The dark and bitter truth was starting to sink in now: this was a well-orchestrated, carefully planned attack, one that they'd very likely rehearsed and trained for exhaustively. In my experience only hard-core jihadi fighters from Iraq and Afghanistan could organize an assault of the scale and complexity of this one. Maybe it was even an inside job, and I was certain that the Libyan "policeman" had been doing a recce.

I knew now how organized and deadly serious these sons of bitches were. The voice was screaming in my head again—*Turn back, turn back, you can't help! You're one man alone and you can't do anything. They're all dead! They're all dead!*

But I was fucked if I was going to.

We approached a left-hand turn that led to the Embassy front gate. There was a pickup parked sideways on to the road with a Dushka gunner blocking the way. Anyone who's ever been under fire from a Dushka knows how fearsome the weapon is: it has a distinctive deep, throaty boom, and the rounds can cut through trees and walls and blow your limbs clean off.

I told Massoud to keep going. "Keep driving. Keep driving. We'll try going around the back. Don't fucking turn, mate—just keep going."

As we shot past the gun truck I stole a glance down the road leading to the Embassy front gate. There was a seething mass of gunmen around the main entrance and all were heavily armed. I saw muzzles sparking in the compound's interior, and I could hear peals of gunfire rolling back across to us. It was maybe twenty minutes into the battle by now, and by the rate of fire pounding through the compound I knew for sure our guys were still fighting.

I had to get in there and help.

The Dushka gunner spotted us and spun his weapon around to follow our vehicle, its gaping muzzle tracking us as we went. His eyes were bugging out, for there wasn't another vehicle on the road now but him and us. His figure was half hidden by the massive machine gun, but I could see that he was dressed half in combats, and half in traditional-style Islamic robes.

I tried to avoid looking in his direction. I sensed Massoud tense for the searing blasts as the Dushka gunner opened fire. Massoud's was a thin-skinned sedan, and the Dushka's 12.7mm armor-piercing rounds would chew it to pieces in seconds. I could hear my heart pounding in my head, beating away like a drum. No doubt about it, I was shit scared and the adrenaline was pumping in bucket loads.

How the fuck was I going to get in there, with so many bad guys swarming the place? Where was the darkest point? Or was it going to be game over before it had even started? Was I going to get shot as I tried getting out of Massoud's vehicle?

One thing was for sure: I was going to have to do this last bit on foot, and no way was I letting Massoud come with me.

CHAPTER FOURTEEN

We were nearing the end of the road, whereupon we'd hang a left to get onto the main highway that ran the length of the rear of the compound. I planned to dismount near the tall building where I'd always feared the enemy would place a sniper. Right now that was the least of my worries: what did they need a sniper for when they'd surged the compound with two hundred Shariah Brigade fighters? From there I'd sneak back east on foot, turn north on the side road, and head for the point where I figured I could climb onto the roof of the gym.

As we neared the left-hand turn Massoud flicked his eyes across to me. "Morgan, you know if we get out of the car we will be killed."

"I don't expect you to get out. Just wait in the car somewhere safe. I'll call you when I'm done."

I knew Massoud well by now and I knew his nature. He was a straight shooter who did everything by the book. I'd once asked him to buy me a water filter. I'd given him the hundred dollars it would cost, plus thirty dollars on top for getting it for me. He'd handed the thirty back. "You pay me a monthly wage. This is my job. It is enough." He was unbending on what was right and wrong and the rule of law. Whenever he saw something that was bad, he'd say: "This is wrong. We cannot move on if people keep doing such things."

I liked and respected him and I did not want to get him killed. Anyway, I needed someone to stay with the getaway vehicle and he was absolutely to be trusted in that role. If I went in there and found all the Americans dead, or that they'd evacuated already, I needed a way to get myself out of here. Or if I found them alive I might even have some of them with me, so I'd need Massoud waiting with his car.

We took the turn leading into the road that ran the length of the rear of the Embassy compound. I breathed a momentary sigh of relief. It appeared to be totally deserted. Then I saw it. Halfway down the main drag there was a vehicle parked across the highway, acting as a roadblock. It was yet another gun truck, the stark silhouette of a Dushka menacing the way ahead.

"Pull in quick, and kill the lights," I told Massoud.

He did as I'd said, the Nissan going dark. We sat there for a second in the comparative stillness, but still the pounding percussions of gunfire from the far end of the compound reached us clearly. The roar of battle punched through the vehicle, each staccato burst reminding me that my friends were in there and in mortal danger.

Massoud glanced at me, inquiringly: *What next?*

"Just give me a second," I told him. "I've got to think about the next move."

My mind was racing. Had the Dushka gunner spotted us? If so and I got out, would he open fire? There was the sidewalk and a patch of open grass for me to cross so as to get to the cover of the Embassy wall. The highway was deserted apart from our vehicle and the gun truck, which was maybe one hundred yards away. Surely they must have seen us? So how did I get from here to the wall?

Every way I looked at it I couldn't see how I could cross that open space without being blown apart by a storm of 12.7mm armor-piercing rounds. But then my words to Dave from the phone call back at the villa flashed through my mind: *Keep fighting. Just keep fighting. I'm on my way.* I had made a promise. I had to try to get to them. I could feel Massoud staring at me. Fair enough: this was decision time.

"Morgan, what are you going to do, my friend? We cannot stay here."

"Give me a second."

I dialed Dave's number. I was going to give him a heads-up. Having seen the strength of the forces positioned around the compound, I was going to have to try to make it over the wall pretty much where I was. There was no way I could make it from here to the gym on foot. It was at the opposite end of the compound, and the streets were crawling with bad guys. After my daily beach runs and gym sessions I'd never been fitter or stronger, and I was going to try to scale the wall using whatever handholds I could find.

Dave's number rang and rang. No answer. *Were they even alive still?* Even worse was the idea that the poor bastards might have been captured.

"Morgan, what are we going to do?" Massoud's voice was laced with urgency now.

"Like I said, I'm not expecting you to do anything. Just wait in the car somewhere safe but nearby."

I reached for the door handle and got out of the vehicle. I squatted in the cover of the Nissan and glanced up the road: still no sign of lights or movement from the gun truck. I got into a crouch and made a move for the wall. But I'd barely taken a first step when there was the bark of a weapon firing and fiery tracer rounds punched through the air above my head. At the same moment I heard the roar of an engine and the screech of tires spinning, and the gun truck surged forward and came tearing toward us.

The truck's lights flashed on, full beam, and instantly I was pinned in the blinding light of their glare. The Dushka gunner had the gaping barrel of the weapon aimed right at us. He'd clearly been waiting for someone to do exactly as I had done—to dismount from the vehicle. The truck skidded to a halt barely ten yards away, the dry dirt swirling in the headlights like gold dust.

It had come to a stop with its side facing us, so the Dushka gunner could bring his weapon to bear, for there wasn't the clearance to do so over the vehicle's cab. One round unleashed from that weapon would likely smash the both of us. *This is it*, I thought. *I've just got us both killed.*

An instant after the gun truck halted I saw Massoud step down from the driver's side, hands very much above his head. The gunner began to scream at us in Arabic. I could tell how pumped up and on edge he was, and while I couldn't understand most of what he was saying I knew he was on the verge of opening fire. To either side of him, perched in the rear of the pickup, were more Shariah fighters, and I could feel their guns and their dark eyes upon us.

Massoud yelled something back at him. I understood only the one word: *Inglesi*—English. The vicious shouting went back and forth some more, as the gunner swiveled the massive barrel from Massoud to me and back again, its flared muzzle gaping at me like the mouth of some alien predator.

Finally Massoud turned his head my way: "Morgan, get your passport out; nice and slow."

I reached down to my cargo pants pocket and pulled out my passport.

"Show it to them," Massoud grunted. "But everything very slow."

I took two steps forward so I was away from the car and fully into the light. I held the passport up, so it was illuminated in the gun truck's headlamps. The emblem on the front of a British passport is a gold-embossed coat of arms, depicting a lion and a unicorn fighting over a crown. Below the crown is the French motto: "Honi soit qui mal y pense"—*Shame on him who thinks evil.*

The emblem and the words glistened in the headlamps of the

Shariah Brigade gun truck as the Dushka gunner stared at it for a moment. The seconds ticked by, each one feeling like a lifetime. Then I saw him twitch the gun barrel toward the east—back the way we had come—and he snarled out a few words in Arabic.

Massoud didn't so much as look at me. "Morgan, get back in the vehicle. But everything very slow."

I inched back toward the Nissan, Massoud doing likewise, and we slid inside. Massoud fired up the engine, did a very careful U-turn, and we started to drive out of there, Massoud making no sudden moves with the vehicle. The Dushka gunner followed our every move until we were able to turn the corner back the way we had come . . . and finally we were out of his line of fire.

I heard Massoud breathe a strangled sigh of relief. His eyes were glued to the front as he drove, his voice tight with adrenaline and fear. "He said if they see us again tonight . . . they will kill us."

"I thought we were dead . . . *Why the fuck did they let us go?*"

Massoud fixed me with this look. "Morgan, these people are *Al Qaeda*. Mostly, they are not Libyans. They are Somalis, Afghans, Pakistanis, and Saudis . . . They came here for one reason only to-night: to kill the Americans."

Fuck me, it was as direct as that. Tonight's attack was about one thing and one thing only: *spilling American blood.* So much so that the very fact I carried a British passport meant that the Shariah mob had let me live, and even though I'd been trying to go to my American brothers' aid. *They have come here for one thing only: to kill Americans.* It was that simple, that dark, and that chilling.

As we headed north parallel to the compound I could see savage bursts of tracer fire arcing into the night sky. I was certain the boys were still fighting in there, and against those who I now knew had come here with the specific aim of spilling their blood. Yet here were Massoud and me sneaking away, like cowards. I had promised to get to them. I had promised Dave, Scotty, and the others help. Instead, I had lost my nerve, or at least that's how it felt to me.

"Honi soit qui mal y pense"—*Shame on him who thinks evil*. That was the motto on the crest on the passport that had just saved my life. But right now the shame felt like it was all upon me.

Only a few days back I'd been having beers with the guys and I'd vowed to Scotty and Dave that I would fight alongside them no matter what. In return they'd promised me they had my back. And now this. I'd done nothing. I'd failed them. I had never felt anything remotely like this before. I had never left a man behind, and I had never been so alone or so out there. I felt like a complete coward.

Massoud kept driving and a few moments later we were heading away from the Mission. Almost as if in a daze—I was close to tears, or maybe I was crying even; I don't know—I dialed the only number I could think of, that of Robert, my boss. It was late in Britain but I needed to speak to someone, and right now he was all that I had. He answered and I blurted out all that had happened.

For a moment Robert seemed shocked into silence. Then: "But what about the Americans?"

"I don't know," I answered. "I can't get near the place."

"Listen, Morgan, under no circumstances are you to try to get into that Mission, you hear me? Under no circumstances."

I hadn't told Robert that I had been trying to, but he had guessed it anyway. He knew my character. He knew I wouldn't take a step back or leave my friends to die. Or at least that was who Robert thought I was. I wasn't so sure myself anymore.

"Yeah. Don't worry," I told him. "I won't try and get in there."

"If need be, get yourself out of Benghazi—go via the safest route on a road move. Give me a heads-up as you go via the satphone—not via your local cell. Let me know where you're making for and I will get you back to the U.K."

The Blue Mountain satellite phone would be a secure means of making comms, as opposed to my Libyan cell phone.

"Got it," I confirmed. "If it proper kicks off I'll head for the Egyptian border, but I'll let you know."

I killed the call.

In reality I had no intention of going anywhere. I had to know where my American brothers were and if they were still alive. I was determined to make at least one more attempt to get to them. If I didn't do that I might survive tonight, but I would never be able to live with myself.

I'd barely finished speaking to Robert when my phone rang. It was Nasir, one of my guards. Nasir had been the guard force supervisor at the moment of the attack, so I'd presumed he was one of those that Omar had said were executed. I snatched up the phone. Nasir was very much alive and en route to the beachside villa, as that was where he presumed I had to be. He had three other guards with him, so Omar must have been wrong when he'd said three had been captured and killed.

I had a thousand questions for Nasir, but as they were almost at the villa we agreed to rendezvous there. It was as good a place as any to do a pit stop and regroup, and Massoud was already halfway there anyway.

"Morgan, I will drop you," Massoud told me. "With all of this trouble I need to get back to check on my family. You will be in good hands with Nasir and the others."

I knew what Massoud really meant here: *There's no way I'm letting you lead me on another kind of a suicide bid like the one we've just been on.* It was fair enough, really. Massoud was a brave and honorable guy and without doubt his quick thinking with the Dushka gunner had saved both of our lives. But perhaps he knew that I wasn't done, for he offered me the use of his Browning pistol—the personal weapon that he always carried, complete with two spare mags.

One Browning pistol. It was better than no weapon at all.

I thanked Massoud for all he had done. He was the Blue Mountain driver, not a one-man war-in-a-box, and over the past couple of hours he had gone way beyond the call of duty.

Massoud dropped me at the villa, urging me to be careful and not to do anything foolhardy, whatever that might mean. Nasir and the others were waiting. Nasir had with him Mohammed and Ahmed—so now I knew that at least four of my guard force had got out alive. The expressions on their faces told a thousand words. They looked utterly petrified. As Nasir explained what had happened I began to understand why.

"Morgan, they shot Majid in the head!" Nasir blurted out. "They executed him! And Mohamed, they shot him in the legs . . ."

"Calm down," I told him. "Did you see this with your own eyes?"

Nasir shook his head. "No. Mutasim told me."

"Right, okay, where did you see Mutasim?"

"Running down the street heading away from the Mission."

"Running away from the Mission instead of putting down the rounds?"

Nasir nodded. "We were heading down a side street to escape, like you told us. There I stumbled into Mutasim also running away."

"No surprises there," I spat. "So, what if anything did the QRF do to repulse the attack?"

Nasir stared at me, like it was a stupid question. "Nothing. They ran away without firing a shot. Mutasim was running *away* from the Embassy when we ran into him."

I was cursing under my breath. *Just as I'd suspected.*

"But you personally did not see any of the guards getting shot in the head?" I asked.

"No. I didn't see it."

"Right, we do not talk about anyone being killed until we see the body. Rumors and reports are flying. We believe nothing until we know for a fact that it's true. You got it?"

Nasir and the others nodded.

I needed to put some steel in these guys, if they were going to be able to help me with whatever was coming—hence my downplaying the reports of the executions. In reality, I was very possibly a man down, but I was far more worried about my American brothers. With my guards it was a done deal: they'd either escaped, been captured and injured, or they'd been killed. What I needed now was a better sense of the attack and the fate of the Americans.

"So, tell me, from the very beginning—what the hell happened?"

"There was no buildup to the attack," Nasir explained. "There were no signs of anyone being out there and no warnings. We—us, the QRF, and the Americans—were taken by total surprise. One guard was outside talking through the window to me, when he heard cries from behind. He turned and saw fifty armed men running for the gate. He rushed inside and we hit the duck-and-cover alarm, as you taught us."

The fact there had been one guy outside the gate showed just how dedicated my guards had become. Just recently the RSOs had stopped them from standing duty on the barrier at night, because they felt it was too dangerous for them. The guy on the barrier tonight had gone above and beyond the call of duty, because I'd urged them to be extra vigilant in light of the special visitor to the Mission—the gray-haired American who spoke such perfect Arabic.

It was having that guy outside that had enabled my guard force to detect the attackers early and raise the alarm. Otherwise, we'd have had an RPG through the guardroom window, and the alarm would never have been raised.

"Having hit the alarm we ran and hid in the bushes," Nasir continued. "I saw the attackers. They had lots of weaponry: RPG, AK, PKM. They had chest rigs and ammo pouches. Some were not Libyan—they were dressed in Afghan style with traditional robes. Two of the guards tried to run to the muster point at the canteen, but they were caught. They were told to kneel and were beaten . . ."

Nasir broke off. I could tell he was close to breaking down himself. The others looked terrified: they were reliving in their minds what had happened.

"They made the captured guards kneel and pray," Nasir continued. "They had guns held to their heads. Then one of the attackers announced: 'We are not here to kill fellow Muslims; we came here to kill Americans only.' So they shot the first of the guards in the legs. At that moment we decided to make a run for it. As we left, more of the attackers were streaming in: maybe a hundred were there."

"What about the Americans?" I asked.

"The Americans were fighting," replied Nasir. "The Americans fired the first shots at the attackers."

I felt a kick of adrenaline-fueled hope. From the very first the guys had been slamming out the rounds.

"Too right as well—that's American soil in there! That's Dave 'n' Scotty for you! And the QRF? Just so we're clear—what did they do?"

"They ran away as soon as the attack started. They ran down the street to save themselves."

"With your own eyes you saw Mutasim running away with the rest of his guys?"

Nasir glanced at the others. "Yes. We did."

"All four of the bastards were running away?"

"No, three. Hannibal wasn't there. He'd just resigned, 'cause he said he couldn't work with Mutasim anymore."

Hannibal had been about the most capable of the QRF, and it was no wonder he'd had a bellyful of Mutasim.

What a nightmare the Americans had been left in. They'd had hordes of gunmen pouring into the compound and no one had stood by them. But what struck me most was this: the Shariah Brigade fighters had slipped into the compound and *held their fire*. They'd displayed the kind of fire discipline that only well-experienced and combat-hardened fighters possess. A mob would have unloaded on the first targets seen: the SUVs parked by the VIP Villa, or the villas themselves. Instead, the attackers went in there silently on the hunt, and they'd held their fire until they could ID their targets—the Americans they'd come there to kill.

It was chilling.

"To be clear, let's confirm: no warning of the attack; over one hundred hit the compound; you don't know the fate of the Americans?"

"Yes, that's correct."

I trusted both Nasir and the others. They were straight shooters, and at least now I knew the worst.

"Right, so if we haven't seen any Americans killed they may well still be fighting. As you ran away the last you saw of the Americans was what?"

"I saw them putting down fire from the VIP Villa roof," said Nasir. "But by then we were all running, so that was the last we knew."

"Right: if the last you saw of the Americans was them on the roof, then they're very likely still fighting, in which case we've got to get back in there to help. Or at least I have."

The guards were staring at me. "But, Mr. Michael, you don't understand," said Nasir. "These are professional killers. Terrorists. No one will survive in there."

"Dave and Scotty might. Sean and Alex might. That's if someone gets in there to help."

"No, no, Mr. Michael, *you cannot go back there*," Nasir insisted. "Right now you have to get out of here. The compound is gone, taken; and soon the attackers will come looking for you. If they know one *feringhi*—foreigner—has escaped, they will come looking."

I told him I wasn't going anywhere—least not until I found my American brothers. Right now we had no evidence to suggest they were killed or captured, in which case we had to work on the presumption they were still alive and resisting. Amazingly, Nasir and the others said that if that was the case, then they would stick by me. Their loyalty and friendship were humbling. But still my mind kept drifting to thoughts of Dave and Scotty and of their young families.

At that moment Nasir's phone ran. It was the brother of Mansour, one of the two guards who had been captured. He'd been shot in both legs, Nasir confirmed, and he was in what the Libyans call the "Twelve-Hundred-Bed Hospital." The hospital was a massive, sprawling complex in downtown Benghazi. It got its name from the number of beds the place contained. Because the Shariah Brigade attackers sought only "to kill Americans," they had apparently taken Mansour to the hospital, along with scores of their own wounded.

That last news was music to my ears. If the Shariah Brigade had serious numbers of injured, then the Americans had to be putting up real resistance. In which case it was time to get in there. Two more of the guard force joined us, as we prepared to move out. One was a guy called Hamid, the other Zahid. Zahid was one of the sharpest of my guards, and he had actually lived in England for several years. I knew him to be both streetwise and worldly-wise.

Zahid looked shocked at what he had just witnessed. He and Hamid had just completed a drive-by recce of the Embassy, passing by the rear of the compound, where Massoud and I had narrowly escaped death-by-Dushka. Even from there they'd been stunned by the level of fighting that they'd seen and the wanton destruction already wreaked upon the Mission.

"The entire compound is gone," Zahid told me, half in a daze. "Everything is gone."

"What d'you mean—*gone*?" I demanded.

Zahid threw me this haunted look. "Everything is on fire. Everything is burning. All the villas . . . Everything. Burning. Gone."

"So, to be clear—the fuckers have torched the place?"

"Yes. Everything is burning." Zahid paused. He was a good guy and I knew he had my best interests and those of the Americans at heart. "Mr. Michael, you need to get out of here, 'cause if they know of you they will come looking. We need to get you out of Benghazi."

"No, Zahid. I'm not going anywhere until I find the Americans."

Zahid stared at me for a moment, then glanced at the others. "Then in that case we will be staying with you."

This wasn't what I'd expected, this solidarity. My guards genuinely wanted to protect me. Their phones were going constantly as worried family kept calling. I asked them to use their networks and try to find out any intel they could on the Americans—but there was nothing. Zero.

For an instant my mind wandered to Sean, the unarmed IT guy I'd befriended over the last few days. I'd told him that he would be okay, that we'd never been attacked before; and now this. It was eating away at me.

I grabbed Zahid's arm. "Right, you, me, and Hamid—let's go." I turned to Nasir and the others. After the trauma of what they'd been through I figured they were best kept out of whatever was coming. "The rest of you guys—go back to your families and let them know you're safe. I'll call you with a heads-up later."

Nasir and the others didn't object. They knew that with Zahid and Hamid I was in good company, and in truth they were finished.

"Right, guys, into Zahid's car," I announced. "Let's get going."

CHAPTER FIFTEEN

We set off driving. Zahid's vehicle was another shitty white Toyota or Nissan. I had Massoud's Browning with me, tucked into the rear of my waistband and with my shirt hanging over it. That way it was invisible to a casual observer, but I could still draw and bring it to bear swiftly. I had the two spare mags in my cargo pants pocket. Brownings use either a ten-, thirteen-, or fifteen-round magazine: I had a maximum of forty-five rounds and a minimum of thirty.

One pistol. Thirty to forty-five rounds. It was better than nothing.

I'd count as I fired, to try to work out exactly what ammo I had remaining.

We'd been on the road for about five minutes when Zahid's phone rang. I saw the color drain from his face as he listened to the caller.

"What is it?" I demanded, as soon as he'd finished talking.

"Mr. Michael, that was my friend," Zahid replied, exhaustedly. "From the Twelve-Hundred-Bed Hospital. Two Americans have just been brought in there."

I fired a series of questions at him: who, when, how? He phoned his friend back and they spoke some more.

"There is one black American and one white," Zahid related, as he spoke to his friend at the hospital in Arabic, "but he says that the white guy is already dead. The black man is injured, but the white is dead."

I felt a jolt like an electric current surging through me. The black guy had to be one of the Ambassador's close protection team, but who was the white guy?

"Ask him what the white guy looks like," I told Zahid.

He spoke a few more words then ended the call. "He cannot say. He has to go. He works at the hospital and it is very, very busy. He says lots of Shariah Brigade wounded."

My mind was reeling. How messed up was this? The victims of the attack and the killers were being taken to the same hospital. But how on earth had two Americans ended up there? Who had taken them? Or were they from the Annex? Shit, nothing was making any sense anymore.

"Zahid, are there any Americans at the hospital with the wounded men?" I asked.

Zahid shook his head. "No. My friend said only Libyan doctors."

I was desperate to know who the dead guy was. I was sick with worry. But another thought struck me now. If we had dead and wounded Americans at the hospital, yet it was crawling with Shariah Brigade fighters, who was there to help or protect those Americans? What was to stop the Shariah killers from grabbing the wounded from their beds? I remembered Massoud's words to me: *Morgan, they came tonight for one thing only—to kill Americans.* Shit, this was all just so fucked-up.

"Zahid, can we get to the hospital?" I asked, voicing the thought that had crashed into my head. "Can we get there in any safety?"

"We drive by," Zahid suggested. "With us, you should be okay. But if there are Shariah Brigade there we keep going and don't stop."

I didn't know what to do. I was torn. Embassy or hospital— what the hell should I do?

I tried calling Robert. He'd promised to stick by the phone all night long if I needed him. He answered and I blurted out the news about the hospital.

"Is it confirmed there are dead Americans?" he asked.

"No, but it's a bloody good source."

"Right, then, the shit's going to hit the fan big-time. Stay at the villa. Your flight is booked business class Benghazi–Doha–London tomorrow. That's the earliest I could get you out." He paused. "Morgan, I am ordering you to stay at the villa. Do not leave the villa, you hear me?"

I told him I understood.

Robert was making the right call, of course. He had a clear head. Mine felt like it was about to explode. In fact, my heart was ruling my head now—and I knew exactly where I was going to go. I was going to the hospital, for I just had to know who was injured or dead. Robert didn't need to be informed, I reasoned. If I got killed, so be it. This way, it wouldn't be his responsibility.

"Zahid, change of plan," I told him. "Head for the hospital."

As we drove across downtown Benghazi I tried to phone Scotty and Dave again. Still no answer. I sent them a text: "I'm hearing one American dead in 1200 Bed Hospital. Sorry. I'm still trying to get to you guys." I didn't get a reply. I wasn't expecting one, to be honest, but I had to keep trying.

Shortly after I'd sent that text a call came through on my cell phone. It was a caller ID that I didn't recognize. I punched the answer button, hoping maybe it was one of the Americans on a number I didn't have. Instead, there was a distinctly Libyan-accented voice on the line. It turned out it was the local fixer from the British Embassy in Benghazi, a guy I knew and rated highly.

"I've been told to call you and ask if you're okay," he said. "The British Embassy in Tripoli wants to know where you are and if you are all right."

"I'm still in Benghazi," I confirmed. "More importantly, any news of the Americans?"

"Nothing. Sorry. We have no one here now, as I think you know?"

"Yeah."

"I've been told to tell you that if you need somewhere to lie low tonight you are welcome to come to the Residence." I knew exactly where he meant: they had a villa about five minutes' drive from the U.S. Mission. I now had a fallback option if my beachside villa got compromised. "I am here if you need to come."

"Thanks," I told him. "I'll call you if I do."

We were nearing the hospital. What I was dreading most was seeing the body of the dead American. I knew there might be Shariah Brigade here. I knew they'd told me if they saw me again tonight then I'd be killed. I was sick with worry, but not because of that. It was finding out who the dead American might be that was twisting my guts tight as a vise. What would I do if it was Dave, Scotty, or Sean? I just didn't have the slightest idea . . .

I'd seen many friends dead. You do in this line of business. But this was different. With all the others I'd known who it was and exactly how they'd died. Mostly, they'd gone down fighting and with their brother warriors at their side. Right now, I had zero idea who was at the hospital, or how they might have been killed.

"Okay, Zahid, here's the plan," I announced. "We get there and see the bad guys, we don't stop. If it's all clear, we go in. Hamid, you stay with the vehicle, but keep your eyes peeled. You see any Shariah Brigade turn up, you call us. It's a massive place and must have loads of fire exits. There's no way the Shariah lot can lock them all off. We'll find one that's free and exit that way, then RV with you in the vehicle. Got it?"

Zahid and Hamid grunted their acknowledgments. We had a plan.

My adrenaline was pumping as we swung onto the dogleg access road that leads into the 1,200-Bed Hospital. I could see the three massive wings of the place lying before us arranged in an E-shape, the serried ranks of windows throwing off the muted glow of hospital wards semi-lit in the depths of night. The place looked almost peaceful, and I couldn't believe for one moment that there were injured and dead Americans in there.

"What d'you reckon?" I asked Zahid. "Does it look okay?"

"Yeah, yeah, it looks okay. But stay close."

Hamid pulled to a halt and Zahid and I got down from the vehicle. I reached behind me instinctively and tapped the butt of the Browning, just to be doubly sure it was safely tucked into my waistband. The bulk of the thing felt oddly reassuring and I had to remind myself it was only one pistol with thirty-plus rounds.

I glanced at Zahid. "Let's go."

As we headed for the main entrance this horrific screaming began. It sounded like someone was being operated on without an anesthetic, it was that bad. But I knew this place to be a reasonably modern, functioning hospital, so it couldn't be that. It had to be wounded—though whether Shariah Brigade or Americans I couldn't tell. People don't tend to scream in any particular language.

"Here we bloody go!" I remarked to Zahid, as the screams became more and more intense and spine-chilling. "If it's Shariah wounded they'll have their people in here, that's for sure."

"No, no, it's okay," Zahid reassured me. "Just stay close."

We entered, and Zahid stopped the first guy he saw wearing a white doctor's coat. "Is there an American in here?" he asked, in Arabic. "We heard there were Americans?"

The doctor glanced from Zahid to me and back again. "Why? Why do you ask? Are you Americans?"

"British Embassy," I cut in. He looked me up and down as if he didn't believe a word. I fished in my pocket and flashed him the out-of-date Embassy ID card.

He looked it over briefly. "Okay. Please, follow me."

He started walking, Zahid and I falling in behind him. I was trying to keep note of the twists and turns, as he hurried along a seemingly endless series of corridors. But each looked exactly the same as the last and all the signs were in Arabic, so I had no idea what wards we were passing. The place was a total maze.

"How many Americans?" Zahid asked, as he hurried to keep up with the doctor.

"Just the one."

"We heard a white and a black guy?" Zahid probed.

The doctor shook his head. "No, no, just the one. A white. No black guy."

The doctor looked harassed and I knew instinctively he was telling the truth—so either there was only one of the guys in here, or the doc didn't know about a second one.

We rounded a right-hand corner, and Zahid's phone rang.

"Tell them to fuck right off," I snapped. "We're busy."

I was wound tight as a spring by what was almost upon us. I couldn't handle any interruptions from worried family members, or any more wild rumors from across this benighted city.

Zahid shook his head. "No. I answer. It is Hamid."

I watched his eyes grow wide with fear as he listened to Hamid's hurried call. "The militia are here! Shariah Brigade!"

For a moment we locked eyes. I was convinced now we could check on the body and still get out of here. There were scores of fire exits that we'd passed, and no way could the Shariah Brigade have them all covered.

"Mr. Michael, we need to get out!" Zahid urged. "Now!"

"No way, Zahid. I've got to see the body."

"But we have to leave. It was Hamid, phoning through the warning."

I turned to the doctor. "Doc, how much farther?" I asked him, in Arabic.

He gestured ahead. "We are more or less here."

I eyed Zahid. "Let's keep going. We see it, we're gone, okay?"

We hurried ahead, all three of us close to running now. We rounded a right-hand corner, and before us was a private-looking room with a long picture window looking out onto the corridor.

The doctor gestured to the window. I stepped forward, dreading what I was going to see. I peered inside.

Lying on a trolley was a body. It was covered in a white sheet from the chest down, but the head and shoulders were bare and the face was turned toward the window. I froze. I felt as if I was going to vomit. I gripped the windowsill in an effort to stop myself from losing it. The face was horribly scorched and soot-blackened, but above that the gray hair was all too visible. I knew who it was instantly, but I simply could not believe what I was seeing.

I felt Zahid staring at me. "What's wrong?"

I could feel my heart thumping irregularly, like the shock was going to fell me. I gripped the sill harder and forced myself to speak. "Zahid, get in there, and get a photo of the face with your cell phone."

I couldn't move. I couldn't bring myself to go in. My mind was reeling. How on earth could this be possible? The repercussions of this were going to be incalculable.

The doctor started trying to interrogate me. "Who is it? You know him? The American—who is it? Give me a name!"

My mind was in utter turmoil. If I told the doc who it was, there was no way the hospital staff could protect his body, which had to mean it was better not to say. We still had Hamid screaming down the phone at us to get the hell out before the Shariah gunmen got to us. If they realized who this dead man was, they'd take his body as a trophy and parade it to the world—of that I was certain. Suddenly I knew what I had to do. But first we had to get out of this maze of a place, and without running into the Shariah mob, or their gunmen. Zahid emerged phone clasped in one hand.

"It is done," he confirmed. He flashed me the ghostly picture. "Now, we go!"

I led the way to the nearest fire exit, retracing our steps to one that I'd memorized as we'd passed. Behind me I could hear Zahid asking what had happened to the American. How had he died?

"He was brought in here unconscious," the doctor explained. "He was unconscious upon arrival. We tried to resuscitate him for thirty minutes, but he had inhaled too much smoke. We could not reach him. Finally, we had to give up and accept that he was gone."

I heard the doctor trying to get a name out of Zahid, but thankfully Zahid didn't have a clue who the dead man was. The doctor hurried after and caught me. He started trying to pull me by the shoulder. He spoke pidgin English and he kept on and on with the same questions.

"You—you know who it is! Tell me! You know who it is! Tell me the American's name!"

"Look, I'm the British Embassy guy. He's American. I don't have a sodding clue."

We reached the fire exit and I booted it open. An alarm started blaring. I drew the Browning and slipped outside, hugging the shelter of the wall. Zahid was right behind me. I scanned the terrain immediately to our front, but there was nothing: no Shariah gun trucks for as far as I could see. We'd emerged at the rear of the hospital, and it looked as if there was no vehicular access around this side.

I sheathed the weapon, flopped my shirt back over it, and eyed Zahid. "Let's go," I rasped. "Call Hamid. Tell him to RV with us over there."

We turned right, heading for the very end and turning point of the hospital access road. We climbed some banking, jumping over a low-lying hedge that barred the way, and made our way onto the tarmac.

Not two hundred yards to our front I could see the enemy now. There were half a dozen Shariah Brigade gun trucks clustered around the main entrance to the hospital. I saw figures hurrying inside, carrying the bloodied forms of their injured. It struck me as being the ultimate sick irony: the Shariah mob were bringing their injured to be treated at the same place where the American that I'd just seen had been brought—*and he was their chief target.*

If Zahid and I ran into that group we were finished. After what the Americans had clearly done to their number—shot them all to hell—they wouldn't be very happy coming face-to-face with me. That, I figured, would be game over.

Not a moment too soon Hamid pulled up beside us and we dived into the vehicle. He moved away, driving carefully so as not to arouse suspicion. I sank lower in the seat so as to hide my presence. A few moments later we were out of the Shariah Brigade's sight and their line of fire. I sat back in the seat shocked into total silence. I still could not believe what I had just seen.

I glanced at my watch: it was just after 2:00 A.M. Libya time, 8:00 P.M. in Washington D.C.

The dead man was J. Christopher Stevens, the American ambassador to Libya.

Ambassador Stevens was a man who had spoken fluent Arabic and who loved this part of the world and its people. He was a man who had done so much to bring the U.S. administration over to support the Libyan rebels, as they had battled Gaddafi loyalist forces. And this was the thanks he had got—to be burned to death and left in some shitty Libyan hospital, alongside those who had killed him.

I had never felt so angry or enraged in my life.

I was burning up inside.

I didn't know what to do. It was the worst moment of my entire life. I was beyond reason. I did the only thing I could think of: I pulled out my phone and called Robert. He was my boss, but more important, he was a father figure and a man of unrivaled experience. Plus I knew we could converse in Welsh, so that if anyone was listening in they wouldn't have a clue what we were on about.

"Listen, it is one hundred percent confirmed that Ambassador Stevens is dead," I blurted out, just as soon as he'd answered. "The U.S. ambassador has been killed."

It took a lot to shock a man such as him, but all there was now was a ringing silence on the other end of the line. "Are you absolutely fucking certain?" he asked, eventually. He seemed unable or unwilling to believe it.

"One hundred percent certain." I told him we had the photo to prove it, and that I'd send it on from Zahid's phone.

Silence again. Then: "What about all the other Americans?"

"I figure they've all got to be dead. I can't get hold of anyone. The main man is dead. Surely, that must mean all of them are dead. They'd have fought to protect him to the last man . . ."

"Right, you've got to make a run for it," Robert told me. "If you don't hear anything either way within thirty minutes get the hell out. Stay in the villa in the meantime, stay calm, but be ready to run. Let's see how things unfold in the next thirty mins, okay?"

"Yeah. Okay."

Robert presumed I was still in the villa. I'd chosen not to tell him that I was in a car with two of my guards driving away from the hospital.

And I didn't tell him that lying low was the last thing I had in mind.

CHAPTER SIXTEEN

I got off the phone to Robert, then sent a text message to every American I could think of—a bunch of RSOs, special operations forces guys, and other assorted operators—alerting them to the shattering news: *Confirmed: your No. 1 guy is in the 1200-bed Hospital, dead. Priority get your people there now to retrieve him.*

I didn't get a single response, but I had to hope the message was getting through and that they'd get a team to the hospital to retrieve the Ambassador's body. He'd had a tiny cut on his forehead, but otherwise he'd appeared unharmed. He didn't look as if he'd been beaten or manhandled, so how the hell had he died, and from smoke inhalation of all things? His death just didn't make the slightest bit of sense, as so many other things didn't on this crazed and messed-up night.

I had a million questions searing through my mind. How on earth had the Ambassador ended up there and *alone*? Where was his close protection team? Had they died with him? Where were Dave, Scotty, and Sean? I knew that not a man among them would have let the Ambassador be taken while they still had fight in them, so presumably all were dead. Where were the guys from the Annex? With their number-one guy abandoned in a Benghazi hospital I had to presume they had all been killed, but surely that was impossible . . .

As thought after thought fired through my head I knew that I was close to cracking up. In desperation I tried phoning Dave and Scotty again. The last communication I'd had with them was the call with Dave on the roof of the VIP Villa: *There're too many. We ain't gonna make it, buddy.* There was no answer. I would have given anything—*anything*—to hear his voice; any voice. But nothing. I tried all the RSOs' numbers, then Sean's—but still not a thing.

Then a thought struck me like a punch to the gut: *If all the Americans are dead, am I the last good guy left in this fucked-up city?* I had to presume that I was. If so, where were the American reinforcements? Where were the teams of Special Forces flying in to the rescue? If the city was littered with American dead, they needed teams in here fast to extract the bodies. But I couldn't raise a soul, and their top guy was lying dead and apparently forgotten in a downtown Benghazi hospital.

I had this one thought running around and around in my head now: *If the Ambassador is dead then all must be dead . . . If the Ambassador is dead then all must be dead . . .* It kept going around and around and around. I tried to think of scenarios whereby the Ambassador could end up killed but those around him survived. Maybe he'd tried to make a run for it and been captured? But his CP guys were bound to have locked him into the safe room in the VIP Villa—a kind of fortress within the heart of the villa itself— so how did that make any sense?

The safe room was more like a prison cell, or at least a set of steel bars that separated off a section of the villa. The Ambassador would have been shut away in there so the bad guys couldn't get to him, while the RSOs were up on the roof fighting them off. But even with him confined to the safe room, his CP guys should have stayed with him absolutely glued to his side. But maybe they'd been driven out by the smoke and lost the Ambassador in all the confusion? I just didn't know.

I'd done some training in smoke-filled environments: they are utterly horrendous and terrifying. I'd had an oxygen mask on my face as they'd pumped the smoke into the room until it was so thick I couldn't see the hand in front of my face. Even when breathing pure oxygen and with no risk of smoke inhalation I'd still found it horrific. By contrast, these guys would have been in a room filled with thick, choking smoke, unable to see or to breathe properly and with rounds flying everywhere, and the bad guys desperate to kill them.

It was the ultimate nightmare scenario.

The only way to stand any chance of survival in a smoke-filled room is to get down on the floor, where there might still be some oxygen, as smoke rises. But if you left someone in a smoke-filled room for three minutes, you could more or less guarantee they would not survive. Zahid had given me those eyewitness reports about the villas being on fire, and I could only assume that was how the Ambassador had died, plus presumably all the others who had been with him.

What an unspeakable way to go.

I was torn away from my dark, murderous thoughts by Zahid. He'd just taken another call.

"There is a massive firefight at the far side of the Embassy compound," he explained, "maybe a kilometer away, at some other building."

The Annex. It had to be. So at least it seemed there were some Americans somewhere still fighting. According to Zahid's news the Shariah Brigade had launched a further massive assault. It was mind-boggling. Their intelligence must have been so good they knew where that supposedly top-secret base was situated—something that even I hadn't known—and to hit both locations.

They'd launched a two-pronged assault employing hundreds of fighters and in total secrecy. My intel network was tight in Benghazi—yet neither Massoud nor any of my guards had picked up even a hint of the coming attack, and neither had the Americans. The ramifications of this were deadly serious. If the Annex was under attack, the Shariah Brigade would have hit it to prevent any QRF getting to the aid of those at the Embassy. As if this night weren't dark enough, it had just become one hell of a lot darker.

"What is this other building?" Zahid asked, confusedly. "Who is there? Is it Americans, too?"

I gave an exhausted shrug. "I've no idea."

He stared at me for a long second like he didn't believe me.

"Zahid, mate, I do not know. Whatever that place is I've never even been there."

"Then shall we go take a look at what is happening?" Zahid suggested. "I can phone the person who alerted me and we can get directions."

I shook my head, emphatically. "No bloody thanks. We've got enough problems at the Mission without getting into another cluster fuck."

Zahid shrugged. "So what next?"

"I tell you what's next," I shot back at him. "Let's go to the Mission. Let's fucking go there! *Now!*"

Zahid's eyes grew wide: "To the Mission? Are you sure? But there are hundreds of bad people up there."

"You know what—I don't care anymore. *Let's go.*"

After discovering the Ambassador's corpse I just had to know the truth. I *had* to know about the rest of my American brothers, and the only way to know for sure would be to go see for myself. I didn't think that I'd get in and out of the Mission alive, but I owed it to my buddies at least to try.

Zahid told Hamid to set a course for the Embassy.

The die was cast. I was going back in.

And now that the decision had been made I felt suffused with this strange, all-encompassing calm.

Zahid and Hamid were the cover to get me close enough in the car and to help me blend in. From there I'd be going ahead alone. I wished I had some of my buddies from the world of private soldiering with me—maybe Shane, my ex–Paratroop Regiment mate; Cat, who was ex–Royal Green Jackets; and Ceri, who was ex–Welsh Guards. Guys alongside whom I'd worked and fought hard in Iraq and Afghanistan. With four or five top guys and some good weaponry—Colt Diemaco assault rifles, M49 SAW light machine guns, and a shitload of grenades—we'd stand a half-decent chance.

But right now it was me alone with one pistol and I'd have to think very differently. Instead of going in all guns blazing, I'd be a lone operator going over the wall covertly. I'd head for the gym insertion point hidden away on the northeast corner of the compound. It would be dark there, and once inside I'd have the advantage of knowing the ground like the back of my hand. I'd pause on the rooftop and survey the compound, and maybe I'd spot Dave, Scotty, and the others still fighting—what I was hoping and praying for. That at least would give me a point to head for.

As I approached the Mission for the second time in the one night the entire sky above it was lit up a fiery orange. It seemed as if there was a massive bonfire burning inside the compound. I told Zahid to bring us in from the northeast, to try to get me close to the point where I planned to go over the wall. We neared the final corner and there were vehicles everywhere blocking the road.

I told Zahid to stop. "Park up. Get in among those vehicles where you won't stand out. I'm walking in from here."

Zahid got Hamid to pull over. "Morgan, let me go ahead and see," he volunteered. "Just to where I can see the main gate."

I knew that Zahid would blend in on the streets, and that he was clever enough to talk his way out of trouble. He was gone for a good minute, during which time I rechecked the Browning and the mags. Zahid came back looking pale and visibly shaken. He slid back into the vehicle.

"Morgan, everything is burning," he told me, his eyes wide with shock. "*Everything*. And there are gunmen everywhere. Hundreds of them."

I shrugged. It was nothing that we didn't know already. For a moment I considered trying to brazen it out and walk through the front gate, with Zahid at my side for company. My "local" look might well get me through. But all it would take was one word of a challenge from the bad guys and I'd be dead, plus Zahid would be in a whole world of trouble. No: it was best to stick to Plan A. I asked Hamid to wait in the vehicle ready for my call, while Zahid tried to find out whatever intel he could on the Americans.

"Right, it's shit-or-bust time," I announced, speaking more to myself than the guys. "Let's get going."

I checked the pistol one last time, making sure I had a round chambered, and tucked it into my belt at the back. I had the two spare mags in different pockets so they didn't clank against each other as I walked or scaled the wall. I switched my cell phone to silent mode. That was it: *ready*. I told the guys to wait for my call and slid out of the vehicle.

I set off on foot into the semidarkness. I was hoping to blend in with all the gunmen and killers who were milling about in the wild, flame-illuminated chaos. I flitted through the darkest parts of the streets, boots crunching on the gravel road underfoot as I went. I could hear long bursts of gunfire sparking off from inside the compound, but still I didn't know if this was a two-way battle going on, or if it was the Shariah murderers "celebrating" their "victory."

All around me the air was thick with smoke and it reeked of the smell of burning rubber. The sky above the compound was burnished a violent, boiling orange. Making like a local and sticking to the darkest areas, I got to my intended entry point without being challenged. My heart leapt: there near the wall was an old oil drum, something that the construction crews had used for mixing cement. It was exactly what I needed to give me a leg up over the twelve-foot-high perimeter.

I rolled it closer, until I had it right against the wall. I climbed onto it and reached for the top. The apex of the wall was just out of reach so I bent at the knees, sprang upward, and made a grab for it. My hands made contact with the tiles that formed the flat upper surface of the wall, and I held fast, dangling there for an instant or two. Then I was pulling myself upward and a moment later I had my elbows hooked over the apex of the wall.

A roll of razor wire was right in my face, topping off the security fence that ran just inside the wall. I used my hands to push the razor wire backward so as to give myself enough room to get my body onto the top of the wall. I managed to get myself up there squeezed into a crouch, but I knew I couldn't afford to delay. I was silhouetted, and someone was bound to see me. I knew where the outhouse/gym roof was in theory, though in the pitch dark I could barely make it out.

I made a guesstimate as to the distance and jumped. I sailed over the razor wire, landed awkwardly on the flat roof, and sank down low. I was hoping that the noise of my arrival had been drowned out by the gunfire. I was down in the prone position and stayed down, taking my time to make sure that no one had seen me. I strained my ears, listening hard for any cries of alarm, but there were none. All I could hear were the sharp bursts of gunfire reverberating through the darkness.

Cautiously, I lifted my head so I could peer inside. I could not believe the scene that met my eyes. Everywhere I looked the compound was aflame. It was like a scene from some movie, like it wasn't for real. This was the place that I'd worked so hard at guarding and protecting for six long months, and now it was completely finished. Everything that could burn was being burned to the ground.

Right in front of me was a small patch of orchard, but on the far side of that lay the Mission's canteen—or at least what had once been the canteen. Right now the entire complex was awash with flame. Even at such a distance the heat on my face was intense: burning hot. Great showers of sparks and glowing embers kept whooshing up into the sky like erupting volcanoes. The canteen roof was still intact, but otherwise the place was in the process of being burned out completely.

I flicked my eyes farther westward. The main body of Shariah fighters was on the far side of the compound, and from my vantage point I could just see them milling around in the distance. I felt talons of fear ripping at my guts: that was where I had to get to, for that was where the VIP Villa was situated—the last known location of Dave, Scotty, Sean, and the others.

I got my head down again. Stay up too long and I'd be spotted.

My heart was thumping like a machine gun, and I could feel the fear monster slavering in my stomach. The voice was back in my head again: *Go any further, Morgan, and you're dead.* I was having difficulty breathing—whether from the heat, the smoke, or the sheer animal panic I wasn't sure. No ifs or buts, I was shit scared now. But I forced the voice of terror to shut it, and I peered over the edge of the roof to scope the way forward.

The ground below seemed close enough and clear of obstructions. I turned around, hung my legs over, lowered myself, and dropped the last six feet or so. I was thinking: *It'll be just my luck if I twist an ankle.* But I landed on the concrete fine, the soles of my desert boots making a soft plop. I scurried across the few yards of open dirt to the orchard and got into its cover. I stayed low for a good minute, hidden among the darkness and the foliage.

Still, there was no particular shouting or yelling in my direction, and no gunfire apart from the odd stray round. It seemed as if I hadn't yet been seen. I tapped the bulge at my back a couple of times, to make sure the Browning had survived the clamber over the wall. Thank God the pistol was still there. Being an older design of weapon, the Browning is a heavy lump of solid steel, as opposed to a modern Glock, which is mostly lightweight plastic.

Whether from the heat, the fear, or the adrenaline I was sweating bucket loads. It was dripping into my eyes. I wiped them clear and started to move at a low crouch. I made my way slowly through the orchard, tracking due west in the direction of the main gate.

Even here, in among the shelter of the trees, I could feel hot blasts of fire breath gusting past me. The wind kept blowing thick ash and choking black smoke into my face.

A savage burst of gunfire rippled through the air. I froze. *Was that some Shariah fighter targeting me?* I couldn't seem to get my legs to move anymore. *Come on, you bastard, move.* I kept telling myself that I had to move more quickly, or I was in danger of crapping out and losing my nerve completely. *Come on, Morgan: Your friends might still be in there fighting for their lives. Get moving.*

I reached the edge of the trees, and just to my south the TOC hove into view. This was where the Embassy's sensitive communications equipment, documents, computer gear, and weaponry had been stored. The building was a mass of burning, flames licking out of windows and gutted doorways. I could smell gasoline in the air, and I figured the attackers must have used it as an accelerant to firebomb the buildings.

This was pure and utter savagery. If any of my American friends had still been in there mounting a last-ditch resistance, they'd have been burned alive by now.

I'd crossed maybe a quarter of the Embassy grounds, and still I hadn't been spotted—but I'd done it all from the cover of the orchard. Ahead of me the canteen block was a raging inferno, gouts of flame licking out yellow and hungry from the windows. All around me the leaves on the trees had been scorched black from the heat, and the ground was crunchy with ash underfoot.

I crouched lower in the cover of the trees, as figures darted back and forth silhouetted by the firelight: *Shariah Brigade gunmen.* Some were passing no more than a dozen yards away from where I lay in the shadows. The wind was blowing the smoke and flame eastward, so away from me, but if it changed direction I was going to get roasted. I'd seen enough here anyway: anyone in either the canteen block or the TOC would have been burned out, killed, or captured by the enemy.

I turned toward the west—the direction of the VIP Villa. The smoke was thick and getting into my throat and my eyes. I heard gunshots, and wild chanting. I could make out the odd cry of "Allahu akbar"—God is great!—but the rest was gibberish to me. What I didn't know was whether the gunfire was actual fighting still, or the Shariah killers dragging out the surviving Americans—or maybe even their corpses—for their sick celebrations.

If it was fighting, there was just a chance that my buddies might still be alive. The very thought spurred me on. I forced myself to break cover. I flitted across a short patch of open ground leading from the orchard to the bushes that lined the nearby wall—the one that divided the Embassy compound into two. I made for its cover, caught my breath for an instant, and then began to track south along the wall's edge. I was darting from one patch of cover to another—that provided by the dense, ornamental-type bushes lining the wall.

I could hear more gunfire and yelling coming from the opposite side of the wall now—the direction in which I was heading. Whatever was happening, the Shariah fighters were working themselves up into some kind of crazed frenzy. I dashed forward to another patch of cover and felt my boot collide with something soft and hollow-sounding. I crouched lower and saw that it was a body.

Fearing the worst—*God forbid, my second dead American*—I moved in so I could peer into the corpse's face. Half the head was missing, from where it had been blown apart by gunfire. In my head I congratulated Scotty and Dave: *nice shooting*. The dead Shariah gunman still had an AK-47 clutched in his hand. I glanced at it for a second before reaching down and scooping it up. It was a good piece of firepower, and it was great for the disguise. Bushy beard, baseball cap, and AK: who would ever know that I wasn't one of the Shariah killers now.

I pushed south, sticking to the cover of the wall. The wild shooting and yelling from the direction of the VIP Villa was growing more extreme by the second. The voices didn't even sound human anymore. I'd come across this Arabic gang mentality before—where they work themselves up into a murderous frenzy against "the infidel." If they found me here I had zero doubt what they would do to me: if they took me alive they would tear me limb from limb.

I had to presume a good number of their fighters had headed over to join the battle at the Annex. But from what I could hear and from the volume of the gunfire, they were still very much in residence at what remained of the Embassy. Was this Shariah fighters doing battle with the Americans, I wondered, or was there someone else here that they were now fighting? There was only one way to find out: keep pushing south, and get eyes on the VIP Villa itself.

I kept going nice and low to the end of the wall, squeezing myself between the vegetation and the blockwork. Every second I was tensing to hear a challenge ring out in Arabic, or for bullets to smash into the masonry at my side. I couldn't believe I had made it this far. Using the wall as cover, I'd traversed more than half the length of the compound seemingly without being seen.

The very idea that an American, or a friend of the Americans, might have penetrated the compound had to be anathema to the bad guys, for they didn't seem to have any of their number standing guard. But presumption is the mother of all fuckups, as they say in the military. I had to remain one hundred percent vigilant.

In any case, what I'd done so far was the easy part. Ahead of me lay the most dangerous leg of my mission. To get eyes on the VIP Villa I had to cross over the side track—the one that branched off the main driveway and ran to the TOC—and push into the open ground to the west of there. I'd then try to get into the vineyard or the rear orchard, depending on how far north I'd drifted as I made my way through. Either way, I was going to be totally exposed as I crossed over that dirt driveway.

I paused at the edge of the cover and took a good look around. There were dozens of gunmen directly to my west—maybe thirty or forty yards away. Several were dressed in traditional Afghan-style robes and headdress, but none seemed to have noticed me yet. I figured if they did see me they weren't close enough to realize that I wasn't one of theirs. I had no option but to bluff it. A mad dash across the driveway was sure to draw attention—and then they'd come hunting. A slow easy stroll was the only way to do it.

I straightened up from my crouch position and took a step into the open. All around me the Shariah gunmen seemed too hyped up and high on their "victory" to notice my presence. I forced myself to walk slowly across the expanse of track, as if I had all the time in the world. But I was feeling neither cool nor calm. My pulse was hammering away, and inside me I tensed for a bullet. I forced myself to keep moving, putting one foot in front of the other, and then I'd slipped into the cover of the trees on the far side.

I went down low again. I was right smack in the center of the Mission compound now—in the heart of the savagery, the burning, and the chaos. A thought struck me: *God, but it was going to be a long way out again.*

I made the cover of a row of dog kennels, which were just to the front of the orchard—the ones that should have had guard dogs in them, had the State Department listened to any of our demands, instead of denying them. I hunkered down behind one and tried to get my breathing and my heart rate under control again.

Right now I needed a few seconds' breather. The kennels were made of concrete and designed for big, ferocious German shepherds. I crawled inside one, the concrete walls providing both cover from view and reasonable cover from fire. In here I was relatively safe. I leaned back against the wall, brushed the rivulets of sweat from my face, and tried to get my breathing under control again.

I knew I'd have to show myself and move forward, for I still couldn't get eyes on the VIP Villa, which was my key objective. Vicious stabs of gunfire echoed across to me. Maybe Scotty, Dave, and the others were still in action, taking out yet more of the bad guys. If they were, how was I going to approach them? I had to link up with them somehow. If I saw the guys still fighting I'd try to call them on the cell phone. I couldn't think of anything else I could do.

I hefted the assault rifle and prepared to move. At least I had a proper weapon now—the scavenged AK-47—plus several mags. I risked movement. I crawled out of the kennel, stood, and walked "calmly" out of cover and into the glaring light thrown off by the fires burning all to my front.

Finally, the VIP Villa hove into view.

CHAPTER SEVENTEEN

For the barest moment my heart leapt for joy. At first glance the VIP Villa seemed more or less untouched, for there were no flames visible. Maybe Dave, Scotty, and the rest had managed to fight the attackers off? But then I saw why there were no flames anymore. The Villa windows were fire-blackened and gutted. The inferno here had been so intense it had burned itself out almost completely. Even the villa beyond it—the one that had housed the so-called QRF, the *Quick Runaway Force*—was a blackened, burned-out, gutted ruin.

Thick smoke still billowed from the VIP Villa's shattered windows, but there were no flames anymore. If, as I suspected, the Ambassador had been trapped in the Villa's safe room, there was no way he would have survived the firestorm that had swept through this place. In that kind of inferno he'd have lasted no more than a few minutes, before the heat and the fumes overcame him.

Yet the doctor at the 1,200-Bed Hospital had said that he was still conscious when he arrived. Maybe when the fire had hit, his close protection guys had got him onto the roof, where Dave and Scotty were making their heroic stand. I scanned the rooftop, searching for signs of life. I was dying to see just the hint of a head popping up with an M4 and loosing off a burst of rounds.

But with the heat of the inferno below them, just how hot would that concrete roof have become? Presumably unbearably so, especially if you were crouched low or lying prone and trying to fight off the bad guys. So maybe Scotty, Dave, and the rest had been driven off the roof by the fire and the heat, and into the very arms of the enemy? Maybe that's how they'd lost the Ambassador? I just didn't know.

I stared at that rooftop willing for a head to bob into view. This was the exact place where I'd said to Jeff they should site a .50-caliber heavy machine gun, to put down fire onto the main gateway. *The exact spot.* One .50-cal up there would have been enough to cover the entire compound. It might not have saved the Embassy from being overrun, but its raw firepower would have bought the guys time to evacuate the Ambassador, and maybe even get reinforcements in.

I scanned for movement. I prayed for something. Anything. But there was none. My thoughts now were the blackest they had ever been. I kept watching the roof, praying for a figure to pop up and put down fire onto the Shariah gunmen below. The cowardly bastards seemed more intent on looting some sick "souvenirs" right now than in doing any fighting. I just couldn't believe that all of the Americans were dead, or worse still—*taken captive.*

I knew it was suicide to do so, but I pushed onward through the orchard to my left, then moved out even farther into the open. I needed to get a look into the Villa entrance itself, the place where I presumed the Ambassador had all but met his end. I don't know exactly why, or what I hoped to achieve. I was clutching at straws here, unable to accept that very likely my American friends had all been killed, and that I had done nothing to stand with them.

There were loads more gunmen here, and gunfire. Muzzles spat fire among the eerie glow of gutted buildings. Shadowy figures were loosing off long squirts of tracer into the night sky, presumably to "celebrate" their "victory." *The fuckers.* I was burning up with hatred and with rage. I wanted to level my scavenged AK and start dropping them—double taps to their heads until I ran out of rounds.

I took several more steps until I was at the very entrance to the VIP Villa. The heat was scorching, the doorway a mass of thick, roiling smoke. The huge ornamental vases that had lain to either side of the doorway had been smashed to pieces, their remains trampled underfoot. There was no way that I could push any farther into the wall of heat and smoke. There was nothing more I could do here.

I turned to leave, but as I did so I froze: a savage cry rang out in Arabic: "Hey! You! We kill them all! Death to America! Kill them all!"

I'd been so focused on searching for any survivors, I'd missed how close some of the Shariah fighters had got. The figure was yelling at me from no more than ten yards away. The evil bastard seemed to be waiting for me to join in the chanting. *Well, fuck that.*

He stared at me, his eyes wide with bloodlust. He seemed drunk on the power of the gun. He thrust his weapon toward me: "Tal! Tal! Tal!"—*Come here!*

I had a split second in which to make a decision. My only possible exit route was back the way I'd come, which would involve running one hundred yards or more across the compound and over terrain that was crawling with the enemy. There was no way that I could make it, especially as so much of it was open ground. I'd be a dead man if I ran.

I turned and started walking toward the Shariah gunman. *Calm it, Morgan, calm it,* I told myself. *He doesn't have a clue who you are.*

He was silhouetted against the fire, and I had the glare in my eyes. My face would be fully illuminated, and I had to pray he didn't notice I was a foreigner. He had his AK grasped in his right hand, but hanging by his side. I figured I could get the drop on him. That wasn't my main worry. It was all the other bastards yelling and shooting it up behind him—those who would come to his aid.

"Temam," I called out to him. "Temam"—*You okay?*

I was trying to sound as calm as I could, but I was having to yell to make myself heard above all the gunfire. His eyes were bulging and I could tell how hyped up he was and how very much on edge. I had to seize the initiative.

"Gitlag. Gitlag," I called across to him—*Let's talk*.

We stepped closer, maybe three paces separating us. For a split second I stared into his face. He was young, in his early twenties, but his features were obscured by a thick growth of beard, plus some kind of head wrapping. His robes seemed to be soaking wet, and I could only imagine he'd doused himself in water so he could dash in and out of the flames. *Searching for my friends, to try to find and kill them*.

As we eyeballed each other I could detect the first signs of suspicion creeping into his gaze, the first hint of worry that I wasn't one of his kind.

Without a moment's warning I brought my weapon around in a crushing blow, striking him exactly where I wanted—on the side of the face, just above the eyes. The butt smashed into his temple. It was a noiseless blow, but I felt his bone crumple and crush under the impact. With barely a whimper his legs buckled and he fell, almost as if he'd been shot.

Luckily his finger hadn't been on the trigger, for he might have fired off a few rounds involuntarily as he went down—and then the Shariah mob would have been upon me. A thick pall of smoke blew across us. I bent to inspect him. One side of his face was caved in; his eye socket was broken, and most likely his jaw, too.

I was about to turn for the cover of the orchard when I realized that maybe I could use this guy. I could question him. Gain vital intel. *Where the fuck are the Americans? What have you done with them? Where the fuck have you taken them?*

I squatted down, but there was thick blood pouring from the guy's face and ears now. He looked halfway dead; unconscious, certainly. There was no speaking to this one, that was for sure. I'd been with him for maybe thirty seconds, and I had to get going before I was spotted. I stepped away and melted back into the shadows of the trees.

As I did so I practically fell over something on the ground. I glanced down. Another body. This one was wearing a proper chest rig, complete with pouches for extra ammo, magazines, and grenades. For a moment I feared it might be Scotty, Dave, or Sean. I used my boot to roll the corpse over. I saw the thick black beard, plus the Afghan-style robe beneath the chest rig. It was another of the Shariah fighters, and his body was riddled with bloodied bullet holes.

Dave, Scotty, and the others knew how to shoot, that was for sure. I hunkered down beside the body in the shadows. It felt good to know one of my guys had got the better of this bastard. I had a sense of what I had to do now. I couldn't believe the Shariah Brigade had slaughtered all of the Americans. They'd want to take some at least alive as high-value hostages. They'd parade them on the Internet. Use them as bargaining tools to push for some sick concessions from the U.S. government. Maybe ask for $50 million in ransom.

It made sense that they'd have taken at least some of my American friends alive—and that meant I had to take one of them at least alive and beat some answers out of him. I lay in the dark and waited. Gunfire echoed back and forth across the compound, but I figured it was the wild eruptions of celebratory fire, not sharp aimed bursts. I couldn't just shoot one of the enemy. I needed him alive, and my aimed shots would draw the rest of them.

Figures flitted back and forth, some drifting closer to me in among the smoke. I tensed to strike, readying myself to bring the butt down on one of their skulls, then drag him into the bushes. But just then a wave of thunderous sound rolled across the compound. It sounded as if an entire convoy of Dushka-toting vehicles were pouring fire into the Embassy via the smashed gate at the front. I saw big chunky rounds tearing down walls, slicing through metal and ripping trees apart.

Once you've heard a Dushka, you never forget it. I knew who these new attackers *weren't*: they weren't an American Special Forces unit come to the rescue. Only rebels and militias used the Dushka. *What the hell was happening?*

It sounded as if a rival force was trying to take the Embassy. As the fire tore into the ground and ripped into the exposed fighters to my front, they started breaking for cover and coming my way. Firing short, aim bursts I started to fall back through the trees. I kept hammering away with the AK and melting backward until I was almost out of rounds.

The intensity of the incoming fire from whoever was attacking just kept increasing. They seemed to be drawing closer. I did the only thing I could now: I turned in the opposite direction and began to race through the cover of the orchard. Bullets chewed up the trunks and branches all around me as I tore along, but I wasn't stopping to see who was doing the shooting anymore.

I had one last objective to achieve before I could get the hell out of here. I headed for the rear gate—the one that lies to the southern end of the compound, behind the VIP Villa and the dog kennels. I was pounding through the trees, ducking under low branches and with leaves whipping my face. I knew if I stuck close to the dividing wall that ran down the center of the compound it would lead me directly to the rear entranceway.

It came into view.

My heart leapt: the gate was open.

It was wide open, and one of the Embassy evacuation vehicles— an armored Toyota Land Cruiser—was gone. *At last.* At last a real, tangible glimmer of hope. If one of the Embassy escape vehicles was gone, maybe some of my American friends had made it out of here alive? Who else would have known how to disable the fuel cutoff, so as to start the vehicle? But how could anyone have escaped in the Toyota, if the Ambassador was lying dead in the 1,200-Bed Hospital?

I'd seen several of the Embassy vehicles shot up and burning fiercely at the front of the QRF building, but I hadn't bothered to count how many there were. My mind had been on other things. Even so, I now knew that at least one of the Mission escape vehicles was gone, and after the hell that I had witnessed here I finally found cause for a glimmer of hope.

Since the rear gate was open and unguarded I grabbed the opportunity and slipped through onto the road. I was now back at the position where Massoud and I had been challenged by the Dushka gunner a few hours earlier—but right now all the action was at the opposite end of the Embassy compound, and the entire highway appeared to be deserted.

I turned right and headed west, away from the Mission. After fifty yards I found some cover: the rear gate of a neighboring compound. I sank into its shadow, taking up a position behind the small concrete barrier that blocked the gateway. I pulled out my mobile, called Zahid, and told him to drive around to where I was.

My legs felt like jelly and I knew the adrenaline was pissing out of my system now. I told Zahid to put his four-way hazard lights on, so I could see him coming, for his sedan looked like any other vehicle in this city. As I waited I kept watching my arcs for the enemy. But as I scanned the night, half my mind was on that SUV evacuation vehicle that had exited the Embassy's rear gate, and who might have driven it out of there.

Three minutes after I'd exited the rear gate I spotted Zahid's vehicle. I dashed out from my place of hiding, they saw me, accelerated, and I ripped open the rear door and dived in.

"Thank God," Zahid exclaimed. "We thought you'd been taken."

"No, mate, I'm still here," I panted, breathlessly. "But let's get going. There's nothing more we can do."

As we drove away from the danger zone Zahid had news for me. While I'd been fighting my way into the Embassy compound, he'd managed to speak to some of the Shariah Brigade gunmen who were milling around outside. No doubt about it, I couldn't fault the guy's bravery or his front, not to mention his loyalty to us all.

"They said all the Americans are dead," Zahid remarked, quietly. "They have all been killed."

I felt my heart lurch. "Did they give any numbers?"

Zahid shook his head. "No, no—no numbers given."

"Well then, they're talking shit," I snapped. "Total bollocks."

I was trying desperately to keep up a brave front here, for in spite of what I was saying I was starting to believe it myself now. After all that I had witnessed inside the compound, I couldn't believe that any of my American friends had escaped alive. But I really didn't want to believe that they were finished, hence my venting on Zahid.

"Listen, Zahid, I would not want to be a Libyan when the Americans wake up to all this tomorrow morning."

"What do you mean?" he asked

"I mean I wouldn't want to be a Libyan when the Americans realize their Ambassador has been murdered. America helped you get Gaddafi out. You'd never have done it without them. And you've just gone and slaughtered some of the key people who helped you do that. A lot of Libyan bad guys are going to go very missing very soon now, 'cause the Americans will have their Special Operations forces on the way . . . And you know what, I'll be the first to cheer them on."

Zahid had gone very quiet. I knew I was venting, and very much taking it out on the wrong person. Zahid was one of the good Libyans, as tonight's events had proven. But I was in a very bad place in my head right now; I was burning up inside.

The car was quiet the entire drive back to my beachside villa. We pulled up and Zahid and Hamid dismounted and came as if to join me.

I held up a hand to stop them. "No, no, guys. That's it for tonight. You need to get home to your families, and I need to be on my own."

The two of them watched me all the way to my villa entrance. I went inside, and without a backward glance I closed and locked the door. I slid onto the floor, my back to the wall, buried my head in my hands, and started to cry. My emotions were tearing me apart. In my heart I just knew that all the guys had to be dead, just like Ambassador Stevens. I cried for each and every one of them, and for all the other good people who had died on this dark and fucked-up night.

The worst thing was that there were no bodies—apart from that of Ambassador Stevens—so I presumed the Shariah Brigade had got them, and that they'd parade them through the streets come daylight. Either that or some of the guys had to have been captured. I dragged myself off the floor and onto the sofa. Between the tears I began to relive all the memories, as images of the good times flitted through my head.

I remembered the time Dave, Scotty, and Silvio had caught me speaking Welsh. I was on the phone to Robert about something and they'd overheard.

"Hey, man, what the fuck's that you're speaking?" Scotty had demanded.

"Yeah, what is that shit?" Dave had asked.

"It's my mother tongue, Welsh. Like people who come from Wales speak Welsh."

"Oh, man, is that like Gaelic? Like they speak in Ireland?"

"Is it the fuck like Gaelic! Breton, Cornish, and Welsh are similar, but Gaelic it is not. Welsh has got bugger-all to do with the Paddys."

Welsh has such a distinctive sound to it, it's impossible to confuse it with Italian or French or Spanish or just about any other European language. I was pretty much used to people staring at me whenever I was speaking it. But the reaction of the guys at the Mission—it had been priceless.

Silvio knew all about Wales and the Welsh language. He called it "the Land of Myths and Dragons." But he'd never actually heard anyone speaking Welsh before.

"Anyhow, guys, don't you worry so much about Welsh," I'd told them. "You lot need to learn to speak English first. I'll give you a lesson later on today. Let's get you up to speed on the Queen's English, so at least people can understand you."

"Fuckin' asshole," Scotty had growled.

But everyone had been laughing.

Amazingly enough, Scotty had a degree in Mandarin, which was part of the reason I loved teasing him about his English. Dave had taken a good few days to work me out and get accustomed to the British sense of humor, but once he'd done that, we'd been inseparable. Dave had told me how he'd served alongside British soldiers in Iraq, and he described how wrong their humor had been. At first he'd thought they were all messed up, but by the end of that Iraq tour he'd learned to laugh at the humor, even though it was way out of line.

One night the guys had watched a London gangster movie called *RocknRolla*. When we met the next morning Jeff and Scotty kept going: "All right, guvnor, you mug?" It was obviously some Cockney slang they'd picked up from the movie. I'd told them I didn't have the faintest clue what they were talking about.

Dave had been chuckling away at it all, but when the kidding was done he'd said to me: "So, buddy, tell me some more about Wales." He'd seemed fascinated by the country, its long history of struggle and its ancient traditions. And it had been a quintessentially British greeting—"All right, mate?"—that had become our collective catchphrase. That's how the guys had greeted me in the mornings.

The recollections tortured me, yet in a strange way they also seemed to help. With memories like those I couldn't believe that the guys could really all be gone. I flicked on the TV news. There on BBC World was a breaking news story, the bulletin flashing across the screen: "U.S. Consulate in Benghazi Attacked by Protesters."

I exploded. I started ranting at the TV set in Welsh and yelling insults. *Protesters! Protesters! Try Shariah Brigade Al Qaeda killers, more like it!* I knew I was losing the plot here. No news agencies would be sending anyone onto the ground in Benghazi right now, so the BBC were likely reporting what they'd been told down some shitty phone line, which meant it was hardly their fault. But where the hell had they got that bullshit line from: *protesters?*

In the midst of me pacing back and forth across the room and yelling at the TV, I felt my phone vibrate. I figured it had to be Zahid checking that I was okay. I glanced at the caller ID: *it was Dave.*

I clicked it open, my hands shaking violently. Part of me feared one of the Shariah fuckers had got hold of Dave's phone and was sending out some sick, evil text message.

I read it with fearful eyes: "MESSAGE: preparing to EVAC Benghazi NOW!"

Oh my God—it looked as if some of the guys at least were getting out of this hellhole alive. I didn't think it was Dave who had sent the text. He'd have made it more personal and put more information into it, knowing it was going to me. But I figured it had to be genuine. I could only imagine that Dave had asked one of his fellow Americans to send me a message, to put my mind at ease.

I texted back: "Hope to God you, Scotty and the others are okay. If you can, let me know."

After all that had happened tonight, the surviving Americans would be on a total communications blackout here in Benghazi. Someone had broken protocol by sending me that text, and in my heart I thanked them a thousand times over for doing so. God, it felt so good to read those words.

I could only presume they'd sent it from the Annex or maybe Benghazi airport, for I knew no one was left at the Mission. It had to mean they were evacuating the country. I just hoped and prayed they'd got the message about the Ambassador, and that they weren't about to leave his body behind.

I'd sent my text about the Ambassador to everyone, including a couple of the Special Operations guys at the Annex, so they had to know. I didn't sign my texts "Morgan," but their phones were sure to have me on their caller ID. They must have known it was me who sent the message: *Confirmed: your No. 1 guy is in the 1200-bed Hospital.* I presumed that someone at the Annex had decided that since I'd gone the extra mile for them, the least I deserved was a heads-up on the status of Scotty, Dave, Sean, et al.—hence the text message they'd just sent me.

Either way, I felt like someone had thrown me a lifeline; this felt like my death reprieve. For the last hour I'd truly been on the bones of my ass—literally falling apart. But the very thought that at least some of the guys were getting out of this alive had galvanized me into action. I knew now exactly what I had to do.

I powered up my laptop and logged on to my email, to check the details of the flight that Robert had booked me. 1300: Business Class, Benghazi–Doha–London, on a packed Turkish Airlines flight. I presumed Robert had pulled a few strings to get me on it, for every man and his dog would be trying to get out of Benghazi right now.

I read the email he'd sent: "Listen, no messing: get on that flight and get out of Benghazi."

I sent him a short reply saying that I'd make the flight. I didn't tell him what I was planning to do in the meantime. I was so full of anger, and no way was I prepared just to slink away. I was going back to the Embassy first, to finish what had been started.

Amazingly, there were emails already from some of the former RSOs: "Morgan, what the hell is going on? We're seeing the news . . ."

"Hey, brother, hope you got out okay, let me know what's goin' on if you get a chance."

I banged out the same reply to all: "I'm okay. Too many attackers. We didn't stand a chance. Mission is gone. Cannot say much more, but from what I've seen it doesn't get any worse."

I wasn't going to be the one to get the news broken that the American ambassador to Libya was dead. The last thing I wanted was for his family to learn of his death over the TV news or the Internet. I just hoped and prayed someone from officialdom was giving his family a heads-up even now, so they would hear it first privately, and before the screaming headlines blew the world away: *U.S. Ambassador to Libya Murdered* . . .

And that right now was the key focus of my intentions. The U.S. ambassador to Libya was dead, and that made the Embassy compound—the place where they had killed him—*a crime scene*. In fact, it was the scene of one of the biggest and most horrific crimes of the past few decades. With whatever surviving Americans there were evacuating, I had to presume I was the only good guy left in this city, and that meant I had to go back in there and document that crime scene before all the evidence was destroyed.

I also needed to check the Embassy for bodies, or weaponry or any classified papers that might still be there, while at the same time securing the evidence of every aspect of what the attackers had done. I hadn't been able to save even one of my American friends, but maybe this way I could help their countrymen hunt down their killers.

The decision made, I sent Massoud a text: *"Get here for first light. Bring AKs plus ammo. We're going back in."*

Massoud was truly one of the good guys. He confirmed that he was on his way. There was no point in my returning to the Embassy before dawn, for I'd need light in which to work.

All I could do now was wait for Massoud and for sunrise.

CHAPTER EIGHTEEN

I set about packing and sanitizing the villa. I had a big board with all the photos of my guards pinned on it, in part so I could organize shifts, in part so I could remember all their names. I pulled the photos off, went outside, and burned them. It was dark and silent out there, with just the faint roar of the waves carrying softly across the sand. In the east I could see the barest hint of dawn.

I stamped the ashes into the sand.

I packed up the laptop, the satphone, the company cash, and my few personal possessions. I was pretty much done. I flicked on the TV news again. The story had broken that two Americans were dead. I knew who one was: the Ambassador. Thank God that hadn't hit the news yet. I had no idea who the other might be.

A text bleeped through from Massoud. *"I am outside waiting for you."*

I stuffed the Browning down my pants, the spare mags in my pocket, grabbed my camera, and headed out the door. The first light of dawn was breaking red and angry across the sea. I slid into the passenger seat of Massoud's Nissan.

Massoud glanced at me. "Morgan, it is good to see you still alive. But you know that two Americans have been killed?"

"Yeah, I know."

"Do you know who?"

I shook my head. "No."

"You know a second compound was attacked?"

"Yeah, I heard."

"Word is they were hammered for hours by the Shariah Brigade but they managed to hold out. Finally, American reinforcements turned up on a flight from somewhere."

"That's good." So that must have been how they'd broken the siege at the Annex and evacuated their people. But it didn't shed much if any light on what had happened at the Mission.

I could feel Massoud's eyes upon me. "Did you know about this other compound, Morgan?"

"Nope. No idea."

I knew Massoud knew I was lying. He probably knew why as well.

"So, they must all have been spies in there," Massoud probed.

"Don't start," I snapped. "Not today. Not that whole fucking American spies bullshit. I don't care who was in there."

The "American spies" line was a daily refrain with the Libyans. *How come you can speak Arabic—are you an American spy? How come you speak this Welsh that no one else can understand—are you an American spy? Why do you know so much about the Koran—are you an American spy?* Maybe they'd had this drilled into them during the Gaddafi years—that every foreigner is an American spy—but either way I did not need this shit today of all days.

"I'm British, remember," I told Massoud. "I'm the British security manager at the Mission. That's all. Now drive."

Massoud got us under way. "You really think you will get into that place this morning?" he asked me.

"No, probably not. If your countrymen are any good they'll have security there out the asshole. The Libyan police and military should have the entire Mission surrounded and cordoned off. But in this place you never fucking know."

"Morgan, it is not wise going back," Massoud remarked. "We

tried once last night . . . You will not get in. And what do you hope to achieve this morning?"

"Just drive."

The Libyans didn't get it. They didn't grasp why I was so tight with the Americans. They didn't understand it. They thought I was the Guard Force's champion, not that of the Americans. In truth I was both. They thought the Americans told me what to do and I instructed the guards in turn, so I probably resented the Americans. They didn't understand how there could be such a special bond between two nations so far apart—America and Great Britain.

Massoud's phone rang and he gabbled away in Arabic for a minute or so. He ended the call and there was a heavy silence. He wouldn't look at me.

"Morgan, now it is four dead Americans."

"How do you know?" I demanded.

"My friend at the airport has just seen four bodies turn up and get loaded onto an aircraft."

"Ask him what their names are. Ask him who they were."

"I have. I have asked. He doesn't know. But he can see Americans are there loading up their dead."

"So ask him to find out who the fuck they are!" I snapped. I was desperate for information.

"Morgan, he can't. No one will tell him. He's not able to."

I'd known that two were dead and I had accepted that fact. One was the Ambassador and I figured one was most likely one of his close protection guys. But now it was four dead Americans, and I just knew in my heart that the number would keep rising.

My phone rang. It was Phil, another of my security mates now working out of Tripoli. "You okay, mate?" he asked. "I'm watching the news."

"Yeah, well, I'm living it."

"What do you need, mate? Anything? Cash? How are you getting out? Where are you right now?"

"I'm fine. I'm keeping moving."

"If you need anything just get in touch. If need be, mate, I'll fly down there for you."

"Thanks."

"Let me know when you get home, okay?"

I killed the call. We turned the last corner and hit the approach road to the Embassy. I simply could not believe my eyes. There were no police. No cordons. No military. No roadblocks. No security at all. Nothing. The place looked wide open. I let out a string of curses.

"You have got to be kidding! One of the biggest atrocities ever and there's no one fucking here!"

I told Massoud to pull over and to wait in the car. I got out, checked my weapon, and made for the battle-scarred entranceway. As I strode ahead Massoud appeared beside me. He told me there was no way I was going in again alone. I guessed he sensed how close I was to losing it, so he was here as much to protect me from myself. Either way, it was good to have some company.

As we moved toward the main gate a white Toyota Corolla pulled to a halt just in front of us. A guy got out dressed in a Libyan policeman's uniform. Bearing in mind that we'd had a "Libyan policeman" doing the pre-attack recce of the Embassy, I was sorely tempted to draw the Browning and put a bullet in his head. Massoud must have realized as much, for he moved quickly and started talking to the guy.

The three of us stepped inside the gates. The smell of burning and the smoke caught in my throat. My God, it looked a whole lot worse in the daylight. It looked as if the place had been flattened in a series of air strikes. As he surveyed the scene Massoud's expression was one of pure horror. He looked shocked beyond words.

He glanced at me. "Morgan, I am so sorry."

I gritted my teeth against the rage. "It's not your fault, Massoud. You didn't do this."

Some random Libyan guy emerged from the smoke. He ran up to me. "This is disgusting. I cannot believe they did this. I am sorry. I lived in the U.S. for nearly twenty years. How can they have done this? I am so sorry . . ."

I gave a curt nod of thanks. We had work to do. As there was zero security around the place, that meant the Shariah killers could return at any moment, especially if they learned that I was here. I gave myself twenty minutes max to get this done.

"Let's get moving," I said to Massoud.

We headed in and to our right was the row of gutted vehicles. I pressed on toward the VIP Villa. Twenty-four hours ago this was a luxury building, decorated beautifully and full of fine furniture. I walked through the scorched entranceway—the place where I'd got challenged a few hours back by the bad guys. The interior of the Villa was totally and utterly fire-blackened and destroyed.

I needed to take photos of everything, but I told myself to concentrate on the grim remains of the "safe room"—the place in which I had to presume the Ambassador had met his end. I walked through the steel gateway that led into the complex of bedrooms that made up the "safe room." The furniture in this place had been like nothing I had ever seen before. Whether it was genuine or repro I didn't know, but it was the kind of stuff you'd expect to see in a French chateau or an English castle. But it was all burned, looted, gone.

I checked what I presumed had to have been the Ambassador's room, or maybe it was Sean's. Weird. Clothes were still hanging in the wardrobe almost completely untouched by the flames. I presumed the killers hadn't been able to throw the gasoline this far inside the building, because of the steel bars, and as a result it wasn't as badly firebombed as the rest of the place.

I checked the way out onto the roof—the place where Scotty, Dave, and the others would have been making their last stand. It was via a large window protected by reinforced steel bars. The window was hanging open, the bars swung wide. Who had opened it? Why? Was this the way the bad guys had tried to get in, or was this the way the good guys had tried to escape the hell of the inferno?

My attention was drawn outside. I could hear muffled shouts

and yelling from behind the villa. Massoud and I looked at each other: *What the hell was going on?* We moved around to the back of the building, and there was the lone Libyan policeman getting abused by five armed men. They spotted the two of us and started leaping about and shouting and doing their V-for-victory signs, as they took photos of each other posing by the burned-out building.

All except one were in full combat dress, and I could see two at least had AK-47s slung over their shoulders. The lone policeman made his way back toward us, clearly making an early escape. No surprises there: the Libyan cop was moving swiftly out of the danger zone. As he passed Massoud he muttered something.

"What did he say?" I grated.

"Shariah Brigade militia," Massoud replied.

My blood was boiling.

This is it, I told myself. *People are going to die now.*

I reached behind me and felt for the Browning. The heavy steel bulge was right where it should be. They started walking toward us, strutting and cocksure in their "victory" and their strength of numbers. *Morgan, lad, this is going off big-time. Get the fuck ready.*

They still had their AKs slung over their shoulders, and I figured I could get the drop on most of them. I'd hit the two I could see with the guns first, then deal with the others.

One started shouting: "You American! You American!"

And what if I am?

He was jabbing a finger at me now. "You American! You American! Death to America!"

The five of them kept coming. *Bring it on. If you think I'm an American why are your weapons still slung, assholes?*

Massoud uttered a few words in Arabic, then: "Inglesi. Inglesi."

"Inglesi?" the lead Shariah guy hesitated. "Inglesi okay. Manchester United. Wayne Rooney. English football good!"

That tipped me over the edge. "Is it? Is it good? Is this shit behind you good? You killed all the Americans and you murdering bastards want to talk *fucking football*?"

I couldn't stop yelling at them. I was shaking with anger. *Seething*. I had never wanted to kill anyone as much as I did these guys. I knew they were probably low-level Shariah, but still I was dying to drop the whole lot of them. They'd come here to take their sick souvenir photos in front of the burned-out wreck of a building where the American ambassador—a fine friend of Libya—had met his end, and most likely to show their mates what good, strong, brave jihadists they were.

And for that in my book they deserved to die.

I saw them exchange glances. They could sense my hatred, even if they couldn't understand all that I was saying. All I needed now was an excuse. I wanted them to have a go. I needed them to make the first move. I knew the lead guy would have to pull his weapon off his shoulder, cock it, aim, and fire. All I had to do was grab the Browning, push it out front, and go. I was more than ready and I was convinced I could drop them before they could drill me or Massoud.

Of course, they wouldn't know for sure that I had a weapon. The Browning was well hidden. I guessed that made my aggression and my staring, killer gaze incomprehensible to them. To them, it had to seem as if they were being challenged to fight by one lone Brit who was unarmed.

The mouthy one spat some words in Arabic at Massoud.

I flicked my eyes across to Massoud. "What did he say?"

"They are asking what your problem is. Easy, Morgan. Take it easy."

"Fuck taking it easy." I fixed the lead Shariah fighter with a stare. "I tell you what my problem is, asshole: you murdered some good people here tonight. Friends of mine . . ."

"Man United," the guy tried again. "Inglesi football good."

"Be careful, Morgan," Massoud muttered. He tried placing a restraining arm on me.

I shook it off. "No! Fuck them! Let's get it on!"

One thought was racing through my head now: *Do I shoot them?*

Do I shoot them? Do I shoot them? I couldn't be the one to move first. I needed them to.

"You fucking people are so fucking stupid," I spat out. "You idiots are being watched right now by the Americans—don't you know that? There will be a drone or satellite watching this compound right now. Don't you get it?" I started laughing. "Don't you realize the Americans are on their way? And you guys—you're dead men walking. All of you. You're all of you fucked."

These guys seemed to understand enough basic English to get the gist of what I was saying. I saw fear replace the bluster and arrogance in their eyes.

"If I was you guys, I'd fuck off right now . . . Even I don't want to be around here when the Americans arrive."

Massoud translated those last words. The five Shariah Brigade fighters didn't seem so brave now. As they made to shuffle past us Massoud started berating them about how they'd brought shame on Libya.

"Shame is the least of your problems!" I spat after them. "You got the Americans on your ass now, and they'll hunt you to your fucking graves."

They tried to walk to the front gate, but once one had started running they all did. Just as I had thought. They were cowards, the lot of them.

We made our way to the main consular building, but still I was shaking with rage. The pool was full of debris: smashed-up chairs, computer gear, desks, a TV. There was Arabic graffiti scrawled all over the white walls. I made sure to photograph every last bit of it. Maybe the evil bastards had been dumb enough to sign their own names, or maybe the names of the factions of the Shariah Brigade they belonged to, or maybe even the names of their commanders—those who had masterminded this night of savagery.

From there we turned left onto the gravel track leading to the TOC. I rounded a corner and there was the burned-out wreck of the canteen. To my utter disbelief two skinny guys came hurrying out laden with gear, and they started to make their way to a rusty pickup truck. They were carrying what looked like a metal filing cabinet. The bastards were still looting.

"WHAT ARE YOU FUCKERS DOING?" I exploded.

Massoud made a run for them. He too was beside himself with rage now. He was screaming at them in Arabic. They dropped their loot, ran for the pickup, and jumped in. I saw him trying to yank the driver out of the window by his hair. This had really pushed Massoud over the edge. Americans were dead, the Embassy was in ruins, his job was gone, and Libya had been shamed in the eyes of the world—and yet there were still guys here looting.

I stepped into the canteen. Everything here had been burned or looted or smashed to smithereens. I searched among the ashes and the debris, and at least there were no bodies. I crossed over to the TOC. Unbelievably, there was still smoke billowing out of the windows—that was how fierce the conflagration had been here.

I stepped inside. It was boiling hot and awash with smoke. I guessed maybe this was the last place that the Shariah killers had managed to torch. If so, maybe it was from here that some of the Americans had mounted their last stand—and that meant there could well be bodies.

I steeled myself to go on.

I pushed farther inside.

The political officer's room was still burning. It was totally trashed. Filing cabinets and desks were overturned and lying on top of each other. I checked where all the classified documents were stored, but there was nothing left that I could see. The weapons locker was on the floor, and it had been busted open. All the M4s, the pistols, and shoguns were gone. Most of anything that was left here was too hot to handle, but my greatest relief was that none of my friends were lying among the debris here as burned and scorched corpses.

I got out, having spent a good five minutes in there photographing everything. I gulped in big lungfuls of fresh air. I wiped the sweat from my eyes. My hair was soaked and plastered to my scalp. I had one thing left to do now: check the vineyard and the two orchards for bodies. I glanced at my watch. I was worried that those Shariah fighters might have rushed off to fetch their friends. We'd been here a good twenty-five minutes already. I told myself to hurry.

I started to run now, dashing from one patch of vegetation to another, my eyes scanning the ground for any dead Americans. There were none that I could see. Even the scores of Shariah corpses appeared to be gone, so I presumed they must have been in here collecting their dead.

I came to the flagpole, the one on which only the day before the flag had been flying at half-mast, in memory of 9/11. I had a lump in my throat just at the thought of it, and this place being hit on that momentous anniversary. Maybe we should have seen it coming, but we'd had not the slightest sniff of any intel about the kind of attack that hit us. I wanted to retrieve the flag, so I could hand it back to whichever of my American friends had survived, but even that was gone.

I raced through the last patch of cover—the orchard next to the outhouse/gym where I'd come over the wall—then back toward the main gate. I caught sight of Massoud waiting for me. He must have wondered what the hell I was doing, tearing around the complex like a madman. But I couldn't have lived with myself had I missed one of the guys and his body had been left behind.

As we headed out the gate someone grabbed me by the arm. It was an older Libyan male and I recognized him instantly. It was the owner of the compound.

He gestured at the destruction all around us: "The Americans will give me money, yes? They will pay?"

I stared at him, struggling to keep my anger in check. "Not if I have anything to do with it they won't."

I walked to the car. I was incandescent with rage. I saw Massoud and the lone policeman start to whack some more looters around the face, using open-handed slaps.

"Come on!" I yelled over at him. "Let's go!"

We set off. All the way back to the villa the silence lay heavy and oppressive between us. I kept thinking of those who had died, not that I knew exactly who it was yet. The not knowing was the worst. It was eating away at me. I told Massoud to wait as I went into the villa and grabbed my gear. I just wanted to get to the airport now and get out of this horrific, messed-up city—and to get out with the photographs that I'd taken this morning very much intact.

We set off for the airport. As we drove through downtown Benghazi I glanced around at the familiar sights, ones that were somehow now so alien to me. I knew for sure that I would never return to this place: it would be too much for me ever to come back. Beside me Massoud seemed very somber and shaken.

"What's wrong?" I asked him.

"I feel very bad for the Americans," he answered. "What has been done here is a shame on our country. And I regret because I know I will never work for you any again."

I was all choked up. I liked Massoud. He didn't deserve any of this. Like my guards, Massoud was one of the good guys.

As we neared the airport I felt as if my world was about to explode. I feared they'd stop me and take the camera; or shove me in front of the hordes of reporters who had to be flooding in to try to get the story right now; or arrest me and throw me into some cell. Massoud must have sensed what a mess I was in. When we got there he told me to wait in the car. He went and talked to some of his Army friends who were manning the airport. Via them I was ushered straight into the first-class departure lounge—bypassing passport control and security.

Fox News was playing on the lounge's TV set. The Benghazi Embassy siege was headline news, and the death of Ambassador Stevens was now being openly reported. I sat there glued to the screen, knowing that I had to look like absolute death: I hadn't slept for ages; my hair and beard were caked in sweat, dirt, smoke, and grime; and I was quite literally stinking.

An elderly-looking Arab man approached me. He held out his hand. "Sir, I am so very sorry for what happened to your friends last night."

I took his hand and shook it. "Shōkran"—*Thank you.*

He'd been speaking educated, fluent English. I had never seen him before, but I presumed he wanted to apologize on behalf of his country, and as a Westerner I was the first person he had seen to whom he could do so. A lot of Libyans would be like this man, and like Massoud: they would be full of shame and outrage.

Two Western-looking guys entered the lounge. I saw them pointing at me and whispering. I felt paranoid, like my head was about to detonate in a shower of brains and goo. They came over and started trying to introduce themselves. They had French accents and one pulled out a notebook. Reporters.

"So, you are an American?" he asked.

"Nope. Welsh."

"Oh . . . Pays de Galles."

"Yeah." Pays de Galles is the French name for Wales.

"What were you doing in Benghazi?"

"Working."

"What can you tell us about the attack on the Benghazi Embassy last night?"

That was it. I lost it. "LISTEN: YOU'D BETTER FUCK OFF BACK TO YOUR SEATS WHILE YOU STILL CAN!"

Massoud came sprinting over. "Yala! Yala! Yala!"—*quickly.* He grabbed them and led them away.

He came back. "Morgan, are you okay?"

"Yeah," I grunted. "Just keep those fuckers away from me."

Massoud got some of his Army friends to throw a cordon around me, keeping everyone away. I was in my own little world now. It was somewhere very close to hell. *Are they all dead?* I kept asking myself. *Should I have tried to shoot the guy with the Dushka, and gone over the wall at the first attempt? If I'd done so, might I have saved them? Should I have got the Ambassador's body and taken it back to the villa? Should I be dead alongside all my friends?*

The same thoughts kept swirling around and around in my head, like a dark storm. I was on the verge of a breakdown.

Massoud crouched beside me and showed me a video clip on his mobile phone. It showed what I guessed had to be some of the good Libyans carrying Ambassador Stevens out of the VIP Villa. Massoud explained that as the battle for the Mission had ebbed and flowed, some of Benghazi's many good citizens—people of a similar mind-set to him and Zahid—had managed to get into the Mission compound and pull the Ambassador out of the VIP Villa. It must have been those guys who helped get him to the hospital. In the video footage it looked as if they were genuinely trying to help him, but I prayed that his family hadn't seen any of those images.

I imagined how terrifying it must have been for him, locked in the safe room but with all the noise of the assault hammering in from outside. Then the heat and the flames. I felt anger burning through me again. Such a lovely man. Such a shitty way to die. *You poor bastard.* This was fucking my head up even more.

My flight was called.

Massoud and I embraced. "Shukran, habibi"—*Thank you, my brother*—I told him. I had tears in my eyes.

So did he. "You will come back to Libya, Morgan? You will come back?"

"Yes. I'll be back," I lied.

I would never return to this place.

I took my bag and walked away without a backward glance. I couldn't take it anymore.

As I boarded the plane all I could think of was getting a long way away from here, and back to my family.

CHAPTER NINETEEN

The two-hour flight to Doha, Qatar, passed in some kind of a daze. We landed and I had a good couple of hours on the ground before the connecting flight to London. I turned on my cell phone and there were scores of missed calls. Almost immediately a call came in from Robert.

"Yeah, it's me," I answered. "I'm in Doha."

"Good to hear it. Listen, the State Department people will be calling you shortly. There will be a shitload of people listening in and it'll be a conference call."

"Who exactly will be listening in?"

"High-ups. That's all I know."

"Well, fuck me, I guessed that much."

"Morgan, watch what you say and don't drop yourself in it. It'll be the usual crowd: CIA, FBI, DIA, and State. Maybe others. And remember, right now everyone is a suspect as far as they're concerned."

Jesus, this was the very last thing I needed right now.

Almost the instant that Robert ended the call my phone rang. It was a "001" number, so I knew it was the United States. I couldn't bring myself to answer. My mind froze. I let it go to voice mail. I wandered through the Doha terminal until I found a quiet, deserted corner. I sank down on the floor, my head in my hands. Tears streamed down my face. I did my best to keep my head down and hide them.

I wasn't heaving or sobbing, so no one could really see or hear, but the tears were simply uncontrollable. I was in a bad place mentally. I didn't even know if I could make it to my next flight, let alone take a call from every American three-letter agency under the sun. I understood why they needed to talk to me. I was the last man out. I'd found the Ambassador. They had no one else. Plus I had the photos and the evidence. But that didn't mean that I was capable of doing this.

I sat there and cried for a good thirty minutes. I tried to compose myself. I put a call through to Laura, the one person other than Robert I really wanted to talk to right now.

"Are you okay?" she asked me.

"No, I am not. I wish I was dead. I'm finished."

Laura talked me down a lot, and just the sound of her voice made me feel a little better. I tried to move on. I tried to lift my day pack, but it felt inconceivably heavy. It didn't weigh more than a few pounds, and it brought home to me how utterly exhausted I was—both emotionally and physically.

I made my way to the business-class lounge. Doha is a plush, space-age kind of an airport, and the lounge was full of swanky-looking international businesspeople and other assorted professionals. I could feel them staring at me like I had horns growing out of my head. I was so wired that I knew if one of them said the simplest word, I would smash their face in.

I took a stool at the bar and ordered a beer. The barman was a really good guy, and he kept refilling my glass as quickly as I drained it. After a good half-dozen beers I was feeling a fraction more human. I checked my phone. Four missed calls from America. I knew they needed to speak to me. No one else had what I had.

I thought: *Right, come on then—next call, let's do it.*

Barely minutes later my phone rang. "Morgan Jones."

"Mr. Jones, this is Sam Peterson from the U.S. State Department. I think you were expecting our call."

"Yes. I'm good to talk."

"Right, thank you, sir, because right now we really do appreciate it. Stay on the line: it'll take a few moments to get everyone patched in and seated and listening."

I supped some more beer as I waited.

"Okay, we're all in now. So, Mr. Jones, please tell us everything that you have seen and heard over the last forty-eight hours."

Fuck me, where did I start? I began relating the lead-up to the attack, then moved on to the events of the night just gone. I found myself reliving it all, and at one moment I found myself breaking down again and the words just wouldn't come. I heard another voice break into the call.

"Look, this guy just isn't up to this right now." Pause. "Sir? Mr. Morgan, we can get someone to that airport to sit with you until your flight is called."

"No, no. It's okay. I'm fine."

"If you want out of that place we can get you to the Embassy."

"No, I'm okay. I just want to go home."

"Understood, sir. Well, if you think you're able to continue?"

I said I was. I talked them through the events leading up to now, and somehow I got through it all. Then the questions began.

"How many attackers were there?"

"I don't know, but I was told two hundred minimum. Maybe as many as six hundred."

"What time did you find the Ambassador dead?"

"Sometime around two in the morning."

"Who were the attackers?"

"Shariah Brigade."

The questions went on and on. When they were finally done, I mentioned the fact that I had the photos from the compound, those that I'd taken when I'd gone back to document the crime scene.

"Hell, we need those ASAP. We have zero. We got nothing."

"I'll email them as soon as I get home. I'll need an email address."

"We'll get one to you. We would really, really appreciate those photos."

"You know about the Libyan policeman taking the recce photos?"

"Say again."

I related the story about the Libyan cop—or the guy posing as a cop—who'd taken all the shots of the Mission's front entrance the morning before the attack.

"No shit. We gotta get someone over to the U.K. to talk to you. Are you up for that?"

I told them that I was.

"So first priority is to email us those photos," the guy from State summarized. "Then we'll see about getting our people to you for a face-to-face."

That was the call. I downed a few gin-and-tonics just for the extra peace of mind, then made my way toward the gate. I'd barely settled into my seat before I'd fallen into the sleep of the dead.

It was a good nine or ten hours later by the time I finally reached home. Robert was waiting for me, and he warned me that the media had started hounding already. He told me that my default response should be "No comment." I told him that I didn't need this shit. I just wanted to be around those I loved in peace and in quiet.

I emailed all the photos that I had taken to the guy I'd spoken to at the State Department. I got a response back almost instantaneously: "Thank you very much for all of them. Brilliant. This is all we have."

That evening the four dead Americans were named on the news: Ambassador Stevens, Glen Doherty, Tyrone Woods, and Sean Smith. Hearing of Sean's death was heartbreaking. He'd been there only a week and he wasn't even a soldier. He was the IT man and a State Department guy through and through. I remembered telling Sean just a day or so before not to worry, for we'd never had a serious attack at the Mission. I'd said it just to put his mind at rest. Now he was dead, and there was a grieving wife and two children in The Hague.

I still had the fifty-euro note that Sean had given me to change into Libyan dinar so that he could buy some silk scarves for his wife. I pulled it out of my wallet, but I couldn't even bring myself to look at it. I locked it away in a drawer.

Glen Doherty and Tyrone Woods I didn't know if I'd met. I'd run into guys from the Annex, but we'd never properly swapped names. Both men were ex–Navy SEALs, and they'd been working at the Annex as private security guys. Their acts during the Embassy siege would turn out to be utterly selfless—the deeds of true heroes. I still didn't know exactly what had happened to Dave or Scotty, or the Ambassador's close protection team, and there was little peace to be had at home.

An FBI team was due to fly in from the States to speak with me. Every agency from America kept calling and asking me to tell them my story, and while I knew how important this was, repeating it over and over and over was cracking me up inside. Laura and Lewis were with me, but I didn't feel as if I was with them. I was in a dark and shadowed place, and mostly they were leaving me well alone.

I decided that I'd do what I had to do, and then I was going to go get myself gone. I was going to go incommunicado. I phoned a maritime security—antipiracy—company that I'd worked for a lot and asked if they had any jobs going. They said they had a ten-day transit starting in forty-eight hours, sailing from Dubai to Jeddah. I signed up to be team leader on the job.

I'd been home for less than forty-eight hours when a pair of plainclothes Special Branch officers turned up at our door. It was a guy and a woman, and they were actually as polite and helpful as can be.

"We just want to make you aware that the FBI has asked if they can come to see you," they explained.

"What d'you mean?" I asked. "They're coming at twelve mid-day tomorrow. It's all arranged."

"Are they fucking really?" the guy responded. "Just give me a minute, will you."

He stepped outside and I could see him making a phone call. He came back in. "Are you happy for them to come?" he asked.

"Yeah. Of course. Nothing to hide."

"Do you want us to be here with you?"

"No. I'm okay."

He handed me his card. "Any time you're not happy with their line of questioning or anything, you phone me and I'll get them the fuck out of here."

"Thanks."

He glanced at me: "Phone and emails . . ."

"Yeah, I know. They'll be monitored."

He nodded. "Yeah."

A little later I had a call from a guy named "Bill," who said he was phoning from the U.S. Embassy in London. "So, this FBI team flying in—hey, you sure you can't make it down to London?"

I could not believe what I was hearing. "Listen, mate, they either come here or they can fuck off."

"Okay, no problem," he responded, hurriedly. "They'll come to you."

"Why did you ask then? Hear this: I am not coming to London."

The following day a five-person team turned up at my house. Three were FBI guys, one was State Department, plus there was a lady in her late fifties who introduced herself as a head prosecutor from New York. They'd caught the train to the nearest station, then a taxi from there. We paused in my garden as they took a second to admire the view. Living on a Welsh mountaintop the scenery is stunning, with an avenue of majestic, windblown oaks marching off into the gray-green distance.

"Hey, man, it sure is beautiful up here," one remarked.

"Yeah. It's nice and quiet. Normally."

They'd paid their taxi driver to wait. I could see him staring at the lot of us, thinking: *What in God's name is going on?* I showed them to the living room, then made coffee for all. The questions began, with the senior of the FBI guys leading. We talked through the attack and the lead-up to it. We talked through the previous security incidents. Then he asked me what I thought of the QRF.

"Utterly fucking useless," I responded. "Cowards who ran away. Not a man among them could use a weapon, and they turned their backs and ran—just as myself and the RSOs had warned they would."

"So did you trust the QRF in any way?"

"*Trust them?* I wouldn't trust those fuckers as far as I could throw them."

The FBI guy asked me a bunch more probing questions about the QRF. I could understand the gist of his inquiries. He was trying to ascertain if I thought the attack on the Embassy could have been an "inside job"—that the QRF had been in league with the Shariah Brigade attackers. I told him it wouldn't surprise me, but I had no evidence either way. All I did know was that the QRF were useless, untrustworthy cowards who ran at the first sign of any trouble.

"What did you think of the RSOs?"

"Utterly faultless. They were brilliant and they worked tirelessly in tough, shitty conditions. They continuously asked for more manpower, weaponry, and equipment and they were continuously denied." I caught the eye of the guy from the State Department. "If they'd got it we wouldn't be here now, obviously."

"Right, okay, this is all important stuff."

How the hell could they not know this, I found myself thinking. Lee, Rosie, Justin, Jeff, and the others had sent through the same feedback, repeatedly: We need to get rid of the QRF; we need U.S.

Marines to replace them; we need more physical defenses; we need more firepower. *Did none of these people ever talk to each other?*

"So who do you think carried out the attack?"

"I don't *think*. I know. I saw them. It was the Shariah Brigade militia."

"Did you have any other concerns about security prior to the attack?"

"Where d'you want me to start? We had fucking loads of concerns. We—or rather the RSOs—detailed those concerns in numerous emails to the State Department. Nothing was ever done." I paused. "And you know what—I feel guilty as fuck because we failed to get the security sorted, and because on the day of the race I let the RSOs down . . ."

The woman prosecutor stepped in now. "No, no, no—let's be clear on one thing: you let no one down."

"Dead right," the FBI guy added. "Without you we'd have no information at all right now. Since the attack no one has been on the ground in that compound apart from you, and we cannot thank you enough for all those photos."

"I still feel guilty that I didn't make it over the wall the first time I tried."

I went to make them all another coffee. The lady prosecutor came into the kitchen.

"Hey, you know, Morgan—you did a good thing," she volunteered. "You did the right thing. Do not beat yourself up over this, okay? You're a good man. A good man, you hear me?"

I was tearing up. She was the motherly, kindly figure that I needed right now, and it was good of her to say those words. She stayed with me as I made the coffees, but in the background I could hear the guys firing questions back and forth at each other in hushed voices. *You ask him . . . No, you ask him . . . Who knows how he'll take it . . . Yeah, but that's what we need to know . . .*

I took them in the tray of drinks. "Guys: Listen up. I heard you whispering. I heard you saying *ask him this; ask him that*. You have something you want to ask me, or that you think might upset me or is insensitive—*just ask*. Let's get it out there. I will not be offended."

"No, no, man, everything is okay," the FBI guy who'd led the questioning reassured me. "And hey, thanks for the coffees."

I went to see if the taxi driver wanted a cup. Apart from anything else it was an excuse to get some air.

He stared at me for a long second: "Who the hell is that lot? And what the hell are they doing here—five scary Americans on the top of a Welsh mountain?"

I shrugged. "They're just some people I work with."

"Fuck off."

I started laughing. He was, too. "Come on, tell me. What the fuck are they doing here, bud?"

"I can't. They're just friends. Kind of."

Three hours after they'd started their questioning the team was finally done. They asked me if I had any questions for them.

"Three," I told them. "First: Scotty and Dave—are they okay?"

"They're both badly injured, but they should pull through okay."

Shit. Well, at least they were alive. "Tell them from me: I'm sorry, but I tried."

I could see that they were choked up. "Yeah, yeah—they know."

"Two: Sean gave me fifty euros to change into Libyan dinar." I handed the note across to them. "I can't look at it. Please, just take it—maybe give it to the family."

They were even more choked up now. "Jeez. Yeah. Thank you very much."

"Three: Did my guard force definitely press the duck-and-cover alarm at the start of the attack?"

"From the people I have spoken to—yes, they did," the FBI guy confirmed.

That was a massive weight off my mind. It was crucial to me. If they'd hit the alarm at least it meant the Americans had had warning, and a bit of time to do something—if only to grab weapons and body armor and get into fire positions.

It was time for the team to leave. They thanked me for all that I had done in Benghazi. I asked them to pass my warmest regards to Scotty and Dave. They told me they'd need me to fly to the United States at some point, to give my side of the story in full. I said I'd be happy to go. Whatever it would take to try to right the wrongs perpetrated on that hellish night, and to ensure the lessons would be learned.

The lead FBI agent gave me his card: "You ever need anything ever, you just call me."

The guy who was the most choked-up among them embraced me. The lady prosecutor gave me a hug as well.

"You did the right thing," she told me again. "You did the right thing."

They got into the cab. The driver leaned out of his window with an odd expression on his face. "You're not going to believe it, bud: they want me to drive them up the mountain!"

They did just that, heading on up the track toward the summit of the hill. As I knew fully well, it was beautiful up there. Fifteen minutes later they passed back down again. I waved from the window and they waved back, and then they were gone.

I put a call through to Robert. "The FBI are done, mate."

"Was it okay?" he asked.

"Yeah, they were fantastic." I told him I was off on the maritime security job the very next day.

"You can't do that," he objected. "You can't just disappear. There are loads more people need to talk to you."

"Listen, mate, I'm done talking. I'm all talked out. They need to start talking to each other and sharing info. I can't do it anymore."

I packed my bags and the next morning I flew out of London to Dubai. I was looking forward to getting on the ship and getting under way, for hopefully that would put an end to the phone calls, not to mention the endless TV news reports about the Benghazi attack.

I boarded the floating armory where antipiracy crews like my own pick up weaponry and prepare to join their ship. I was grabbing some food in the galley and the news came on the TV: it was yet more about Benghazi. There were other teams in there waiting to board their ships, and a guy made a comment.

"Fucking how could they let the Embassy get taken? If I'd been there I'd have shot every last one of the bastards."

The voice was clearly British. I turned around. It was a big, fat oaf of a bloke. "Would you fucking really?" I snarled. "And what the fuck do you know about it?"

The guy could tell that I was that close to murdering him, and he shut his mouth very quickly. I turned back to my food, but the guys on my team were giving me the look now. I could tell what they were thinking: *Christ, we've got some kind of a psycho for a team leader.*

Luckily, the operator directly under me, Dai, was a fellow Welshman, and with twelve years' experience as a Royal Marine I knew he had to be well capable. Just as soon as we were under way on the ship we were guarding I called him into my cabin.

"Listen, mate, there's something you need to know," I explained. "I am struggling here and I don't think I'm going to cope." I explained to him all that I had just been through. He couldn't believe it, and I could tell that he was genuinely concerned for me.

"No problem, mate," Dai said. "I can take over as team leader, and we'll keep it just between the two of us."

From then on Dai did all the meetings with the ship's captain, and all the briefings with the crew. I stood my watches, tried to stay alert for any pirates, and otherwise was locked away in my cabin, brooding. I had some seriously dark thoughts during some of those long nights alone on the ship, standing watch. I wondered what the point was of it all. Of life. On a night like that of the Benghazi Embassy siege, who or what had determined who lived and who died?

It crossed my mind to jump. What stopped me were the thoughts of Laura and of Lewis waiting for me back at home. But I knew I would never be the same again. I made it through that antipiracy trip and headed for home, hoping that I was on the mend. I'd been away for twelve days, but just as soon as I was in the United Kingdom again my phone started to ring. It was a woman from the U.S. Embassy.

"Mr. Jones, you cannot simply disappear overseas when we want to talk to you, willy-nilly, and of your own free will."

"Where are you based?" I asked her.

"London. At the American Embassy."

"Right: Listen here. I am fucking British. I do not answer to you and I will go wherever I fucking please. I told your people everything I fucking know. If you lot had listened to the RSOs in the first place we wouldn't be in the pile of shit we are now."

Silence.

"We'll leave it there then."

I'd had two good American friends badly injured as a result of that ill-fated night—how badly I would only learn in time—and I'd had one good friend killed. I had discovered the American ambassador lying dead and abandoned in some shitty Benghazi hospital. Self-important, deskbound pen-pushers like her did not have injured and dead friends to mourn. *Who the hell did she think she was?*

Over the coming weeks and months I was haunted by images of those who had died and were injured during the Benghazi Embassy siege. I was tortured because I had broken my promise by not getting to them in time. If I could have got into the Embassy before the attack, I would gladly have stood side by side with Dave, Scotty, and the others. I don't leave my friends hanging.

I had tried, but not hard enough, and I can't ever forgive myself for that.

POSTSCRIPT

I n the nine months since the attack on the Benghazi Mission of September 11, 2012, I have managed to piece together the bigger picture of what took place on that fateful night, while I was hell-bent on trying to get to the aid of my American friends.

It seems likely that the team from the Annex went over the Mission wall—as I did later in the evening—as opposed to going in via the obvious route, the front gate. That at least is the story as it is related in the e-book *Benghazi: The Definitive Report* and as some ex–Special Forces members have related the events to me. Using their SUVs as a springboard, they climbed onto the vehicle roofs and hauled themselves onto the wall, over the security fence, and inside.

No one opened fire from their position inside the Embassy until all six were in. Ty Woods had radioed Alex in the TOC to warn him that a team from the Annex was coming in, and what direction from which he was to expect them. That done, they began to fight their way into the TOC. Between them they had one MK 46 MOD 1 light machine gun and some Heckler & Koch 416 assault rifles complete with underslung 40mm grenade launchers.

Using well-placed bursts from the light machine gun, highly accurate assault rifle fire, and unleashing 40mm grenades, they battled their way into the compound, killing scores of enemy en route. Having fought their way inside, the team from the Annex split up—some heading for the TOC to retrieve Alex, who was there manning communications, the rest heading for the VIP Villa.

Dave Ubben, the Ambassador's two CP guys, and the new arrivals from the Annex now redoubled their efforts to search the burning building for the Ambassador and Sean Smith. Finally, they managed to drag Sean out, although he appeared unconscious due to smoke inhalation. In spite of making repeated searches of the Villa's smoke-filled interior, they still could not locate the Ambassador. Sadly, Sean Smith would later that night be declared dead, the cause being the inhalation of toxic smoke.

Lead RSO Alex and the Annex team from the TOC fought their way through to the VIP Villa, at which point all the Americans were reunited, except for Ambassador Stevens. Further efforts were made to locate him. With attempts via the rear window being frustrated by thick smoke and heat, Alex tried to go in through the charred and burning front entrance. As he did so, the ceiling all but collapsed on him, due to fire damage. At the same time, enemy fire had begun to sweep across the compound as the Shariah fighters launched a counterattack.

The American force was again in danger of being overrun. They were running low on ammunition and facing a massive number of enemy. At the urging of the team from the Annex, Dave, Scotty, and Alex plus the two CP guys took one of the Mission's surviving SUVs—the escape vehicle parked at the rear exit—and made good their evacuation of the Embassy, leaving the Annex team to make one last attempt to find and rescue Ambassador Stevens.

As their vehicle left through the rear gate, they came under intense fire, and they noticed roadblocks manned with scores of gunmen. They accelerated past, and at one stage they were taking fire from small arms and grenades at very close quarters, with bullets pinging off the armored skin of the SUV and grenades exploding beneath it. With tires blown out, they continued driving, although the enemy fire had all but penetrated the vehicle's bulletproof glass.

They pressed onward for the Annex, completing the last stage of that desperate journey having crossed the central dividing line of the highway and driving against the traffic as a way to escape from vehicles in pursuit. By the time they were nearing the Annex, the two vehicles that had been following them, both with their lights off, had been lost. On arrival at the Annex, they made it safely inside the gates, which were closed and secured behind them.

Those who were able joined the force manning a security perimeter around the Annex to repel any attackers who might target this complex. Back at the Mission the team led by Ty Woods was embroiled in an intensive firefight as the enemy targeted them with machine-gun fire and repeated rocket-propelled grenade (RPG) strikes. Sharp stabs of fiery tracer pierced the darkness above the burning buildings. In danger of running out of ammo, and having made repeated attempts to find Ambassador Stevens, they were forced to abandon the search.

Carrying Sean Smith with them, they conducted a fighting withdrawal, using fire and maneuver tactics to retrace their steps to their vehicles, fighting off more of the enemy as they went. The team from the Annex left the Mission at around 11:30 P.M., with all of their number still alive and having evacuated all the Mission personnel—apart from the Ambassador.

They came under fire as they exited the compound, and they basically had to fight their way out through the streets they had used as they fought their way in. They were driving armored SUVs and as they exited the area of the Mission they were hit by crowds of Shariah fighters gathered in ambush and blocking positions. Despite this they made it back to the Annex with no loss of life.

At just after 11:00 P.M. an unarmed American drone had been placed over the location of the attack on the Mission, and it was able to relay live imagery to Washington of the drama unfolding below. The then CIA director, General David Petraeus, was apparently in the CIA Operations Center overseeing the rescue for the entire duration of the Benghazi siege, and until all Americans were accounted for.

The Annex itself now came under serious assault from fighters wielding AK-47s, RPGs, and heavy machine guns. Dave Ubben and the Ambassador's two CP guys joined those mounting the defense at the Annex—a defense that was again going to be led by Tyrone Woods, the ex-SEAL. Scotty was in a bad way due to all the smoke he had inhaled, and he was being treated for his injuries.

However, the Shariah Brigade attackers were taking on a very different target at the Annex than they had at the Mission. There were thirty Americans based there, including many battle-hardened elite operators. There was also a sizable Libyan guard force that was highly paid and motivated. Most important, that force was properly armed, presumably because those at the Annex didn't think that having an unarmed guard force was a very sensible idea. The Annex itself had good defensive positions, complete with the type of heavy weaponry required to defend such a compound.

While the fighting was every bit as intense as it had been at the Mission, the defenders killed scores of Shariah fighters and weren't yet in serious danger of being overrun. They also had high-intensity floodlights illuminating the scene, which proved blinding to the attackers and helped the Americans to pick them off. The fighting continued for a good hour, by which time the Shariah Brigade commanders must have realized they needed heavier weaponry to stand any chance of taking out the Annex. There was an ominous lull.

By now it was well after midnight, and Dr. Saif Eddin al Zoghbia, a general surgeon at the Benghazi Medical Center (BMC)—the formal name of the "Twelve-Hundred-Bed Hospital"—was the duty doctor working the 8 P.M.–2 A.M. shift in the ER. From the outside, the desert-brown BMC building looked like a modern, efficient hospital complex, complete with all the various wards and departments that such a facility should possess. In reality it was woefully ill-equipped and understaffed at all levels. Only one of the three wings functioned properly, and of the twelve hundred beds only a third were being used. A surgeon such as Dr. Zoghbia earned eight hundred Libyan dinar a month, the equivalent of six hundred dollars. The ER lacked the basic necessities of such a unit—including proper sterilizing equipment, lifesaving drugs, and oxygen and respiratory equipment.

There is no emergency medical service in Libya, so no ambulances or ambulance crews. Any injured are normally brought into the hospital by distraught relatives or bystanders. The ER department was receiving a lot of road accident victims, due to the chaotic nature of the city after the downfall of dictator Muammar Gaddafi, plus a lot of gunshot victims due to lawlessness and killings on the streets.

At 1:30 A.M. Dr. Zoghbia was taking a break by the exit to the ER unit when he heard frantic shouting. A group of young men came running toward him carrying a makeshift stretcher. They were panicking and he could hear them shouting: "This man is going to die! We found him at the Embassy!" The first thing Dr. Zoghbia did was check the man's carotid pulse. There was none that he could detect. He took the man inside and started to do cardiopulmonary resuscitation while yelling out "Code Blue!"

"Code Blue" was the alert for any spare doctors or nurses to come to the ER and lend assistance in a life-threatening emergency. Dr. Zoghbia had no idea who the man on the stretcher might be. He couldn't even tell if he was a foreigner or a Libyan. The man was clothed, but he was smoke-blackened and some of his clothes seemed to be singed and burned. He was wearing running shoes, and one of the young men commented again that he was a "foreigner from the U.S. Embassy."

Dr. Zoghbia ignored him and concentrated on trying to save the patient. A nurse connected a monitor to check his vital signs and applied an oxygen mask. One of the young men who had brought the patient in said they had found him at the Embassy, and that he believed he was the U.S. Ambassador. Dr. Zoghbia didn't believe him: it was inconceivable that this man whose life he was trying to save could be the American Ambassador to Libya. He continued to give CPR, compressing the man's chest in an effort to get him to start breathing again.

He was joined by two other doctors, and together they worked on trying to revive the patient. They tried to intubate him—to open his airway by placing a tube down it, to enable oxygen to enter the lungs—but the airway was completely swollen and constricted. They switched to using a bag valve mask—a handheld ventilator that pumps air into the lungs—with additional oxygen. They continued to give CPR for nearly twenty minutes, but there was no response from the patient.

Dr. Zoghbia was greatly frustrated at their failure to revive him. It was then that he checked the man's pupils, and realized that he had gray-blue eyes—suggesting he might well be a foreigner and from the U.S. Embassy, as the young men had claimed. He still could not believe that this man could be the U.S. Ambassador.

The man's pupils were dilated and fixed and showed no reaction to the light at all. The doctor then checked his entire body for any signs of trauma or injury, but there were none. He concluded the patient had died from smoke inhalation, and very likely before he reached the BMC. He noted the time of likely death, disconnected the monitor, and signed off on the paperwork.

Ambassador Stevens's body was then covered in a sheet and wheeled out for transfer to the morgue. After his ER shift was done, Dr. Zoghbia spoke to one of the young men who had brought the body in. He learned that he was one of a group of young Libyan men who had seen the Mission on fire and had gone to try to help. They had found a locked and barred room. They'd gone around to the rear of the building and found a window they could force open. One of them had jumped into the room, which was hot and filled with smoke.

That man had stumbled upon a body, which he and others had proceeded to pull out of the burning villa. At that moment they believed the man still to be alive. They carried him across to the nearest private car and that was how they had got him to the hospital. Dr. Zoghbia heard the young man's story but still could not believe that the man now lying dead in his hospital might be the American Ambassador to Libya.

Some three hundred miles to the west of Benghazi, a Quick Reaction Force had been mobilized at the U.S. Embassy in Tripoli. It consisted of five Americans, including ex–Navy SEAL operator Glen Doherty, who was on contract to the CIA as one of their Global Response Staff (GRS), plus two Delta Force operators. Doherty was a close friend of Tyrone Woods, having served alongside him in SEAL Team Three, and he was determined to get to the aid of those at the Annex.

When serving as a SEAL, Doherty had responded in October 2000 to the terrorist attack on the USS *Cole* in a harbor in Yemen, and he had completed tours of duty in both Iraq and Afghanistan. Doherty had left the military in 2005 and had since served as a private security operator. He was in Libya as part of the U.S. team hunting down MANPADS—shoulder-launched missiles that had fallen into militia, and hence perhaps terrorist, hands.

A hastily rented private aircraft—the pilots were reportedly paid thirty thousand dollars in cash to undertake the flight— carried the Tripoli QRF down to Benghazi. Their aim was to reinforce the defense at the Annex, where some thirty Americans were now holed up. The five-man team touched down at Benghazi airport sometime between 11:00 P.M. and 1:00 A.M. (CIA and Pentagon accounts differ over this timeline).

The QRF who had flown down from Tripoli had been told there would be "fast movers" over Benghazi by the time they got there—fast movers referring to American military fast jets (F15s, F16s, or F18s). However, no U.S. airpower was deployed over Benghazi to assist U.S. forces in the defense of either the Embassy or the Annex during the long night of the siege—apart from the two drones (one replacing the other) that were put over the scene and held there until the battles were over.

The five-man QRF were detained upon arrival at the Benghazi airport—presumably by whichever militia were running "security"—and held for a good five hours. The Libyans maintain that this was because of the need to assemble a Libyan Army force powerful enough to escort the Tripoli QRF to the Annex, and this may well be true.

While held at the airport the Tripoli QRF tried to verify where Ambassador Stevens was, as he was now the lone American missing. Learning that he was very likely dead and at the BMC, the decision was made not to go and retrieve his body, but to go to the aid of those at the Annex. This was made in part because they believed security at the hospital to be uncertain, especially since the Shariah Brigade had taken their wounded there.

Either way, as a result of the delay at Benghazi airport the QRF did not get to the aid of those at the Annex until around 5 A.M.—more than seven hours after the attack began. They reached the Annex safely and joined the defenders. With the Shariah Brigade having ransacked the U.S. Mission and driven the Americans out, the full focus of their attack now shifted to the Annex. The defenders at the Annex racked up dozens of kills as the Shariah Brigade tried to overrun it—as they had done the Embassy—by sending scores of their fighters to scale the walls.

Tyrone Woods led a bunch of elite operators—now including fellow ex-SEAL Glen Doherty—plus Dave Ubben, in a fierce defense from the Annex roof. Scotty was apparently already out of action, due to smoke inhalation and other injuries suffered at the Mission. Having realized they couldn't storm the Annex, the Shariah Brigade brought up what is believed to be a French 81mm mortar—one that had very likely been airdropped to the "rebels" during the fight to topple Gaddafi.

At around first light the enemy mortar team started to rain down mortars onto the Annex, targeting the rooftop position occupied by the main body of defenders. Very quickly they had their target "bracketed"—with a mortar round dropped to either side of the rooftop defensive position. The mortar tube was zeroed in on its target, and ready to hit those rooftop defenders.

It would take a British or American mortar team many months to learn to fire a mortar with such accuracy in such a busy urban environment. To get accurate mortar rounds onto such a small target as the Annex roof so quickly was a major feat of gunnery. It suggested several things. One, that the Shariah attackers must have recce'd the Annex and worked out a set of GPS coordinates and grids for their targets. Two, that they had a highly trained mortar team in-country—most likely a foreign team, one with widespread battle experience and probably from Iraq or Afghanistan.

The first accurate mortar round dropped on the rooftop position and fatally wounded Tyrone Woods. His body shielded much of the blast from a second GRS agent, but that man was nonetheless seriously injured from shrapnel and blast. Glen Doherty tried to reposition himself and take cover, but a second round dropped in quick succession and killed him instantly.

Dave Ubben was hit in the same mortar strike, suffering shrapnel injuries and broken bones. It was only due to the heroic actions of the medic-trained operators based at the Annex—who sprinted up to that roof to give first aid—that Dave's life was saved. Tyrone Woods did not die immediately as a result of being hit, but apparently bled out over several hours and died from his injuries.

The wounded—Dave Ubben, Tyrone Woods, and the GRS agent—were taken down from the roof using ladders. The American MQ1-Predator drone now orbiting above the Annex was relaying live feeds to those based at the Annex, and to headquarters and command. Via the feed to their Rover terminal—a small computer-like screen that played live video feeds from the orbiting Predator—those in the Annex could see large numbers of Shariah Brigade fighters converging on their position for what appeared to be a major assault. At that moment the decision was made to evacuate the Annex completely.

The Annex had taken an absolute pounding. The one thing the American operators based there had in their favor was combat experience and tactical awareness. Their weapons were also far superior to those of the Shariah fighters. Still, it was a numbers game now, and there were simply too many enemy massing to attack. The decision to evacuate the Annex was without doubt the right one.

At around 6:30 A.M. Libyan Army vehicles escorted the thirty-odd American personnel out of the Annex and the siege was finally broken. The Predator followed that convoy as it made its way to the airport to evacuate. At 7:30 A.M. a number of evacuees, including all the wounded, were flown out of the Benghazi airport on a chartered jet and landed in Tripoli, where they were met by Embassy staff, including medics. The wounded were transferred to a Tripoli hospital, where the rapid access to full medical care doubtless saved the lives of the two most seriously injured Americans—Dave Ubben and the wounded GRS agent.

A Libyan Air Force C-130 Hercules transport aircraft was made ready to carry the remainder of the Mission and Annex staff from Benghazi airport to Tripoli. Alex and others present worked with local contacts to get the Ambassador's body retrieved from Benghazi Medical Center. It arrived at the airport at 8:25 A.M. under escort from Libyan Army personnel, whereupon Alex was able to verify that it was indeed Ambassador Stevens's body.

At around 9:00 A.M. all surviving U.S. personnel in Benghazi—that's everyone from the Mission and all from the Annex—evacuated the city on that C-130 Hercules headed to Tripoli.

At that stage I was the last Westerner from the Mission or Annex remaining in the city.

The Annex was actually about a ten-minute drive from the Mission—so less than a kilometer away. My mission once all the Americans had pulled out of Benghazi was to check the Mission for the bodies of my friends and to document the scene at which the American Ambassador to Libya had been killed.

At 7:15 that evening the wounded from the Benghazi attacks were airlifted out of Tripoli in U.S. Air Force C17 and C130 aircraft, along with most of the Benghazi Embassy and Annex staff. They were flown to Ramstein Air Base, in Germany, on aircraft equipped with military doctors and nurses providing medical care en route. The aircraft touched down at Ramstein at approximately 10:30 P.M. (Libya time)—so some twenty-four hours after the attacks in Benghazi had begun.

At least two elite American military teams had been readied to fly into Benghazi the night of the siege, but neither actually made it. One was a contingent of some fifty U.S. Marines, forming up a FAST—Fleet Antiterrorism Security Team—force, based at Rota, in Spain, a short flight across the Mediterranean from Benghazi. That team was hindered in its response because it lacked "dedicated airlift"—in other words, air transport—at its location (air transport was in Germany). Even if airlift had been available, it's unlikely the FAST force would have been able to arrive in time to save the lives of those killed in the attack.

A team of Special Operations forces was sent out from Fort Bragg, North Carolina, and one was on standby in nearby Croatia— but neither team was given clearance to enter Libya, even though at least one was only a short flight away in Europe. There were also U.S. warplanes based at Aviano Air Base, in Italy—again just a short flight away across the Mediterranean—but the only U.S. air assets deployed over Benghazi the night of the Mission and the Annex attacks were the Predator drones.

The Libyan surgeon who treated Ambassador Stevens learned

of the man's true identity only when he saw it revealed on the TV news later that morning. Dr. Zoghbia still could not believe that the American Ambassador to Libya had been killed and ended up on his treatment table. He wondered then, if there had been a properly equipped ambulance at the scene—one with oxygen and breathing apparatus—could Ambassador Stevens's life have been saved? He felt frustrated that he'd been unable to save him and angry that this could have happened.

While the doctor found it hard to comprehend how the American Ambassador had ended up in his hospital dying or already dead, he, like many Benghazians, had known that security at the U.S. Mission was lacking, that the Mission was inadequately protected. Moreover, employing the 17th February Militia as the Embassy's guard force was seen as nonsensical—for the Militia was known to be connected to extremists like the Shariah Brigade. Most Benghazians were mystified as to why the U.S. Embassy would have hired such people to "protect" their diplomatic mission.

One thing that I have learned over the years working with Americans is that they do not leave their fellow countrymen to perish. How those from the Annex managed to get to the Mission compound at all amazes me—for the attackers would have spotted them immediately and hit them hard, and as I knew from my own experience, there were scores of gun trucks surrounding the Mission sporting Russian-made 12.7mm Dushka machine guns. The team from the Annex may have been driving armored SUVs, but the Dushka fires armor-piercing rounds: it would have torn apart their vehicles like a can opener.

Tyrone Woods and his team must have had balls of steel, for they were initially up against one hundred Shariah Brigade fighters. However, the number of attackers was increasing at an alarming rate, and the highest number I heard on the ground was five hundred to six hundred, and those numbers were reliably confirmed.

To attempt such a rescue mission under those circumstances was suicidal—but they did it anyway, and I knew for sure they would be on their way just as soon as they got the call.

They would have had one advantage over the enemy: they would have known the layout of the Mission compound and would have known where the staff had barricaded themselves in and taken up defensive positions. However, the villas would have been well ablaze by the time they arrived, and they went in taking heavy fire—from PKM light machine guns, AK-47s, RPGs, and very possibly Dushkas. To have got in and out as they did and to have recovered and rescued all the surviving Americans except one is an incredibly brave and courageous achievement.

One of my main fears while trying to gain access to the U.S. Mission that night was bumping into the Annex team, for I knew they'd be dropping any bad guys that came anywhere remotely near them. I was on my own carrying the terrorist weapon of choice—an AK-47—and I knew that if they spotted me I'd be finished. I'd met only a few of the Annex guys briefly, so in the heat of battle and the darkness they would have been unlikely to recognize me—and I would have been finished.

Needless to say, they are the true heroes of the Benghazi 9/11 story.

EPILOGUE

The September 11, 2012, attack on the U.S. Embassy in Benghazi was not the first time such a catastrophic event had occurred in that city. On June 5, 1967, a mob had laid siege to, taken control of, and burned down the then–U.S. Consulate in Benghazi. A quote from a first-person account of that event is chillingly reminiscent of what took place forty-five years later.

"The mob finally battered its way in. They pushed themselves in through broken windows and came at us cut and bleeding . . . Dropping tear gas grenades we fought our way up the stairs and locked ourselves in the second-floor communications vault. There were ten of us in there including two women. The mob set fire to the building."

That testimony is from the lead Diplomatic Security agent at the time, John Kormann, paratrooper and a World War II veteran of behind-enemy-lines missions, who had joined the State Department Foreign Service in the 1950s. The ten Embassy staff remained locked in the vault, as the flames and heat drove the attackers out of the building. They set about burning secret documents, as a British armored column tried to get through to them, but it was beaten back by gasoline bombs.

At one stage the attackers were on the Embassy roof and tried to tear down the U.S. flag. Kormann ordered the flag raised again, which an American Army captain managed, to the rage of the attackers. Fearing that the Americans were being burned alive in the building, a British armored column eventually did get through to the Embassy building and all were rescued.

The main difference between the 1967 attack on the U.S. Mission in Benghazi and that of 2012 is that no Americans lost their lives in 1967. But there are other key differences. The 1967 attack was a spontaneous uprising by a mob, one that had become enraged by false reports that the U.S. Navy was attacking the Egyptian capital, Cairo. That which occurred forty-five years later was a carefully planned assault by a group of battle-hardened fighters.

The 1967 attackers were largely unarmed: they hit the embassy with rocks and boulders and firebombs. The attackers of 2012 were heavily armed—wielding assault rifles, light machine guns, grenade launchers, and vehicle-mounted heavy machine guns. The 1967 mission wasn't relying on a Libyan militia for its armed security as was that in 2012. And while the 1967 siege was broken by a column of (British) armored vehicles, no such major armored force was able to come to the aid of those in 2012. That rescue was mounted by six extremely brave and principled former elite forces operators.

The makeup of Libya in 2012 was also markedly different from that of 1967. In 1967 there was a strong central government and rule of law, with a functioning military and police force. In 2012, especially in eastern Libya—the birthplace of the revolution—central government held little sway. The city of Benghazi, like much of the east, was controlled by a mishmash of militias. Those militias—which were nominally government-aligned and -controlled—supposedly carried out most of the duties that the military and police would do in a normal, functioning state, but they did so following their own often violent and lawless agendas, and in some cases driven by Islamic extremism.

As the Libyan revolution had gained momentum during 2011, there was an ever more worrying trend witnessed on the front line of battle. Bit by bit, the frontline units were being taken over by jihadists, most of whom were Salafist in orientation— ultra-hard-line Sunni Muslims who sought to turn Libya into an Islamic state ruled by Shariah law. In effect, an uprising that had been born out of the desire for freedom and democracy had been hijacked by those with a very different agenda. Fellow Islamists flocked to the cause in Libya from all over the world.

With many being international jihadists—ones hardened in battle in Iraq and Afghanistan—they had a natural ability to command frontline units. They began to transform amateur revolutionary fighters into jihadi fighting units. The turning point in the struggle for control of the revolution between the jihadists and the secular revolutionaries came with the assassination of rebel leader and former Libyan Army general Abdul Fatah Younis. During the 1990s General Younis had conducted Libyan Army campaigns against the rising forces of Islamism in the east of the country. Consequently he was hated by the Islamists, but revered by the people of the revolution.

As the revolution gained pace, General Younis realized the extremists were receiving the bulk of the weaponry that was arriving in covert air shipments from Qatar, Abu Dhabi, and Saudi Arabia, ones being flown into Benghazi or Derna airports. General Younis raised his voice to complain about this: *sophisticated weaponry was falling into the wrong hands.* An attempt had already been made on the general's life. During one frontline operation his vehicle had been hit by RPGs.

In response to his opposition to the covert weapons drops, General Younis was seized by Islamists in Benghazi and taken to a 17th February Militia/Shariah Brigade base. General Younis was a highly experienced Special Forces soldier and a man of bravery and principle. He was tortured and shot to death. His body was dumped outside the city. His eyes had been gouged out; his body was partly burned and was riddled with bullet holes.

After his assassination the front line changed radically—with the Islamists seizing ever more iron control. The Islamists made up only 10 percent of the frontline fighters, but with their battle experience and hard-line fanaticism they exerted far greater influence than their numbers alone warranted. Many of these Islamists hailed from outside Libya: they came from Sweden, Norway, and the United Kingdom. Some spoke fluent Pashtun—a result of having lived and fought in Afghanistan on the side of the Taliban and Al Qaeda for many years.

They were fanatical and proved extremely aggressive toward Westerners even as the revolution was ongoing. A French ex-commando was captured by Islamists in Benghazi and killed by them. It was 17th February Militia and/or Shariah Brigade fighters who captured and killed him. Two British ex–Special Forces operators were very lucky to escape from Benghazi with their lives.

After Gaddafi was toppled, the Shariah Brigade in particular began to exert its control on the streets of Benghazi. Citizens were terrified of their marauding bands of militiamen. They would beat people if they were caught drinking alcohol, or if a man was caught on the streets in the company of a woman. One person was whipped eighty times on the soles of his feet for being caught drinking. Another was cut twenty times on his back for being caught with a bottle of whisky in his car.

This was akin to some of the worst excesses of the Taliban, once they had seized control of Afghanistan. It gave the lie to exactly who the Shariah Brigade were, their background, beliefs, and intentions.

On the morning of the 2012 attack on the U.S. Embassy in Benghazi, twenty to thirty Shariah Brigade gun trucks reportedly left the coastal city of Derna, some 125 miles to the east of Benghazi. Derna was known by Libyans to be a hotbed of Islamic extremism and to be a stronghold of such forces, one more or less completely under the control of the Shariah Brigade. Those Shariah Brigade gun trucks headed to Benghazi to reinforce those fighters already in the city preparing to hit the U.S. Embassy.

Twenty to thirty gun trucks generally hold some 160 to 240 fighters—a good proportion of those who assaulted the U.S. Mission and the Annex that September evening. This is yet another indication of how carefully planned and premeditated was the entire assault. Moreover, the attack took place on the symbolic anniversary of the 9/11 terror attacks on America, and Ambassador J. Christopher Stevens had only just arrived at the Mission.

Ambassador Stevens was a veteran diplomat who joined the U.S. Foreign Service in 1991. He had expressed his "extraordinary honor" at being appointed the U.S. Ambassador to Libya in May 2012. He had held two previous posts in Libya, as Deputy Chief of Mission between 2007 and 2009 and then the American envoy to Libya's Transitional National Council (TNC) during the uprising in 2011.

Ambassador Stevens was reported to have facilitated "nonlethal military assistance" to the TNC during the Libyan revolution. A speaker of French and Arabic, he had previously been posted to Jerusalem, Damascus, Cairo, and Riyadh. In Washington he'd acted as the director of the Office of Multilateral Nuclear and Security Affairs; as a Pearson Fellow with the Senate Foreign Relations Committee; and as an Iran desk officer and a staff assistant to the State Department's Bureau of Near Eastern Affairs.

Ambassador Stevens was an old Libya hand. As early as August 2, 2012, he was making his concerns regarding security in Libya clear to the State Department and requesting additional security. In cables to Washington he described the security situation in Libya as "unpredictable, volatile and violent" and requested further "protective detail bodyguard positions." Throughout August 2012 he sent further alerts, outlining how "a series of violent incidents has dominated the political landscape," referring to "targeted and discriminate attacks."

By August 27 the State Department had gone as far as issuing a travel warning for Libya, citing the threat of assassination and car bombings in both Tripoli and Benghazi. On September 11,

2012—the day of the Embassy attack—Ambassador Stevens had sent cables to Washington including a weekly update on Benghazi security incidents, which reflected ordinary Libyans' "growing frustration with police and security forces who were too weak to keep the country secure."

Bearing in mind the makeup of the armed groups at large in Benghazi post-Gaddafi, the American Embassy should have been provided with a level of security befitting a Mission in a postconflict zone menaced by America's foremost enemies. Extremely reliable and well-placed sources involved in constructing the Benghazi Embassy's physical defense and security measures have told the authors of this book how they warned the Americans that they needed far greater physical security measures in place if they were to ensure the security of the Benghazi Mission.

Those sources—who have asked to remain anonymous due to worries over their security—pointed out to U.S. authorities that the security measures that were *recognized as standard for a U.S. diplomatic mission had not been put in place in Benghazi*. They were stunned when no further security measures were undertaken at the Benghazi Mission, and they raised this with the State Department, warning that the Mission remained vulnerable to attack.

Other "outsiders" also warned those at the Mission what was self-evident to any moderately experienced Benghazi watcher—that the U.S. Embassy was woefully underprotected. Veteran New Zealand ex–elite forces soldier Mike Mawhinney—a private security operator widely experienced in Libya—provided security for Al Jazeera and other news crews during the height of the fighting to topple Gaddafi forces, plus for a number of other private contractors.

He visited the Benghazi Mission and general vicinity on two occasions, and on both he was shocked to witness the woeful lack of proper security measures and manning at the Mission. "I visited the Mission twice between March and September 2012," Mawhinney remarks. "I could not believe how poorly it was protected, to such a degree that I could not at first believe it could be a U.S. Diplomatic Mission."

Mawhinney was shocked to discover that the 17th February Militia had been retained as the Mission's Quick Reaction Force. "Both I and my Libyan friends knew immediately that they had entirely the wrong people supposedly protecting the Mission. The female RSO in charge at the time seemed dynamic, capable and smart, and I presumed the inability to get anything changed at the Mission had to come from on high."

If there was sensitivity about providing U.S. Marines to safeguard the Benghazi Mission—as has been suggested in some quarters—any number of private military contractors (PMC) could have provided such a force. A PMC could have provided a dozen top operators—as indeed the British diplomatic mission in Benghazi had a security team made up of six to eight private contractors. Of course, when a PMC *was* contracted to assist with security at the Benghazi Mission, the British firm Blue Mountain was contracted to provide a local, Libyan guard force who were at all times to remain *unarmed*.

Use of PMCs deploying teams of private operators is far from unusual. In 2006 there were at least one hundred thousand contractors working for the U.S. Department of Defense in Iraq, which equates to a force larger than the entire British military. That amounts to a tenfold increase in the use of PMCs since the Persian Gulf War just over a decade earlier. Today PMCs are contracted to supply security for U.S. military bases; they provide live ammunition and training packages, they maintain complex weapons systems, they escort convoys, and they provide close protection teams for VIPs. They would have been well capable of securing the Benghazi Mission.

A cable quoted in the U.S. media indicates that a meeting was held at the U.S. State Department on August 15, 2012, to discuss security failings at the Benghazi Mission. The cable is quoted as stating: "RSO expressed concerns with the ability to defend Post in the event of a coordinated attack due to limited manpower, security measures, weapons capabilities, host nation support, and the overall size of the compound." The Mission was also aware of "the location of approximately ten Islamist militias and AQ training camps within Benghazi," AQ standing for Al Qaeda. Due to the date of this cable, it would seem likely this was a summation of the issues raised by the Mission's then lead RSO. Of course, nothing was done to address those concerns.

Some have suggested the Annex was the hidden extra layer of security for the Mission. I never went to the Annex, but it seems as if it had up to thirty operators based there, making it a far larger setup than the Mission itself. That raises the question of whether the Mission was a cover for the Annex. No more than seven State Department officials—RSOs and diplomatic staff—were ever based at the Mission, whereas the Annex appears to have had more than four times that number of personnel. It stands to reason that the Annex was therefore a key focus of U.S. activity and interest in Benghazi.

The mass of weaponry that fell into militia hands—both "liberated" from Gaddafi's armories, and provided by the Gulf states and Western nations—was a genuine concern after Gaddafi's fall. Much of that weaponry had disappeared off the radar and was controlled by extremists; some of that weaponry had already fueled conflicts in West Africa and as far afield as Gaza. Hunting down that weaponry was a legitimate and worthwhile aim, and so the U.S. effort in Benghazi may well have been first and foremost a CIA-led operation—the Mission itself being something of a sideshow, providing a veneer of diplomatic legitimacy.

But that in turn raises the question of who was really in charge in Benghazi—the State Department or the CIA? It seems likely that the Annex was somehow "contracted" to provide an added layer of security to the Mission, although few were made aware that this was so. If the RSOs knew of this backup agreement they certainly didn't mention it to me, and they weren't reassured by it, for they shared my concerns and worries over the lack of appropriate security at the Mission.

In any event, whatever security support the CIA-run Annex agreed to provide to the State-run Mission, the policy was a flawed one, as the events of the night of September 11, 2012, proved. Four Americans, the U.S. Ambassador to Libya included, lost their lives, many more were injured, and the U.S. Mission was reduced to a smoking ruin. America was humiliated by a mass of Islamist militiamen. By anyone's reckoning, the policy of having a secret Annex providing covert security backup to the Mission—if indeed there was such a policy in place—was flawed and resulted in catastrophic failure.

Some U.S. officials have claimed that the Shariah Brigade fighters stumbled upon the existence of the Annex, having followed the QRF back to its base. This seems unlikely. The mortar team that hit the Annex rooftop position with several highly accurate rounds would have needed either a set of accurate coordinates—GPS grids—to pinpoint such a small target in a busy, built-up urban environment, or detailed recces and target rehearsals beforehand, to be able to get mortar rounds directly on target. This necessitates having prior knowledge of the existence of the Annex.

In much of the media reporting following the Benghazi siege the Blue Mountain guard force were criticized for running away. The guards were five unarmed men facing fifty-plus heavily armed Shariah Brigade fighters. If they hadn't run away all of them would have been captured, injured, or killed. As it was, two were taken captive and one was shot through both kneecaps. More to the point, their training and their orders were that they were to sound the alarm and then save themselves if the Mission was attacked by an armed force.

The Blue Mountain guard force was also accused of having left the pedestrian entrance open and of "letting the attackers in." Five unarmed Libyan guards faced at least fifty enemy armed with AK-47s, light and heavy machine guns, and RPGs. Attackers ordered them to open the pedestrian gate or get blown to smithereens; the guards opened the gate. Had they been provided with appropriate weaponry with which to defend themselves and the Mission—weaponry that the State Department contract denied them— it might well have been a very different story. Either way, blame does not lie with the Blue Mountain guard force: it lies with those who dictated that they try to hold the line without a single weapon among them.

There have been reports in the media that the State Department refused to have a force of U.S. Marines based at the Mission or to let the Libyan guard force be armed, in an effort to keep the security at the Mission "low profile" and "nonconfrontational." To attempt low-profile and nonconfrontational security in a place like Benghazi and at an American diplomatic mission is misguided, as the disaster that unfolded on the night of September 11, 2012, proves.

By having one Blue Mountain guard outside manning the barrier—something they had been told not to do for their own safety; but which they chose to do because we'd asked them to up their game—the guard force was able to detect the attackers early, which won them the vital seconds in which to hit the duck-and-cover alarm and/or radio warnings to the RSOs. (There are conflicting reports as to whether they radioed through warnings or hit the alarm: but either way, a warning was given.) As much as they were able to they stood by the Americans, and put their lives on the line.

Even I—with all my experience working as a private security operator, team leader, and manager on major American contracts and with senior American clients—was not permitted to carry a weapon at the Benghazi Mission, as stipulated on the State Department contract for all Blue Mountain personnel. In spite of not allowing the Blue Mountain force to be armed, let's consider what that force did achieve on the night of the attack.

Blue Mountain employees were the first to detect the attackers and the first to raise the alarm. Blue Mountain employees—myself, and some of the guards—went back into the Mission when the attack was ongoing, to try to gather intelligence and find the missing Americans. Blue Mountain employees located the body of Ambassador Stevens and alerted U.S. authorities to its whereabouts and the need to secure it. Blue Mountain employees were the only people to go back into the Mission the morning after the attack to check for bodies, and to document the crime scene.

Considering the scope of Blue Mountain's contract with the State Department, all of these actions—apart from raising the alarm—fall well outside of what Blue Mountain was contracted to provide. Only the State Department can provide answers as to why it believed an *unarmed* guard force was appropriate to secure a U.S. diplomatic mission in as volatile and dangerous a place as Benghazi. Either way, Blue Mountain employees delivered above and beyond what was asked of them.

For up to two weeks after the attack on the Benghazi Embassy and the Annex the U.S. administration maintained the line that the attack was a spontaneous demonstration against an anti-Islam video posted on YouTube called "The Innocence of Muslims." On the contrary, this was a carefully planned and well-orchestrated attack by highly experienced and battle-hardened extremist fighters—ones that aimed specifically to target and kill Americans.

Bearing in mind that immediately after the attack I gave my detailed testimony and photographic evidence to an alphabet soup of American agencies—the State Department and FBI among others—and that my evidence was arguably the most detailed the U.S. administration possessed immediately following the attack, I cannot understand how the administration argued that this was a spontaneous demonstration that got out of hand. From my testimony alone it clearly was not.

The testimony and evidence that I provided made it clear who carried out the attack and the organized and highly effective nature of the fighters involved, and that they were specifically seeking to kill Americans. The State Department, FBI, and other agencies were clear in telling me that immediately following the attack my photographs and testimony were "all we've got." In light of this I fail to understand why the attacks were initially portrayed as a "spontaneous demonstration that got out of hand."

The official "spontaneous demonstration" line was the one that was picked up by most of the world's media. However, I was far from being the only source immediately after the attack to state that this was a specifically targeted, carefully planned two-stage attack against two separate targets, involving many hundreds of heavily armed and mobile fighters from the Shariah Brigade, a militia with a worrying history of human rights abuses and extrajudicial executions in Benghazi, and one with known links to extremist groups, including Al Qaeda.

Demonstrations began on the streets of Benghazi and Tripoli about the Benghazi assaults and killings on September 12, so immediately following the attacks. Benghazians carried signs saying "Chris Stevens was a friend to all Libyans" and "Benghazi is against terrorism" and apologizing to America for the attack. That same day Libya's deputy ambassador to London, Ahmad Jibril, told the BBC that Ansar al-Sharia—the Arabic name for the Shariah Brigade—was behind the attacks.

On September 13 the Libyan ambassador to the United States, Ali Aujali, apologized to then–Secretary of State Hillary Clinton for this "terrorist attack" against the U.S. Mission in Benghazi. The Libyan ambassador praised Ambassador Stevens as a real friend to Libya and a hero, and urged the United States to keep supporting Libya through "a very difficult time" and to help "maintain security and stability" in the country.

On September 16 the Libyan president, Mohammed Magariaf, announced that the attack on the Benghazi Mission was planned many months in advance: "The idea that this criminal and cowardly act was a spontaneous protest that just spun out of control is completely unfounded and preposterous. We firmly believe that this was a pre-calculated, preplanned attack that was carried out specifically to attack the U.S. consulate."

On September 21, ten days after the assault on the U.S. Mission in Benghazi, a popular uprising on the streets of the city drove out the Shariah Brigade militia. Some thirty thousand people marched through the streets, and over two days they fought open battles with the Islamist militias, targeting particularly the Shariah Brigade. They stormed several of the militia compounds and purged the city, forcing the militias to flee and seizing their headquarters.

In the aftermath of the Embassy siege, Secretary of State Clinton convened an Accountability Review Board (ARB), as required by America's Omnibus Diplomatic and Antiterrorism Act of 1986. In December 2012 the State Department official ARB report was released. It was seen as being a sharp criticism of officials in Washington for ignoring requests for more guards and safety upgrades, and for failing to adapt security procedures to a deteriorating security environment.

It is worth considering the report at some length. While recognizing that the perpetrators of the attack are subject to ongoing criminal investigations, the ARB report reaches some interesting conclusions. It recognizes the gravity of the events of September 11, 2012, noting that "the Benghazi attacks represent the first murder of a U.S. Ambassador since 1988"—in other words, in more than two decades.

The report states: "There was no protest prior to the attacks, which were unanticipated in terms of their scale and intensity." I'd take issue with the second part of that statement: the single greatest fear of myself and the RSOs in the Benghazi Mission was that we would be hit by a sizable force of extremist and/or Al

Qaeda–allied militia, and that the Embassy would be overrun and everyone killed or captured. This was a repeating theme of our discussions, reflecting a very real fear of all those who served at the Benghazi Mission. Such fears were shared with Washington by the diplomats, RSOs, and others.

The ARB report further states: "Overall, the number of Bureau of Diplomatic Security (DS) staff in Benghazi . . . was inadequate, despite repeated requests from Special Mission Benghazi for additional staffing." DS are also known as RSOs, which is the term they used to refer to themselves in the field. The ARB report found a "pervasive realization amongst personnel who served in Benghazi that Special Mission was not a high priority for Washington when it came to security-related requests, especially those related to staffing."

Unpacking that a little, it basically means there were not enough RSOs at the Benghazi Mission, or armed guards, and requests for more were denied by Washington. This is pretty much my experience and that of the RSOs as revealed in the pages of this book. The report further states: "dependence on the armed but poorly skilled Libyan 17th February Brigade militia members and unarmed, locally-contracted Blue Mountain Libya (BML) guards for security was misplaced."

I'd agree on both counts: employing the 17th February Militia as the QRF at the Benghazi Mission was absolutely the wrong thing to do. Likewise, expecting our guard force to do their jobs *unarmed* was deeply misguided. The report goes on to find "the responses of both the Blue Mountain guards and February 17th to be inadequate." While the report states that it found "little evidence that the armed 17th February guards offered any meaningful defense" of the Mission, it doesn't specify in any detail how the response of the Blue Mountain guard force was "inadequate."

In the recommendations made by the report it does support the deployment of more Marines to such diplomatic missions in future, and suggests the expanding of the Marine Security Guard program, with additional funding. The report suggests more Department of State personnel be deployed to "high-threat posts." In other words, more Marines and more RSOs should be provided to missions like that of Benghazi in 2012, which was exactly what the RSOs stationed at Benghazi—and myself behind them—had repeatedly asked for.

The report also calls the "short-term, transitory nature of Benghazi's staffing another primary driver behind the inadequate security platform in Benghazi. Staffing was at times woefully insufficient considering posts' security posture and high-risk, high-threat environment . . . This staffing 'churn' had significant detrimental effects . . ." In other words, there were too few RSOs on too short contracts, something that I and the RSOs had repeatedly complained about, especially considering how dangerous Benghazi was.

The report states that while a five-person RSO complement was "initially projected and later requested multiple times," it was rarely achieved. When I first worked at the Mission we had one RSO, and there were never more than three permanently based there. Even if five had been allocated, a mission of the size and risk factor of Benghazi should have had eight RSOs allocated to it, in my opinion—an opinion shared by many of the RSOs who served there.

The report noted significant failings in physical security measures at the Mission. Most notably, security cameras provided to cover the exterior of the Mission, and in particular the front gate, had not been installed because "technical support to install them had not yet visited post." In other words, surveillance cameras that would have given early warning of the attack were not in use, because no one had been provided to fit them.

Indeed, the guardroom monitor that provided a view from the camera covering the front gate was out of service on the night of the attack—another reason one of our guard force was stationed outside the front gate, to keep eyes on the area and give early warning.

The report states several times that the responses of Blue Mountain's guards and the 17th February Militia were "inadequate" on the night of the attack. It states that there were "no BML guards present outside the compound immediately before the attack ensued, although perimeter security was one of their responsibilities, and there is conflicting information as to whether they sounded any alarms prior to fleeing . . ."

The State Department report appears to equate the Blue Mountain guard force's so-called failings with those of the 17th February Militia—the so-called QRF. This is mind-boggling. The only responsibility of our guard force in the event of an attack by an armed force was to raise the alarm, which they did (whether by radio, or by the duck-and-cover, or by both). Their only role thereafter was to run and save themselves, for the very reason that they were deployed at the Mission *unarmed.*

By contrast, the QRF were contracted as the *armed* guard with the responsibility of defending the Mission from an armed attack. They were also supposed to call in support from the 17th February Militia, who apparently had a major base not far from the U.S. Mission. In both of these supposed functions they categorically failed. Moreover, the RSOs had reached the conclusion that the 17th February Militia were at best useless, and at worst a danger to the Mission, and had asked for them to be replaced—requests that were repeatedly denied.

To my knowledge no RSO raised complaints about the Blue Mountain guard force or asked for them to be replaced—certainly not in the three months leading up to the attacks. Indeed, the Blue Mountain guard force was praised for doing a fine job in terms of what they were contracted to do, and they had even received State Department commendations for their response to the IED attack on the Mission. For the State Department report to equate the

Blue Mountain guard force and the 17th February Militia as failing on a level somehow equal is unacceptable.

The State Department's criticisms of the Blue Mountain guard force are also wrong in a number of specific aspects:

- According to my guards, we did have one guard stationed outside the main gate—the one who first spotted the attackers—on the night of the assault. He was there because we'd asked the guards to "up their game" security-wise due to the Ambassador's visit, and because the screen via which they were supposed to be able to view the security camera covering the front gate was broken.

- The Blue Mountain guard force was contracted to patrol the interior of the Mission and its boundary—not to provide an external guard force. They were never supposed to be patrolling *outside* of the compound.

- I was told by my guards and by the FBI investigators that the guard force had hit the duck-and-cover alarm. Dave and Scotty have also indicated that the guard force radioed through a warning to them of the attack. Either one or both is true, and either way the Blue Mountain guard force did provide a warning.

Indeed, what is striking from the State Department official report is that there is *no* mention made of the considerable efforts made by myself or other Blue Mountain personnel after the attack began. There is no mention made of my or my guards' attempts to get into the Mission to find the Americans, and to help rescue them and/or locate their bodies. There is no mention made of my and my guards risking our lives to locate and positively identify the Ambassador's body at the Benghazi Medical Center, or of my alerting the U.S. authorities to his death and his body being there and providing photographic evidence of the same.

There is not even any mention made of my and my guard force

driver documenting the crime scene the morning after the attack, when Shariah Brigade fighters were still present on the ground and menacing the Mission, or of my provision of such evidence (photographs and testimony) to U.S. authorities, including the State Department immediately thereafter. In fact there is no mention made whatsoever of any of this in the State Department's official inquiry report into the Benghazi Mission attack. Why this should be so I fail to understand.

The report concludes that there were "systematic failures and leadership and management deficiencies at senior levels within two bureaus of the State Department resulting in a Special Mission security posture that was inadequate for Benghazi and grossly inadequate to deal with the attack that took place." In other words, Washington failed the Benghazi Mission.

However, the report concludes that it "did not find that any individual U.S. Government employee engaged in misconduct or willfully ignored his or her responsibilities, and, therefore did not find reasonable cause to believe that an individual breached his or her duty so as to be the subject of a recommendation for disciplinary action."

In other words, the official report into the Benghazi Mission attack concluded that no disciplinary action should be taken against anyone for all that had transpired. The RSOs had spent six months raising the grave security concerns that we all shared, and requesting more physical security and more staff and armed guards. They were repeatedly denied, and at the end of those six months the attack we all had feared did indeed take place—with consequences that actually went beyond what we had predicted.

No one in Washington seemingly takes the rap for any of this, yet at the same time justice is somehow seen as being done.

In the aftermath of the Benghazi Mission attacks, Rex Ubben, the father of RSO Dave Ubben, went public asking the State Department to own up to its mistakes and release all the information it has about what occurred in the lead-up to and during the Benghazi Mission siege. Rex Ubben said he found it troubling that "they have not owned up to their shortcomings: in government, in the military, and in business, if something goes wrong, you admit it, correct it and move on."

Dave Ubben has been treated at the Walter Reed National Military Medical Center, outside Washington, D.C., for his injuries, which are extensive. His father describes his son as having been blown up twice, and that he kept going after the first time. His son suffered shrapnel damage from head to toe, and five broken bones, one of which was completely smashed, necessitating extensive surgery.

"I was surprised by how many parts of him were injured," Rex Ubben remarked. "I owe a tremendous debt of gratitude to whoever did the first aid the first time, the second time, and maintained the tourniquets until they could get him out of there."

Rex Ubben is a twenty-four-year veteran of the U.S. Air Force, who retired in 1995 as a master sergeant. He said his son had described the events of the night of September 11, 2012, as "obviously an attack and not a riot." Dave had sketched out what appeared to be a sophisticated mortar attack during the assault on the Annex, during which ex-SEALs Glen Doherty and Tyrone Woods were killed.

"The first [mortar] dropped fifty yards short and the next two were right on target," Rex Ubben explained. "This indicates to me that someone was either very, very good, highly trained and skilled, or that the mortar was already set up and pointed at the safe house and only minor adjustments were needed."

Rex Ubben said he was bothered, too, that "people do not seem to realize that this was a much bigger disaster for the people of Libya than it was for us, that they were attacked just as we were."

Of course, Rex Ubben is right. The attack on the Benghazi Mission was an assault on the wider movement for democracy, freedom, and the rule of law in Libya, and a victory for those who espouse fascistic Islamic control in Libya and the rule of Shariah law—as the Shariah Brigade does. As their name suggests, the Shariah Brigade are hard-line supporters of Shariah law.

Sadly, the expulsion of the militias from Benghazi hasn't lasted. Today, the Shariah Brigade is back in Benghazi, and their black flags fly in many of the city's southern areas. They dominate some areas and control city checkpoints. They are a force to be reckoned with. They are well trained, battle-hardened, and well armed—thanks largely to the weapons they seized from Gaddafi's armed forces and the weapons provided to them by the Gulf Arab States.

For these reasons the new Libyan Army is reluctant to take them on, but they know they will have to, and before they consolidate their control, at which stage it will be too late. The Libyan Army was never particularly strong, and many argue it was kept deliberately weak by Gaddafi, to lessen the threat of regime change via military coup. The question remains, which will come out the stronger: the new Libyan ruling regime and its organs of law and order and defense (the police and the armed forces), or the heavily armed militias?

To assist Libya in disbanding such extremists groups, the Obama administration has rightly allocated $8 million to train an elite Libyan commando force. After the attack on the Benghazi Mission, President Obama ordered security to be increased at all such diplomatic missions worldwide, and in Libya itself a fifty-member Marine FAST team was deployed to bolster security.

The FBI was tasked to investigate the attack on the U.S. Mission, and U.S. officials announced that surveillance over Libya would be increased, including the use of unarmed drones to "hunt for the attackers." The effectiveness of such measures remains to be proven: they certainly came too late for those who died and were injured during the Benghazi Mission siege.

• • •

On April 23, 2013—seven months after Benghazi 9/11—the French Embassy in Tripoli, the Libyan capital, was targeted by a car bomb. The blast destroyed the embassy's ground floor reception area and perimeter wall, as well as damaging neighboring homes. One embassy guard was severely injured and another suffered light injuries. As with the United States, France would have had every right to consider herself a friend of the Libyan people: France was at the forefront of the NATO air strikes that helped topple Colonel Gaddafi.

Also in April 2013 a political action committee called Special Operations Speaks (SOS) called for the U.S. Congress to open a new investigation into the Benghazi 9/11 attacks. An SOS letter signed by seven hundred military Special Operations veterans urged support for House Resolution 36, a measure introduced by Virginia Republican representative Frank Wolf, calling for the appointment of a House Special Committee to determine what happened at the U.S. Mission in Benghazi.

"Additional information is now slowly surfacing in the media which makes a comprehensive bipartisan inquiry an imperative," the letter from SOS states. "Many questions have not been answered thus far . . . It appears that many of the facts and details surrounding the terrorist attack which resulted in four American deaths and an undetermined number of American casualties have not yet been ascertained by previous hearing and inquiries."

I hope the lessons from Benghazi 9/11 have been learned by America and her allies. It is important that they are: if the catastrophic failures at Benghazi are ever repeated at another U.S.—or allied—mission, more lives will very likely be lost. As a security expert with decades of experience I am in no doubt that the lives lost on that ill-fated night could have been saved, had the security measures recommended by me, as well as the RSOs and diplomats, been implemented.

If the same numbers of Shariah Brigade fighters had hit the Embassy, but it had had proper physical security measures in place, plus the weaponry and personnel along the lines that we had repeatedly requested, the attackers would have been repulsed, or at the very least held off until everyone was safely evacuated. That is the saddest part of this whole sorry and tragic tale.

Twelve U.S. Marines; one or two .50-caliber heavy machine guns; a team of German shepherd guard dogs with handlers; standard extra-physical security measures: Do the math—what would that have cost, compared to the tragic loss of life and injuries suffered, not to mention the humiliating and shaming of America in the eyes of her enemies?

For all our sakes I hope to God the lessons from Benghazi 9/11 have been learned.

AFTERWORD

Since completing the draft of this book, five House of Representatives committees have issued an Interim Report on the September 11, 2012, terrorist attacks in Benghazi. Those committees: Armed Services, Foreign Affairs, Judiciary, Oversight & Government Reform, and the Permanent Select Committee on Intelligence. Those committees are continuing to investigate the Benghazi 9/11 attacks, their aftermath, and their ramifications. As it stands the Interim Report makes for sobering reading, and it is well worthy of mention in this book, hence the points quoted from it below.

1. Prior to the Benghazi attacks, State Department officials in Libya made repeated requests for additional security that were denied in Washington despite ample documentation of the threat posed by violent extremist militia.
2. The volatile security environment erupted on September 11, 2012, when militia composed of al Qa'ida-affiliated extremists attacked U.S. interests in Benghazi.
3. After the attacks, the Administration perpetuated a deliberately misleading and incomplete narrative that the violence grew out of a demonstration caused by a YouTube video. The

Administration consciously decided not to discuss extremist involvement or previous attacks against Western interests in Benghazi.

4. After the U.S.-backed Libyan revolution ended the Gaddafi regime, the U.S. government did not deploy sufficient U.S. security elements to protect U.S. interests and personnel that remained on the ground.

5. Repeated requests for additional security were denied at the highest levels of the State Department.

6. The attacks were not the result of a failure by the Intelligence Community (IC) to recognize and communicate the threat.

7. On the evening of September 11, 2012, U.S. security teams on the ground in Benghazi exhibited extreme bravery responding to the attacks by al-Qa'ida-affiliated groups against the U.S. mission.

8. Senior Administration officials knowingly minimized the role played by al-Qa'ida-affiliated entities and other associated groups in the attacks, and decided to exclude from the discussion the previous attempts by extremists to attack U.S. persons or facilities in Libya.

9. This singular event (the Benghazi 9/11 attack) will be repeated unless the United States recognizes and responds to the threats we face around the world, and properly postures resources and security assets to counter and respond to those threats. Until that time the United States will remain in reactionary mode and should expect more catastrophes like Benghazi, in which U.S. personnel on the ground perform bravely, but are not provided with the resources for an effective response.

10. Congress must maintain pressure on the Administration to ensure the United States takes all necessary steps to find the Benghazi attackers. Active terrorist organizations and potential recruits will be emboldened to attack U.S. interests if the U.S. fails to hold those responsible for this attack accountable.

11. The decision by the British Embassy, United Nations and the

International Committee of the Red Cross to withdraw their personnel from Benghazi after armed assailants launched directed attacks against each organization were additional major indicators of the increasingly threatening environment.

12. These developments caused Lieutenant Colonel Andrew Wood, who led U.S. military efforts to supplement diplomatic security in Libya, to recommend that the State Department consider pulling out of Benghazi altogether. Lt-Col Woods believed that after withdrawal of these organizations, "it was apparent to me that were the last [Western] flag flying in Benghazi. We were the last thing on their target list to remove from Benghazi."

13. Despite mounting security concerns, for the most of 2012 the Benghazi Mission was forced to rely on fewer than the approved number of DS agents. Reports indicate the Benghazi Mission was typically staffed with only three DS agents, and sometimes as few as one DS agent.

14. The 17th February Martyrs Brigade was one of the militias that fought for Gaddafi's overthrow. Numerous reports have indicated that the Brigade had extremist connections and it had been implicated in the kidnapping of American citizens as well as in the threats against U.S. military assets.

15. Due to security concerns and bureaucratic entanglements among the Department for Justice, State and Defense, the FBI team investigating the terrorist attacks did not access the crime scene until more than three weeks later, on October 4, 2012. During this time the site was not secured and curious locals and international media were able to pick through the burned-out remains of the U.S. facility.

16. The State Department's Accountability Review Board (ARB) highlights "systematic failures" of Washington, D.C.–based decision-makers that left the Benghazi Mission with significant security shortfalls. Yet, the Board also fails to conduct an ap-

propriately thorough and independent review of which officials bear responsibility for those decisions.

17. Despite repeated requests for further security by U.S. officials working in the high-risk, high-threat environment, requests were denied by senior leadership in the State Department . . . Thus, the Administration was willing to provide necessary force to expel Gaddafi in support of the Libyan opposition, yet it simply failed to provide sufficient protection for the U.S. personnel and interests that remained.

While I take no issue with all the points raised above—indeed, I commend the committees on their Interim Report and a set of findings that reflect my own empirical experiences on the ground in Benghazi—I find it strikingly odd that there is not one reference made in this report, or that of the Accountability Review Board, of the role played by any Blue Mountain personnel, namely, myself and my guards, in responding to the Benghazi 9/11 attacks. Under considerable risk to our own safety we located the Ambassador in the Benghazi Medical Center, verified his identity and that he had been killed, alerted U.S. authorities, and provided photographic proof of his death and whereabouts. No mention is made of that in either of the official U.S. reports. We alone returned to the Embassy in the direct aftermath of the attack—again at very real danger to ourselves—to check for any American dead, photograph and document the crime scene, and provide all of that evidence, augmented by my own verbal testimony, to U.S. authorities. Again, no mention is made of that in any official U.S. documents, or at least not ones that I have seen released to the American and world publics.

I have no interest in seeking official recognition for my own sake: it doesn't interest me and is irrelevant. But if a full accounting of Benghazi 9/11 is to be reached, and the right lessons are to be learned, it needs to be truly a full accounting—which raises the question, why have we been written out of the equation? Has it somehow been made an "unmentionable" that a lone British security operator and a handful of Libyan guards managed to do what the FBI failed to do for weeks on end—if at all—and what the State Department made impossible on the night of the attack, by refusing to protect and garrison the Benghazi Mission properly, and if so, on whose orders and in whose interests has this been made an "unmentionable"? When the FBI originally interviewed me at my home, I was asked to go to the United States to tell my side of the story. I said I was willing, but it never happened. Too many people died or were horrifically injured, and America (and her allies) was too badly wounded by Benghazi 9/11 to play politics with the truth, or to suppress any aspects of what took place there. A full and open accounting should be just that, and nothing less.

SOURCES

Documents and publications that proved useful in writing the postscript, epilogue, and afterword of this book include the ebook *Benghazi: The Definitive Report*, written by former U.S. Army Ranger Jack Murphy and former Navy SEAL Brandon Webb; the official State Department Accountability Review Board report on the Benghazi 9/11 events; and the official House of Representatives Interim Report on the Benghazi 9/11 events.

ACKNOWLEDGMENTS

We'd like to thank lead publisher Threshold Editions, and editor Mitchell Ivers, ably assisted by Natasha Simons. Also at Threshold, we thank publisher Louise Burke, publicity director Jen Robinson, production editor Al Madocs, managing editor Kevin McCahill, art director Lisa Litwack, design director Joy O'Meara, interior designer Claudia Martinez, and copyeditor Tom Pitoniak.

We would like to acknowledge a group of former U.S. Navy SEALs who wished to remain unnamed, for their assistance in our telling of the wider story of the night of the Embassy siege, and honoring the heroics of their teammates Ty Woods and Glen Doherty. Guys, your help and your insight were invaluable. Seasoned military veteran Mike Mawhinney carried out invaluable research on the ground in Benghazi and across Libya, including interviewing and facilitating our own interviews with the surgeon who treated Ambassador J. Christopher Stevens on the night of the attack, when he was first taken to the hospital in Benghazi, plus various other key players in Libya connected to the Benghazi Embassy siege. Mike, your work was of massive help to us, your contacts unrivaled, and we couldn't have told the wider story so well without your help. As ever, greatly in your debt.

—*Morgan Jones & Damien Lewis, England, June 2013*

I'd like to say a big thank-you to my co-author, Damien Lewis, for his patience and understanding during a very dark time in my life. I couldn't have done any of this without your continued support.

A special thank-you to my mates for standing by me, and listening over the past twelve months, ones that have proven extremely difficult for me: Glenn, Tom, John, Gwilym, Jason T, Cat, Steve T, Baz, Dave K, Ryan K, Nick F, Ty, Greg, Rhys, Paul T, Dan F, Jason P, Mac, Rouven, Calum, Ade, Fletch, Scotty, Chris W, Lee K, Richie, and Chris H.

Finally, very special love and gratitude to my family, for their ongoing support over the years: Laura, Lewis, Mam, Mogs, and Anna.

—Morgan Jones, England, June 2013

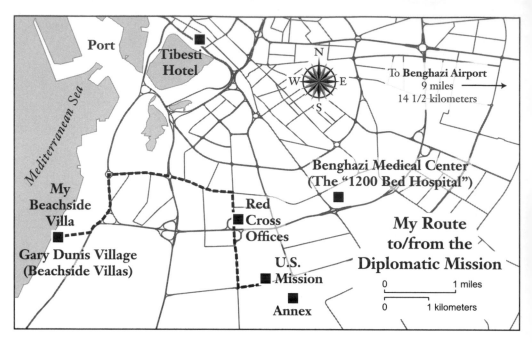

1. Having gone over the wall, I pause on the rooftop position to observe the attackers and scan for any Americans left alive and fighting in there.
2. From the cover of the orchard I see the canteen and the Tactical Operations Centre (TOC) burning where the attackers have fire-bombed them.
3. In the cover of the bushes that line the dividing wall, I stumble into my first dead Shariah Brigade fighter who had attacked the U.S. Mission in Benghazi.
4. Forced to emerge from cover, I bluff my way across the open ground of the side driveway, posing as one of the attackers.
5. I take cover in the concrete dog kennels to watch Villa C (the VIP Villa), the location the Americans retreated to as a last-ditch defensive position.
6. I push through the cover of the orchard to a position where I can see the VIP Villa burning and smoke-blackened. I scan the rooftop, desperate to see my American friends putting down defensive fire from up there.
7. I see no Americans left alive or fighting, but I push on to the entrance of the VIP Villa, where there are scores of Shariah Brigade fighters milling about, chanting and letting off gunfire.
8. I am finally challenged by one of the attackers and forced to break my cover and fight.
9. Realizing that all the Americans must have been either captured or killed, I make a fighting withdrawal toward the rear gate—the last thing I need to check
10. I see the gate is open and that the Mission's armored SUV—the escape vehicle—is gone. A sudden ray of hope: maybe some of my American buddies did get out alive.
11. I exit via the rear gate and use my cell phone to call in Zahid and Akram, two of my local guard force, who pick me up in our vehicle.